JAMES FENIMORE COOPER

JAMES FENIMORE COOPER

THE NOVELIST

by

GEORGE DEKKER

Routledge & Kegan Paul
LONDON

First published 1967
by Routledge & Kegan Paul Ltd
Broadway House, 68–74 Carter Lane
London, E.C.4

Printed in Great Britain
by Butler & Tanner Ltd
Frome and London

This book is for

DONALD *and* DOREEN

CONTENTS

Contents

INTRODUCTION

IF MY OWN EXPERIENCE is representative, Cooper's novels are
taught either unsympathetically or not at all in the American
literature courses which American undergraduates have to
take when they 'minor' or 'major' in English literature. I was
never advised, much less required, to read a Cooper novel;
I do not recall that his name was even mentioned. Later on, as
a graduate student at a different university, I attended a course
of lectures, designed primarily for undergraduates, on the
American novel. From such a course Cooper could not very
well be excluded. The lecturer was a distinguished scholar who
had (I later discovered) written perceptively and not unsympathetically about Cooper's Leatherstocking tales. But in
this course, taking *The Pathfinder* as a characteristic work, he
treated Cooper primarily as a practitioner in the decadent
genteel tradition from which subsequent, more serious, American novelists would have to free themselves. A novel which
moved Balzac to exclaim, 'C'est beau! c'est grand! c'est d'un
immense intérêt'—was presented by the lecturer as an object
for good-natured condescension and ridicule. At the time this
seemed to me exactly what *The Pathfinder* deserved: a bright undergraduate or graduate student could not fail to spot Cooper's
rigid and snobbish adherence to genteel conventions, his
laborious attempts at humour, and his frequent technical lapses.
(Balzac saw them too, but had eyes for other things as well.[1])
Neither did it seem proper, or quite mature, to give Cooper
much credit for being a spellbinding narrator of physical
adventure. His being a 'classic' both of American and children's
literature was decidedly a cultural embarrassment. To be sure,

---

[1] Balzac's review of *The Pathfinder* is collected in *Œuvres complètes* (Paris, 1869–
79), vol. XXIII, pp. 584–90. Other comments on Cooper are to be found in
L. Gozlan, *Balzac en pantoufles* (Paris, 1890).

the lecturer was not half so contemptuous of Cooper as I and most other students were, but we might all have been a little enlightened and chastened had he applied as much intelligence to *The Pathfinder* as he later did to *Moby Dick* and *Light in August*.

Possibly my experience was exceptional. Certainly the numerous cheap editions, not only of the Leatherstocking tales, but even of such comparatively out-of-the-way works as *The Bravo* and *Home as Found*, demonstrate that there is a large academic market for Cooper's works in America today. Then, too, the best critical and scholarly studies of Cooper, most of them written during the past thirty years, are very good indeed: they *must* have penetrated. Nevertheless, my conversations with scholars from both countries lead me to believe that Cooper's strengths are more appreciated in Britain than in America. I do not mean by this that Cooper is 'in' in England and 'out' in America. But it does seem that, because of a number of cultural factors, the mid-twentieth-century English reader is in a better position than his American contemporary to respond freshly and honestly to Cooper's fiction: to respond as did Balzac, Melville, Goethe, Turgenev, Conrad, and, of course, D. H. Lawrence. Lawrence's *Studies in Classic American Literature*, so influential in America, has had even more influence in his own country among those engaged in the advanced study of American literature. Lawrence loved, in some ways misunderstood, but above all took Cooper seriously.

The knowledge that Lawrence took Cooper seriously, and that Yvor Winters and Donald Davie did too, disturbed my complacency somewhat. But it was not until I had to teach an American literature course at the University College of Swansea that I forced myself to read another Cooper novel. Following Marius Bewley's advice in *The Eccentric Design*, I prescribed *The Deerslayer* and then set to work. Reading through it, I paused frequently, sometimes to admire a felicitous descriptive passage, but more often to note a clumsy fictional manœuvre or yet another instance of Cooper's obnoxious class consciousness. What finally mattered, however, and what I found difficult to explain to myself and my students, was that the novel as a whole had, on me, the impact of major fiction. This led me to read other works by Cooper and eventually to undertake the present study, since no other critic had explained to my satisfaction the nature of Cooper's distinction and achievement. In the course of this work I have found, inevitably, that most of his other novels cannot equal or surpass *The Deerslayer*. But a number of them do, and, taken as a whole, Cooper's works of fiction and non-fiction form one of the most varied and consistently interesting bodies of writing in the field of American literature.

A few years ago I supposed that my work on Cooper might help to improve the way his novels were introduced to students, especially in the United States. But having written the book, I have to recognize that my interest in the subject has both deepened and widened, so that what I now have to say about Cooper is, much of it, not immediately relevant to the undergraduate classroom situation. Moreover, in spite of my personal experience, I am now persuaded that Cooper is not the sort of author who wins converts readily. He is not a novelist of the very first rank, and those who do not see beyond his obvious defects cannot allow that he is a novelist even of the rank of Howells or Dreiser. These defects are real and serious and cannot be argued away. What is in dispute is whether his no less real strengths are as great and richly compensating as I believe them to be. I have tried to show that they are. I have tried to show that, on the evidence of the published criticism, several of his best novels have never been read except in a superficial way.

Basically, this book is a critical survey of Cooper's fiction. But since it did not seem useful to discuss this fiction in a historical vacuum, I have devoted a good deal of attention, on the one hand to Cooper's politics, and on the other hand to his assimilation and development of the historical novel as first perfected by Sir Walter Scott. Cooper's debt to Scott was immense. His involvement in politics, European as well as American, was such as we find difficult to conceive of today, but such as seemed natural and proper to many leading writers of Cooper's generation—his friends Bryant, Paulding, and Bancroft among them. It may appear that Scott and American politics are not very closely related preoccupations, and I certainly do not wish to pretend that my discussion of, say, *Guy Mannering* early in this study has any direct connexion with my later account of Whig campaign strategy in the 1840 presidential election. But Cooper was very conscious of being an *American* novelist. Often he used his fiction as a vehicle for advocating or criticizing American political institutions. More important, his major formal innovations in the field of historical fiction were, like Scott's, something more than mere experiments: they were made because American social and political developments differed radically from those of Scott's Europe and so demanded a different formal expression. At the same time, it is only just to add that Cooper's literary and socio-political activities were not always well integrated: as his contemporaries complained, many of his novels are damaged more or less seriously by long, tedious, and extraneous passages of social or political commentary. That too is part of the picture. But what I have tried to show finally—and this appears to me the major task of Cooper criticism today—is that Cooper the romancer and Cooper the social critic were not always or essentially at odds with each other.

One of the pleasures of a student of Cooper is to read the many excellent studies of his work by other scholars. Still the best brief critical survey is Yvor Winter's 'Fenimore Cooper, or the Ruins of Time'.[2] Memorable, indeed indispensable, studies of particular groups of Cooper's novels are those by Mark Twain, D. H. Lawrence, Roy Harvey Pearce, Henry Nash Smith, and Marius Bewley.[3] As especially challenging and illuminating readings of individual novels I would wish to single out those by Donald Davie (*The Pioneers*) and Leslie Fiedler (*The Last of the Mohicans*).[4] Perhaps none of these writers would be classified as a 'Cooper specialist', but their contribution to our understanding and evaluation of his work

[2] Winters, *In Defence of Reason* (London, 1960), pp. 176–99.
[3] Twain, 'Fenimore Cooper's Literary Offenses', *North American Review*, vol. CLXI (1895), pp. 1–12; Lawrence, 'Fenimore Cooper's Leatherstocking Novels', *D. H. Lawrence: Selected Literary Criticism*, ed. Anthony Beal (London, 1956), pp. 314–29 [Lawrence's earlier and in some ways better draft of this essay is collected in D. H. Lawrence, *The Symbolic Meaning*, ed. Armin Arnold (Fontwell, Arundel, 1962), pp. 91–111]; Pearce, 'The Leatherstocking Tales Re-examined', *South Atlantic Quarterly*, vol. XLVI (Oct. 1947), pp. 524–36; Smith, *Virgin Land* (Vintage ed.: New York, 1957), pp. 64–76 and 256–60; Bewley, *The Eccentric Design* (London, 1959), pp. 47–112.
[4] Davie, *The Heyday of Sir Walter Scott* (London, 1961); Fiedler, *Love and Death in the American Novel* (New York, 1960).

has been enormous. It is also more likely to win general recognition than the contribution, no less important, of those scholars who are specialists in this field. Chief among these, surely, is Robert E. Spiller, whose biographical and bibliographical studies provide the basis for contemporary Cooper scholarship.[5] Scarcely less essential is the great edition of the letters and journals, still in progress, by James F. Beard, Jr.[6] All students of Cooper must be grateful for the biographical labours of Marcel Clavel.[7] James Grossman's critical biography, a remarkable achievement in any case, is yet more remarkable for being the work of a professional lawyer rather than of a professional academic.[8] The important pioneer study of Cooper's politics is Dorothy Waples' *Whig Myth of James Fenimore Cooper*.[9] Excellent recent studies of Cooper's fiction are those by Howard Mumford Jones, Donald Ringe, and Thomas Philbrick, Jr.[10]

I owe a more particular debt to my colleagues, past and present, at the University College of Swansea and the University of Essex. My greatest debt is to Donald Davie, Professor of Literature at Essex. His guidance and encouragement at all stages of my work have made this a much better book than it would otherwise have been. Dr Howard Erskine-Hill and Mr Brian Way of Swansea read an earlier, shorter draft of the present book, as did Mr R. W. Butterfield of Essex: their detailed and sympathetic criticism gave me just the help I needed. I am also grateful to Miss I. M. Westcott of Swansea, Dr Simon Collier of Essex, and Dr John Hayden of the University

[5] Spiller's principal works on Cooper are *Fenimore Cooper: Critic of His Times* (New York, 1931) and, with his co-editor Philip Blackburn, *A Descriptive Bibliography of the Writings of James Fenimore Cooper* (New York, 1934).

[6] *Letters and Journals of James Fenimore Cooper* (Cambridge, Mass., 1960–), vols. I–IV so far published.

[7] Clavel, *Fenimore Cooper: Sa vie et son œuvre: La Jeunesse (1789–1826)* (Aix-en-Provence, 1938).

[8] Grossman, *James Fenimore Cooper* (New York, 1949).

[9] Waples, *Whig Myth of James Fenimore Cooper* (New Haven, 1938). Also important as an early and shrewd assessment of Cooper's political attitudes is V. L. Parrington's *Main Currents in American Thought* (New York, 1927), vol. II, pp. 222–37.

[10] Jones, 'Prose and Pictures: James Fenimore Cooper', *Tulane Studies in English*, vol. III (1952), pp. 133–54; Ringe, *James Fenimore Cooper* (New Haven, 1962); Philbrick, *James Fenimore Cooper and the Development of Sea Fiction* (Cambridge, Mass., 1961).

of California, who have given me invaluable criticism of particular passages of this study.

Writing a book on an American subject has its problems if one lives in Wales or England. But grants from the University College of Swansea enabled me to make full use of the rich American literature resources of the British Museum, while an unusually generous grant from the University of Essex made it possible for me to work at the Yale University Library and the library of the New York State Historical Association in Cooperstown. Like every other researcher, I have made huge demands on the patience and knowledge of librarians. To all of them I wish to express my gratitude, but especially to those with whom I have worked at the libraries of Yale University, the University of Essex, and the British Museum. This is also the place to thank Margaret Hine and Marjorie McGlashan, since besides typing the various drafts of this book they have done their best to save me from my unscholarly ways.

Unless noted otherwise, I have used the Red Rover edition of Cooper's novels (New York, n.d.), 33 vols. [a reprint of the Mohawk edition, New York, 1895–1900]. In cases where Cooper is known to have made revisions, I have compared the Red Rover text with the text of the first edition or, where this was possible, of the manuscript.

CHRONOLOGY OF
JAMES FENIMORE COOPER

1754	William Cooper born in Pennsylvania.
1786	William Cooper founds Cooperstown on the edge of Lake Otsego in New York.
1789	James Cooper born (September 15) at Burlington, New Jersey. [Inauguration of George Washington as first President.]
1790	William Cooper's family moves to Cooperstown.
1796–1800	[Period of Federalist supremacy: John Adams as U.S. President, John Jay as Governor of New York, William Cooper as U.S. Congressman.]
1803	James Cooper enters Yale College.
1805	Expelled from Yale because of misconduct.
1806–1807	Sails before the mast on the *Stirling* to England and Spain.
1808	Becomes midshipman in U.S. Navy; service at Fort Oswego (Lake Ontario) and New York City; retires from active service shortly after.
1809	Death of William Cooper.
1811	Marriage to Susan Augusta De Lancey.
1811–1819	Gentleman farmer in Cooperstown and Westchester Co., New York.
1820–1822	Begins participating actively in politics and literature, as Secretary to Westchester Co. Clintonian Republicans and as author of *Precaution* (1820) and *The Spy* (1821).
1822–1826	Moves to New York City and sets up as professional writer: *The Pioneers* (1823), *The Pilot* (1824),

Lionel Lincoln (1825), *The Last of the Mohicans* (1826). [John Quincy Adams elected President, 1824.]

1826–1833   Residence in Europe: based mainly in Paris but with extended visits to England, Switzerland, Germany, the Low Countries, and especially Italy. The period of Cooper's involvement in English, French, and Polish politics through his friendships with such figures as Lord William Russell, Lafayette, and Adam Mickiewicz. [Andrew Jackson elected President, 1828 and 1832.] Publishes *The Prairie* (1827), *The Red Rover* (1827), *Notions of the Americans* (1828), *The Wept of Wishton-Wish* (1829), *The Water Witch* (1830), *The Bravo* (1831), *The Heidenmauer* (1832), and *The Headsman* (1833).

1833–1836   Residence in New York City: period during which Cooper's disillusionment with the American reading public and distrust of the 'oligarchical' (Whig) party, already pronounced before he left Europe, leads him to stop writing novels and to become an active supporter of the Jacksonian party. *A Letter to His Countrymen* (1834), *The Monikins* (1835).

1836   Returns to the home of his father, Otsego Hall, in Cooperstown. Commences publication of five volumes of European travels (1836–8). [Van Buren succeeds Jackson as President.]

1837–1838   Three Mile Point affair leads to publication of *Homeward Bound* and *Home as Found* (1838) and libel suits against Whig editors. [W. H. Seward elected N.Y. Governor, 1838.] *American Democrat* (1838) and *Chronicles of Cooperstown* (1838).

1839   *History of the Navy of the United States.* [Outbreak of Anti-Rent troubles on the Rensselaer estates near Albany.]

1840–1843   Begins writing historical romances again: *The Pathfinder* (1840), *Mercedes of Castile* (1840), *The*

Deerslayer (1841), *The Two Admirals* (1842), *Wing-and-Wing* (1842), *Wyandotté* (1843). [Election of Harrison as President and re-election of Seward in 1840: Tyler becomes President in 1841.]

1844–1847   Supports landlords in the Anti-Rent controversy and President Polk [elected in 1844] concerning the War with Mexico. *Afloat and Ashore* and *Miles Wallingford* (1844). The 'Littlepage Trilogy': *Satanstoe* (1845), *The Chainbearer* (1845), and *The Redskins* (1846). *Jack Tier* (1846–8). *The Crater* (1847).

1848–1850   Supports Compromise measures of 1850 and publishes last novels: *The Oak Openings* (1848), *The Sea Lions* (1849), and *The Ways of the Hour* (1850). 'The Lake Gun', an attack on Seward, published in 1850. [Taylor elected President in 1848, succeeded by Fillmore in 1850; Seward elected U.S. Senator.]

1851   Cooper dies (September 14) in Cooperstown, leaving his last work, *The Towns of Manhattan*, unfinished.

I

COOPERS, JAYS, AND
DE LANCEYS

1. JUDGE WILLIAM COOPER

WHEN AFTER THE French withdrawal from Canada the Western Lands of New York Colony were first opened up to speculators and settlers, they were usually bought by land companies or wealthy individuals, who alone could afford to develop them. Many of these individuals already held large hereditary estates in the older regions of the Middle Colonies. Rich, educated, of good family, and politically powerful, such men were destined to become—depending on the side they chose to support in the American War of Independence—either exiled and dispossessed Tories, or the influential Federalist allies of John Jay and Alexander Hamilton. Some, like General Philip Schuyler, Gouverneur Morris, and the great Albany Patroon Stephen Van Rensselaer, were themselves men of national prominence. In the new state of New York, because they owned so much of it, they often seemed more important than Hamilton or Jay, whose bases of operation were New York City and Philadelphia and whose connexions were with law and commerce rather than with the land. Law, commerce, and land were natural allies in the early Empire State—it was no coincidence that Hamilton was Schuyler's son-in-law. Men like Schuyler, who owned vast tracts of the wilderness north and west of New York City, were quite as keen to develop a canal between the Great Lakes and the Hudson River as were the New York City merchants, who longed to have a direct, short trade route to the heart of the continent. Both groups naturally favoured a government which was energetic and, at the same time, prudent and

I

stable—in fact, the very government that John Jay had provided
for in 1777 when he wrote the New York State Constitution: it
was a republic in which the electors were the state's freeholders
and the representatives were its 'natural governors', i.e. the
great Federalist lawyers, merchants, and landlords themselves.
They were self-interested, aristocratic—some of them lived in
baronial splendour on their estates—and they could not last long
as the ruling party of a state which, like the rest of the nation,
was heading in the direction of Jacksonian democracy. They
were swept out of office, never to return to effective power, by
the Jeffersonian Republicans in 1800.[1]

Not all Federalists were born into the 'governing class',
however, and not all speculators in Western Lands were already
landed proprietors. Especially after the sequestration of land
owned by loyalists, did new men have their chance. Yet what
successful speculator, of comparatively obscure birth and recent
fortune, would not try to win his way into the Federalist
squirearchy? It was nearly inevitable that he should. From the
economic point of view, their cause was his cause. Neither was
there anything effete about men like Schuyler or Morris; though
aristocrats by birth, they had all the qualities of personal
courage, energy, large vision, and resourcefulness of the most
brilliant 'self-made man'. With Washington as their national
and Jay and Hamilton as their state chiefs, they might well be
regarded (whatever the Jacobinical Republicans said) as the
guardians of the *American* Revolution. No wonder then that one
of the most ardent Federalists in the heartland of Federalism
was William Cooper, a man who in spite of early poverty and
poor education had, not long after the Revolution, become the
founder and proprietor of one of the most thriving new settlements in the state.[2] It was almost as much a matter of course that
Cooper should campaign for Jay and Hamilton as that he should

[1] My account of the political, social, and economic life of New York Federalists
leans heavily on two justly famous works by New York historians: Jabez Delano
Hammond's *History of Political Parties in the State of New York*, 3 vols. (4th ed.:
Syracuse, 1852); and Dixon Ryan Fox's *Decline of Aristocracy in the Politics of New
York State* (New York, 1918).

[2] The best biographical accounts of William Cooper are by Lyman H.
Butterfield, 'Judge William Cooper (1754–1809): A Sketch of His Character and
Accomplishment', *New York History*, vol. XXX (Oct. 1949), pp. 385–408; and
'Cooper's Inheritance: The Otsego Country and its Founders', *New York History*,
vol. XXXV (Oct. 1954), pp. 374–411. Though fictionalized and somewhat

build himself a splendid manor house and make sure that his village was named Cooperstown. With Washington and John Adams as Presidents of the Republic and John Jay as Governor of the state, a new man might well nurse dynastic ambitions— the bold pattern was there for all to see, and the materials, mile on mile, were lavishly at hand.

William Cooper was born in Pennsylvania in 1754. Some of his Quaker ancestors had been prosperous farmers and merchants; but his own parents were too poor to give him a good education, let alone to set him up as a gentleman. He was well able to take care of himself. Shortly before the War of Independence, he eloped with Elizabeth Fenimore, the genteel daughter of a well-to-do Quaker; during the war, as co-owner of a produce store, he began to acquire his fortune; and as soon as the war was over, he was ready to take advantage of the lively market in Western Lands. By 1786, aged thirty-one years, he had acquired a tract of some 40,000 acres stretching west from the shores of Lake Otsego, near the middle of New York state. This land he promptly sold, mostly in small parcels to impoverished immigrants from the populous New England states. It is at this point that William Cooper begins to emerge historically, not only as a socially and politically prominent figure, but as a well-documented creature of flesh and blood. So far as the early years are concerned, he appears to us only as a shadowy operator— possibly, at worst, a war-time profiteer who used his Quakerism as a cloak whilst others hazarded their lives and fortunes for the sake of liberty or loyalty; at best, little more than an adventurous capitalist who took care to form the right connexions.

But obscure though his early years are, they are important because they obviously left their mark on him and, through him, on his son James. It is rather to his boyhood days as a wheelwright's apprentice, than to his manhood days on the frontier, that we must trace his fondness for wrestling and other feats of physical strength. It was with the passion of a man who had raised himself from poverty by his own exertions that he persecuted Jeffersonian egalitarians and sought by fair means or foul to keep the Federalists, friends of property and internal

---

idealized, the most vivid portrait of Judge Cooper is that which his son painted in the character of Judge Temple in *The Pioneers*.

improvements, in office.³ Deprived of a good education, he later had little time or appetite for philosophy or the arts. Because he had a clear and vigorous mind, he was able to write a sturdy and fairly correct English prose when he wrote deliberately; but when he wrote in haste, his earlier lack of training showed through:

> I have wrote to him on the Subject Expect his answer wich I shall Shew the with a Copy of Mine. the Man has Paid him ten Shilings pr. acre but apeares to be the most Christianly inclind of Any of those along the River, yet I fully believe the wioming afair Could be Settled Easy by Proper Management. the People in the Bend where of the Same Spirit but they have give Ear to my arguments and Come in to take tiller and Are All on Our Side incorrageing Every One to Doe as they have Done.⁴

No doubt his speech, especially in moments of excitement or relaxation with his family, was equally unpolished. Clearly, though he was entertained socially, and apparently was quite genuinely respected, by all the leading Federalist families of New York and Pennsylvania, William Cooper could not have passed muster as an 'American Gentleman'—not, at any rate, as that idealized figure was to be drawn by James Fenimore Cooper. Yet it might be maintained that he was something better.

Jabez Hammond, a younger neighbour of William Cooper and an equally shrewd observer, commented that 'Judge Cooper was an uneducated man, but very few *knew men* better than he'.⁵ This quality is evident throughout his little book, *Guide in the Wilderness*, an account of his experiences as the founder of Cooperstown and a practical do-it-yourself handbook for the

---

³ Hammond, *History of Political Parties*, vol. I, calls Cooper a 'heated politician'. In 1792 he was accused of coercing many Otsego residents into supporting the Federalist ticket. Later he enforced the Alien and Sedition laws so vigorously against political opponents as to cause a scandal. When through a defect in the Presidential election machinery, Burr and Jefferson won the same number of votes for the presidency (though it was generally known that Burr was the Republican party *Vice*-Presidential candidate), Cooper was one of the many Federalist Congressmen who gave their support to Burr when the election was taken to the House of Representatives.
⁴ Quoted from Libr. Co. Phila., Rush MSS., vol. 32, fol. 100, by L. H. Butterfield, 'Judge William Cooper (1754–1809): A Sketch of His Character and Accomplishment', *New York History*, vol. XXX, p. 394.
⁵ Hammond *op. cit.*, vol. I, p. 143.

prospective investor in wilderness lands.[6] Federalist though he was, Cooper's theme is that the fully successful settlement must be a fully communal venture in which no individual, the proprietor included, enjoys any special advantages or exclusive rights:

But, while we acknowledge the importance of the wealthy undertaker, we must not despise the offer of the poor man. He can never be insignificant who is willing to add his labor to the common stock, for the interest of every individual from the richest land-holder to the poorest settler conspires and contributes to the great primary object, to cause the wilderness to bloom, and fructify; and each man prospers as he contributes to the advantage of his neighbor.[7]

As for the proprietor himself, 'he should be ever in the midst of the settlers, aiding and promoting every beneficial enterprise'.[8] It was by following his own advice, by sharing the troubles and labours of his settlers, that Cooper won their love and respect— and also made sure that they were able to repay their mortgages. Now and then a trace of his native humour appears in the *Guide*: 'I once had a surveyor's chainbearer bitten [by a rattlesnake], but an application being made of pounded water-pepper (or arsesmart), he was relieved in a few hours time.' [9] From other sources we know that he was a jovial, popular figure. After officiating at a marriage

He then gave the bride a good hearty kiss, or rather smack, remarking that he always claimed that as his fee; took a drink of rum, drank health, prosperity and long life to those married, ate a cake or two, declined staying even for supper, said he must be on his way home, and should go to the foot of the lake that night, refused any other fee for his services, mounted his horse and was off. . . .[10]

There is little suggestion here of a man 'unbending'. Squire Cooper, for all his devoutly held Federalist doctrines, was an authentic man of the people. He knew them as no blue blood could, and knew by trial that they deserved his respect:

As to those western counties of New York, which I have been describing, they are chiefly peopled from the New England states,

---

[6] William Cooper, *A Guide in the Wilderness; or the History of the First Settlements in the Western Counties of New York with Useful Instructions to Future Settlers*, introduced by James Fenimore Cooper [II] (Rochester, N.Y., 1897), first published in Dublin, 1810.   [7] *Guide in the Wilderness*, p. 6.   [8] *ibid.*, p. 7.   [9] *ibid.*, p. 27.
[10] Quoted from Levi Beardsley, *Reminiscences* (New York, 1852), p. 51, by L. H. Butterfield in 'Judge William Cooper', *New York History*, vol. XXX, p. 396.

where the people are civil, well-informed, and very sagacious; so that a wise stranger would be much apter to conform at once to their usages than to begin by teaching them better.[11]

But he also knew how much he had done for them. If they were good settlers, he was a good proprietor who had saved them from famine, built them schools and churches, bullied the state legislators into making roads in the area. If they were good farmers, he was a good Judge; and William Cooper was a man who believed, with truly Platonic strictness, in the division of labour.[12] A benevolent paternalism, then, seemed reasonable and natural in Otsego County, so far as the Judge was concerned; and he proceeded, as soon as conditions permitted, to build a residence out of bricks, it being a more durable and, of course, less common material than wood. The imposing new Otsego Hall was ready for occupation in 1799, the year that Cooper was for the second time serving as U.S. Congressman. Although the days of the Federalist supremacy were drawing to a close, he had ten more years during which to consolidate his social, political, and economic position.

After the Republican victory in 1800, he determined to send his youngest son, who was then eleven years old, to a school in Albany. There, with the sons of Governor Jay and Lieutenant Governor Van Rensselaer as his school-mates, James might imbibe sound social and religious doctrines from the British clergyman Thomas Ellison. By this time, William Cooper had decided that Anglicanism, the religion of all good Federalists, was the religion for him and his children too. When John Jay determined to send his son William to Yale in 1803, William Cooper followed suit. Possibly the Judge hoped that James would, as his friend William Jay did, go on to study law: he might eventually become a great Federalist lawyer like Hamil-

---

[11] *Guide in the Wilderness*, p. 41.

[12] A strict division of labour was one of William Cooper's pet theories. In the *Guide* (pp. 14–16) he argues at length that each man should stick to his own trade. Town lots, he maintains, should be kept small, so that the blacksmith or grocer will not be tempted to grow his own vegetables; 'for if he be half tradesman and half farmer he will neither prosper as one nor as the other'. The same doctrine is advanced by Judge Temple in *The Pioneers*. James Cooper, as I shall point out later, possibly recognized a Platonic parallel; but Judge Cooper's source was probably Hamilton, who perceived that division of labour was a necessary precondition of the complex capitalist society which he hoped to create in America.

ton or John Jay. But James was too much his father's son to be
so easily bred into a cultivated Federalist gentleman: it was only
after his father's death in 1809 (from a blow inflicted by a
political opponent) and his own marriage into the Tory De
Lancey family in 1811, that he set out in earnest to become the
complete gentleman that William Cooper never was.

At no time in his life, least of all in his youth, could James
have been ashamed of his father. Men whom he idolized, such
as Governor Jay, welcomed him into their homes precisely
because he was William Cooper's son. He could and did take
filial pride in the Judge's pioneering achievements, as *The
Pioneers* amply demonstrates. And he could find no fault with a
father who, after his rustication from Yale, got him started successfully in his second (and probably much wished-for) career
as a naval officer; who bequeathed him an ample fortune; and
who left him a name with which the snobbish De Lanceys
were not unwilling to be allied. Perhaps the most impressive
testimony to the novelist's affection for his father appears in a
letter written when he was a middle-aged, disillusioned gentleman:

The bridges are pretty and high, and boats are passing almost without ceasing. Twenty certainly went by, in the half-hour I was on
them this evening. I have been up the ravine to the old Frey house.
It looks as it used to in many respects, and in many it is changed for
the worse. The mills still stand before the door, the house is, if
anything, as comfortable and far finer than formerly, but there is a
distillery added, with a hundred or two of as fat hogs, as one could
wish to see. I enjoyed this walk exceedingly. It recalled my noble
looking, warm-hearted, witty father, with his deep laugh, sweet
voice and fine rich eye, as he used to lighten the way, with his
anecdote and fun.[13]

In the same letter, he comments on the civility and intelligence
of the boatmen, and concludes that 'Every hour I stay at home,
convinces me more and more, that society has had a summerset,
and that the élite is at the bottom!' In spite of his own common
touch and informed respect for the people, Judge William could
never have been convinced of such a thing. Yet it was not the
case that, by 1834, James still revered his father as a man but
rejected what he stood for socially and politically. It was, rather,

[13] Letter to Mrs Cooper (12 June 1834), *Letters*, vol. III, p. 41.

that America had changed radically—a change registered concretely in the old Frey house, which once belonged to a close
friend of the elder Cooper. The old Republican simplicity—the
comfortable plain house with mills standing, not inappro-
priately, before the door—had given way to a vulgar concatena-
tion of distillery, a hundred or two fat hogs, and a far finer
house. With a characteristic perception of the symbolism implicit in everyday objects, Cooper records here the change from
Federalist to Whig values. In a mood which is at once nostalgic and Jacksonian, it is the frank, intelligent boatmen who
seem to Cooper closest in spirit to his 'noble looking, warm-
hearted, witty father'.[14]

Yet if the middle-aged novelist found it possible to reconcile
his own recently acquired Jacksonianism with the old-fashioned
Federalism of his dead father, his relationship with that father,
living or dead, must always have been a complex one. As we
have seen, William Cooper was an imperfect mixture of Federalist squire and man of the people; only in a pioneering context
did this mixture constitute genius or provide a satisfactory
model for his sons. Beloved and admired as he was, the Judge
could not have been a satisfactory model for his youngest son,
who was given the education as well as the wealth and social
position of a gentleman. Yet there can be little doubt that the
example of his father greatly influenced the development of
James Cooper's imagination. His social ideal, expounded in
novel after novel, was derived from the social ideal which led
William Cooper to build Otsego Hall for future generations of
Coopers. Unlike his father, James was never truly *of* the people
himself, but there can be little doubt that the Judge's example
and opinions helped him to shape the great proletarian heroes of
The Bravo, The Spy, and the Leatherstocking tales. In fact, the
imperfect mixture of Federalist squire and man of the people
was to be mirrored in his son's fiction and political philosophy
long after the master of Otsego Hall had bit the dust.

[14] For an excellent analysis of the extent to which Jacksonianism, and particularly Cooper's Jacksonianism, was a nostalgia for the old Republican simplicity,
see Marvin Meyers, *The Jacksonian Persuasion* (Vintage ed.: New York, 1960),
pp. 57–100 and *passim*.

2. THE JAY FAMILY

In *The Spy*, after witnessing the death of his father and after rejecting a proposal of marriage, the peddler Harvey Birch stands entirely alone in the world, bereft both of family and property. A lonely outcast figure striding along the ridges at night, he is free to carry out his heroic but secret and unappreciated mission on behalf of American freedom. In the valley below, gathered around their comfortable hearth, are the genteel members of the Wharton family. This stark antithesis between the upper-class family unit and the relationless lower-class hero, is to be found in most of Cooper's novels, though it is more explicit in some than in others. His upper-class heroes and heroines are, virtually by definition, members of some larger family group with a family history which it is their responsibility to carry on into the future. This is true, not merely of the world of Cooper's fiction, but of the world as we know it. But it is not always true in real life, as it almost always is in his novels, that a folk hero, a great man of the people, has no family whatever. The perfect symbolic background for such social isolation Cooper found, of course, in the timeless American wilderness; but the same wifeless, childless figure haunts most of Cooper's landscapes. Almost invariably, he is the character who arouses our interest and sympathy; with few exceptions, Cooper's genteel characters, with their tidy manners and fortunes, their conventional phrases and emotions, are a great bore.

Yet it is probably true that Cooper's imagination worked naturally in terms of major contrasts and that we should not have the great antitypes—Natty Bumppo, Harvey Birch, Old Antonio, Chainbearer, Moses Marble—if he had not believed passionately in his cultivated upper-class families. The trouble is not primarily that they are upper-class but that their chief representatives in most of his novels are their marriageable sons and daughters. The novel as Cooper practised it, a love/adventure story hamstrung by his own and his readers' sexual prudery, was no place to exhibit the virtues of old Governor Jay or his unadventurous but highly distinguished sons. Late in life, in *Afloat and Ashore* and the Littlepage trilogy, he did successfully portray families who, in a somewhat humble way, embodied his most cherished social values; never in his fiction did he draw a portrait of that great family of statesmen which seems to have exemplified, beyond all others, his American social and political ideal.

John Jay belonged to the third generation of Jays in America. His father and grandfather had been wealthy New York merchants who through their marriages allied themselves with the leading families in the Colony. After graduating from King's College (Columbia) in 1764, having studied under the distinguished Dr Samuel Johnson, he embarked upon a highly successful career in law. Ten years later, though conservative in his political as in his social views, he served as a delegate to the First Continental Congress in Philadelphia, where he wrote his *Address to the People of Great Britain*, a work which Thomas Jefferson called 'a production, certainly, of the finest pen in America'.[15] When Independence was declared, Jay became one of the civil leaders of the revolutionary regime in New York. In 1778 he returned to national affairs, acting successively as President of the Continental Congress, Minister to Spain, co-negotiator of the British-American Peace Treaty of 1783, Secretary for Foreign Affairs during the days of the Confederation, co-author of *The Federalist*, and first Chief Justice of U.S. Supreme Court. Though the treaty he negotiated with Britain in 1794 to settle territorial claims, known as the Jay Treaty, was exceedingly unpopular in America, Jay was—with the obvious exception of Washington—probably the most widely trusted man in American public life, and he was one of the small circle of men in whom Washington himself placed most trust. Along with that of his fellow Federalist John Adams, Jay's reputation has suffered from the neglect or vilification of liberal historians. But the facts of his career argue that his contemporaries were more just in their estimate of John Jay.[16]

The Cooper family was first closely associated with John Jay, not in his capacity as a national official, but in his capacity as a Federalist politician in New York state. William Cooper campaigned vigorously (and apparently unscrupulously) for Jay when he ran unsuccessfully for Governor in 1792. A few years

[15] Jefferson, *Autobiography*.
[16] My estimate of Jay as a man and statesman is based primarily on the accounts of Jay in Jabez Hammond's *History of Political Parties in New York* and Frank Monaghan's *John Jay: Defender of Liberty* (New York, 1935).

later, as a proven party stalwart and U.S. Congressman, William Cooper was a welcome visitor at the Governor's mansion, which Jay occupied from 1795 until his retirement from public office in 1801. It was many years later, after his father's death and Jay's retirement, that James Cooper became a frequent guest at the old Governor's home in Bedford, where his son William, Cooper's oldest friend, also lived. James probably resisted any temptation to measure his father against the elder Jay. Indeed, so different in character and personality were the two Federalist squires that no comparison was invited. In *Notions of the Americans* (1828) Cooper described the Jay family and the Governor himself in the following terms:

> I scarcely remember to have mingled with any family, where there was a more happy union of quiet decorum, and high courtesy, than I met beneath the roof of Mr Jay. The venerable statesman himself is distinguished, as much now, for his dignified simplicity, as he was, formerly, for his political sagacity, integrity, and firmness.[17]

In public life, unlike brawling bride-kissing William Cooper, Jay was noted for his Roman austerity and aloofness; only within his family circle, as a much-loving and much-beloved husband and father, did he resemble James's father. To most of us, no doubt, 'warm-hearted' William Cooper is the more attractive, because more spontaneous and vulnerable, human being. Yet if James chose John Jay rather than William Cooper as his model, it was not only because of Jay's 'dignified simplicity' and that 'happy union of quiet decorum, and high courtesy' which he met beneath Jay's roof. These things were important to Cooper, he believed they were valuable in their own right. But he placed a much higher premium on moral qualities, which, as a Christian and son of the frontier, he knew were not the exclusive property of the aristocracy. It was because Jay and, to a somewhat lesser degree, his sons, combined beautiful manners with moral greatness that, for Cooper, they became a kind of paradigm of what an American Gentleman and his family should be.

One of the last episodes in John Jay's political career may be taken to exemplify the whole—the whole, at least, as it appeared to Cooper and many of his contemporaries. In 1800 Jay

---

[17] *Notions of the Americans*, vol. 1, p. 88.

determined to retire from public life. He hoped that his guber-
natorial successor would be the Lieutenant Governor, Stephen
Van Rensselaer; but Rensselaer, like most other Federalist
candidates for state office, was defeated in the election of that
year. Far more momentous changes were threatened as a result
of the Republican victory in New York. For 1800 was a presidential election year; and New York's twelve Presidential Electors, chosen by the state legislature, could tip the scales either
way, in favour of Jefferson or in favour of a Federalist candidate.
Hamilton, Schuyler, and John Marshall quickly perceived that
by recalling the old, heavily Federalist Legislature, which still
had a legal existence, Governor Jay might gain for the Federalists just enough electoral votes to defeat Jefferson. Hamilton's
letter to Jay, urging this action, is a most revealing document:

> The moral certainty . . . is, that there will be an anti-federal
> majority in the ensuing legislature; and the very high probability is,
> that this will bring *Jefferson* into the chief magistracy, unless it be
> prevented by the measure which I shall now submit to your con-
> sideration, namely, the immediate calling together of the existing
> legislature.
>
> I am aware that there are weighty objections to the measure;
> but the reasons for it appear to me to outweigh the objections. And
> in times like these in which we live it will not do to be over-scrupu-
> lous. It is easy to sacrifice the substantial interests of society by a
> strict adherence to ordinary rules.
>
> In observing this I shall not be supposed to mean, that anything
> ought to be done which integrity will forbid; but merely that the
> scruples of delicacy and propriety, as relative to a common course
> of things, ought to yield to the extraordinary nature of the crisis.
> They ought not to hinder the taking of a legal and constitutional
> step to prevent an atheist in religion, and a fanatic in politics, from
> getting possession of the helm of state.[18]

In spite of its apparent equivocations, Hamilton's message was
nicely calculated to appeal to Jay's prejudices; Jay was a deeply
pious Christian; though no monarchist, he had been shocked by
the excesses of the French Revolution. Jay himself, in 1792, had
been deprived of office by Republican electoral chicanery. His
course was clear. On the back of Hamilton's letter he wrote a

[18] H. P. Johnston, ed., *The Correspondence and Public Papers of John Jay* (New
York, 1890–3), vol. IV, pp. 270–2. Hamilton's letter is dated 7 May, 1800.

terse note: 'Proposing a measure for party purposes, which I think it would not become me to adopt.' By this refusal to take an action which was legal and constitutional but unprincipled, Jay the great Federalist assured the victory of the Republicans. Many years later, when Federalism had passed into oblivion, this episode in Jay's career was remembered by the Jacksonian historian Hammond: 'In the history of man, amidst his follies, his vices, and his crimes, there are now and then green spots on which the mind delights to dwell, and this is one of them.' [19]

This exchange between Hamilton and Jay, which Cooper may have known about as a young man, anticipates with uncanny accuracy the many exchanges between the Whigs and James Fenimore Cooper during the 1830's and 1840's. Though he became a Jacksonian, he never deserted his class; his case against the Whigs was that, in order not 'to sacrifice the substantial interests of society', they deserted the high Federalist principles of their class. Cooper's political morality was that of Jay, the Whigs' that of Hamilton.

After his marriage, James may be said to have become virtually a protégé of the Jays, even when he lived at a considerable distance from them. Jay and his sons, as public-spirited gentlemen, were active supporters of the Westchester County Bible Society and Agricultural Society. Cooper, in Otsego County, helped found a local Agricultural Society and gave strong support to the Otsego Bible Society. John Jay was the first Vice-President of the American Bible Society which Cooper helped to found in 1816. When the Coopers settled in Westchester County in 1817, James transferred his memberships and became even more closely associated with the Jays. It must have been during this period that the Governor told Cooper the story which was to form the basis of his second novel, *The Spy*. And it was to John Jay and his family that he read the manuscript of his first novel, *Precaution*, before seeking a publisher. Their approval (of the moralizing, probably, rather than the story-telling) was decisive. William Jay he considered the ideal critic of his work:

I read the book to him and to Mr Aitchison—the latter the best scholar and critic—both *flattered* me I suppose of *course*—but Mr Jay the most—not that he *said* more than *the other*—but *what* he *said*

[19] Hammond, *History of Political Parties*, vol. I, pp. 145–6.

was more to my *taste*—he *understood me*—one is a christian and the other a Deist——[20]

Cooper's first active participation in politics took place during the state elections of 1820. By this time Federalism had been shattered as an effective political force, partly because of the gathering strength of democratic sentiment throughout the country and partly because of the equivocal patriotism which many leading Federalists had shown during the War of 1812. Veterans like John Jay, his elder son Peter Augustus Jay, James Kent, the Rensselaers, and other old friends of Cooper refused to join the party of Jefferson—at most they would call themselves 'Independent Republicans'—but they were willing to join forces with the Republican party faction led in New York by DeWitt Clinton. Clinton, though a Republican whose family had long and often successfully opposed the Jays in state politics, was himself a patrician figure with scholarly leanings and moderate social views, whose great achievement was, ironically, to make a reality of the old Federalist dream of a canal connecting New York City with the Great Lakes. Judge William Cooper had advocated such a canal, and now his son came to the defence of the man who had staked his political career on the building of it. William Jay joined Cooper in his electioneering activities when the latter became Secretary of the Westchester County Clintonian Republicans.[21] That Cooper was then no apostate from the Federalist ideal is demonstrated by the fact that during the State Constitutional Convention of 1821, which greatly liberalized voting rights, he sympathized with the reactionary forces led by Chancellor Kent, Stephen Van Rensselaer, and Peter Augustus Jay.[22] Clearly, in 1820–1 Cooper was on the brink of a political career which, given his energy and ability and the patronage of Clinton and the Jays, might well have been a brilliant one. But he was also on the brink of a career as a professional writer, which, with the sensational success of *The Spy*, led him away from active politics, and established his full independence.

[20] Letter to Andrew Thompson Goodrich (19 or 20 Oct. 1820), *Letters*, vol. I, p. 66.

[21] Cf. Letter to Peter Gansevoort (19 April 1820), *Letters*, vol. I, p. 41: 'I find now I dabble in politics—it is a pleasant thing to find your old Friends on the same side with you—Jay and myself keep together . . .'

[22] Cf. Letter to John Jay (6 Sept. 1821), *Letters*, vol. I, pp. 70–1.

Cooper remained closely associated with the Jay family to the end of his life, though he came in time to disagree with some of their social and political views. Peter Augustus Jay remained staunchly Federalist, long after Federalism had become politically irrelevant and after Cooper had become a supporter of Jackson. William Jay, following in his father's footsteps, became a leading figure in the national Abolitionist movement—a movement which, on political grounds, Cooper viewed with uneasiness. But the Coopers and Jays remained exceptionally close and warm friends. In Cooper's mind, old John Jay was never supplanted as the ideal American gentleman. Washington and, later, Jefferson, he regarded as greater men; but he had not known them personally—and they were, in any case, Virginians. When in such late novels as *Satanstoe* and *Afloat and Ashore* Cooper tried to record and thus to recover a vanished ideal America, he wrote many a passage which recalls this description by William Jay of his father's farm at Bedford:

He disclaimed all intention of converting his farm into what is usually termed 'a seat', regarding expensive rural decorations as inconsistent with the state of American society and fortunes, and too often leading to the alienation of the estate itself. His buildings etc. were therefore constructed with simplicity, and with direct reference to the uses for which they were intended; but no cost was spared in procuring the best materials, and in putting them together in the most durable manner. A friend . . . remarked . . . that Governor Jay, in all his conduct, seemed to have reference to perpetuity in this world and eternity in the next.[23]

3. THE DE LANCEYS

It would be a mistake to suppose that William Cooper's son had an easy passage to gentility. Though James's mother and sisters maintained as best they could an atmosphere of refinement in the Cooper household, the Cooperstown of his infancy was still a raw settlement not essentially unlike the Templeton of *The Pioneers*. And though his education in Albany and at Yale was in some respects a good one—he was a sound Latinist and keen student of chemistry—he was a boisterous youth whose love of pranks eventually got him expelled from college. Neither was

[23] William Jay, *The Life of John Jay* (New York, 1833), vol. I, p.442.

there anything refining about his brief though immensely rewarding experiences, first, as a sailor before the mast during his seventeenth year, and then during his nineteenth year, as a U.S. Navy midshipman stationed at Fort Oswego, a wilderness outpost on the Great Lakes. It was his cruise aboard the *Stirling* that taught him his seamanship and gave him an intimate knowledge of the sea itself; it was on Lake Ontario that, by his own account, he received his first impressions of a truly 'new country'.[24] It was also as a midshipman, first at Oswego and then in New York, that he seems to have developed that acute sense of moral responsibility which was to be so characteristic of him and his writings. His letters of this period suggest that he saw himself as a frank and manly, rather than elegant and learned, gentleman. Describing his courtship of Susan De Lancey to his elder brother, he wrote, 'I loved her like a man and told her of it like a sailor'. [25] But his marriage to her put an end to his naval career.

If the Coopers were upstarts and the Jays were more than respectable, the De Lanceys had been one of the great families of New York. They were allied through marriage with the Schuylers, Heathcotes, and Van Cortlandts; and during the colonial period they had been leaders of the faction favouring the King. When the War of Independence came, they remained loyal, fought against the Continentals, and finally lost most of their property. Susan's Harrow-educated father was one of the Tories who, in time, returned to America and lent his political support to the Federalists. Though reduced in fortune, John Peter De Lancey was still a very affluent gentleman farmer; and, in a state which had changed its political but not its social structure, the De Lancey name was still a great one. When he married Susan Augusta De Lancey of Heathcote Hall, James Cooper of Otsego Hall was making a very good marriage indeed.

And it was a good marriage. Cooper and his bride were both simple souls whose love was to remain warm and true over a period of forty years. His family life was always serene, graceful, rich in fun, loyalty, and shared interests: well that it was, since he spent the last twenty years of his life at war with most other

---

[24] Letter to Horatio Hastings Weld, for the Brother Jonathan (22–25? March 1842), *Letters*, vol. IV, p. 259.

[25] Letter to Richard Fenimore Cooper (18 May 1810), *Letters*, vol. I, p. 17.

people. It remains true, however, that Cooper paid a high price for this happiness. Both because he loved and admired her and because she was a De Lancey, he *had* to maintain and even improve his social and economic position. This became a serious problem when it turned out that William Cooper's estate was heavily encumbered and that only his cash bequests were ever likely to reach his heirs. James was deeply in debt when he achieved his first great success as a writer. And profitable as fiction-writing proved to be, at first, it was only by steady, unrevising labour that he was able to support his large and expensive family. As for Mrs Cooper herself, she seems to have been a singularly amiable and unpretentious woman, whose attachments were to people rather than to ideas or things. If we are to judge from her husband's letters to her, she was fond of scandal and interested in all his interests. At the same time, she was the loyal daughter of a pious Anglophile family whose ideas about female decorum were simple and strict. With a family of four daughters in 1820, she and her thirty-year-old husband had much virtue and little fortune in their charge.

They must have read with solemn approval, even if with deep boredom, the British women novelists then in vogue, whose works they would have purchased themselves or borrowed from Heathcote Hall. A former naval officer and now an officer in the state militia, Cooper was an open patriot and secret dreamer of adventure; and we may be sure that he himself preferred to read Scott, Shakespeare, or Southey. But he was a proud and sensitive man, made more so on account of his high connexions and declining fortune; he was also a man with a somewhat reckless and uncouth boyhood to live down. Accordingly, for his first effort in fiction he chose what, given his talents, was the worst possible model—the English novel of domestic manners. Yet it was the safest model he could find. It is true that he knew but little about English society from personal observation, but he knew a great deal by report and reading. And in any case, his subject was not English society as such, but manners and morals common to the upper classes on both sides of the Atlantic. His topic: the education and marriage of young ladies. His tone: elevated. He could scarcely fail to win approval as a moralist and sound *pater familias*, even if he won no fame for genius or taste.

Precaution is such a self-conscious, synthetic book that it is less a novel than a commentary on novels and their readers. Often the commentary is disconcertingly direct. The heroine, Emily Mosely, rarely reads a book 'unless in search of information'. Her sister Jane, however, practises 'unlicensed and indiscriminate reading'. Emily's virtuous suitor reads aloud to her 'Campbell's beautiful description of wedded love, in *Gertrude of Wyoming*'. 'His ideas were as pure, as chastened, and almost as vivid, as those of the poet . . . The poem had been first read to her by her brother, and she was surprised to discover how she had overlooked its beauties on that occasion.' On the other hand, Jane's beau, who later jilts her, favours Thomas Moore. She too 'had often devoured [Moore's] treacherous lines with ardor . . .'; for 'poetry was the food she lived on, and in works of the imagination she found her greatest delight'. Even *Precaution* itself comes under suspicion:

Books are, in a great measure, the instruments of controlling the opinions of a nation like ours. They are an engine, alike powerful to save or to destroy. It cannot be denied, that our libraries contain as many volumes of the latter, as of the former description; for we rank among the latter that long catalogue of idle productions, which, if they produce no other evil, lead to the misspending of time, *our own* perhaps included.

These passages tell us not a little about Cooper's attitude to fiction and about the society for which he wrote. He is not at all sure that fiction is respectable or that, in itself, it deserves to be taken seriously; but he knows that it must be taken seriously simply because ingenuous young Janes and Emilys will read it. Moreover, they are likely to read it aloud in the presence of even younger Janes and Emilys. At times, indeed, *Precaution* seems to have been inspired, not so much by reading of contemporary English novels of manners, as by a reading of solemn cautionary reviews of them in the *Edinburgh* or *Quarterly*. Though he was to become less self-conscious about the act of writing a novel and more certain of its value, Cooper, the father of four daughters, never lost sight of his impressionable audience.

There is another respect in which *Precaution* reveals Cooper as an uneasy yet probably already addicted author. So far as *Precaution* has any novelistic interest, it depends on the deceptions practised variously by suitors, mothers, and eligible young women on each other and themselves. As Professor Ringe has pointed out, the central theme of the novel is the conflict of appearance and reality—a theme of great importance to Cooper's subsequent fiction.[26] But to say so is perhaps to imply too much about the seriousness of Cooper's intentions when he wrote *Precaution*. The main deception in the novel amounts to no more than an incognito: this creates the mystery, misunderstandings, and suspense which, however feebly, keep the book alive. Cooper himself patently enjoys the fiction that Emily's lover, who is really the gallant and fabulously wealthy Earl of Pendennyss, is plain poor Mr Denbigh. The deception lends a glamour to lives which are otherwise dull indeed. Yet as a moralist Cooper could not approve of deception in any form, and he is obliged to punish Pendennyss-Denbigh before permitting him to marry fair truth-loving Emily. Of course fiction itself is an art of deception: one wonders whether Cooper ever felt entirely easy about the moral and metaphysical status of his art.

[26] Donald A. Ringe, *James Fenimore Cooper* (New Haven, 1962), pp. 24-5.

II

AN AMERICAN SCOTT: IMITATION AS EXPLORATION AND CRITICISM

I. THE EARLY WAVERLEY NOVELS

AMONG THE MANY ANNOYANCES which Cooper had to put up with during the last two decades of his career, one that nettled him most was the title admiring critics had bestowed upon him after the publication of *The Spy* and *The Pioneers*: to the nineteenth-century reading public he was 'the American Scott'. Writing to Samuel F. B. Morse in 1832, he comments on his most recent novels—

> The 'Heidenmauer' is not equal to the 'Bravo', but it is a good book and better than two thirds of Scott's. They may say it is like his if they please; they have said so of every book I have written, even the 'Pilot'!
>
> But the 'Heidenmauer' is like, and was intended to be like, in order to show how differently a democrat and an aristocrat saw the same thing.[1]

But Cooper himself was an aristocrat, or as nearly one as a patriotic American could well be, when in 1820 he began to work on *The Spy*. Scott's nostalgic Toryism, tempered by a healthy respect for the mercantile classes, no doubt appealed to the young friend of Stephen Van Rensselaer, Chancellor Kent, and Peter Augustus Jay. What made it more appealing, Scott's Toryism was also tempered by a generous humanity: his Jeanie Deans and Rob Roy are as sympathetically drawn as any of

---

[1] Letter to Samuel F. B. Morse (19 Aug. 1832), *Letters*, vol. II, p. 310.

Cooper's lower-class heroes. But whatever the shade of his politics, Scott was an irresistible model because he was, at the same time, a major figure in the English literary tradition—with his roots in Shakespeare—and a highly successful spokesman for a quite different national culture. Unlike Scott, who was saturated in German literature, Cooper's literary culture was narrowly classical and English, as was the case with most Federalist gentlemen. Therefore, had Scott and his Anglo-Irish predecessor Maria Edgeworth never written, Cooper would have lacked any readily available models and the American novel might not have been born until much later.

To call Cooper the 'American Scott', then, is to acknowledge a major debt on the part of one English-speaking provincial culture to another. It is true, as Lounsbury once wisely observed, that 'to call Cooper the American Scott in the days of his popularity, and in derision in the days of his unpopularity, was a method of criticism which enabled men to prize or undervalue without taking the trouble to think'.[2] It is true, and yet the greater danger, as in Lounsbury's own case when he dismisses the title, is that men will not take the trouble to think at all about the nature of Cooper's indebtedness to Scott.[3] If we are to understand Cooper and appreciate his originality, we must surely make some effort to understand and appreciate Scott. For this reason, much of this chapter is devoted to a discussion of the Waverley Novels, though in fairness to Scott I should add that I do not pretend to give a full account of his novelistic strengths and weaknesses. My end is to make Cooper's achievement more intelligible; an analysis of Scott's early novels is one of my means.

Scott was a well-established writer of verse narratives when, anonymously, he published his first novel, *Waverley*, in 1814.

---

[2] Thomas R. Lounsbury, *James Fenimore Cooper* (Boston, 1882), p. 59.

[3] Notable exceptions are Donald Davie, *The Heyday of Sir Walter Scott* (London, 1961), and Leslie Fiedler, *Love and Death in the American Novel* (New York, 1960). Mr Fiedler's discussion of the Scott–Cooper relationship is bold, often original—and misleading, because of his concentration on two of the worst, though most popular, works by these authors. To Mr Davie's discussion of Scott and Cooper I am deeply indebted; and I share his debt to David Daiches' discussion of Scott in *Literary Essays* (Edinburgh, 1956), pp. 88–121, and to Georg Lukacs' in *The Historical Novel* (London, 1962, originally written in German in 1936–7). In spite of some factual errors and, I believe, mistaken judgments of particular books, Lukacs is easily the most profound of Scott's critics.

Whatever we may think of the intrinsic merits of the novel, there can be no doubt that its publication was a literary event of the first magnitude. Unlike *Precaution, Waverley* was a finished work of art which, however, embodied major formal innovations—innovations which were to make Scott the master of Cooper and (to name no others) Pushkin and Manzoni.

The main action of *Waverley* begins on the eve of the Jacobite rebellion of 1745 and ends shortly after the rebel leaders are tried and executed. Edward Waverley, the hero of the novel, is a youth whose English Tory upbringing and childhood addiction to Froissart and romantic fiction make him peculiarly susceptible to the charms of the Stuart cause—in spite of the fact that he holds a commission in the Hanoverian army and that his father is a Whig minister. Rather a guileless dreamer than a political adventurer or single-handed man of action, Waverley, though never ridiculous, is more like Candide than like one of Froissart's knights. He is therefore one whom the Jacobites will readily win over with tokens of friendship and trust but whom the Hanoverians will later regard indulgently. In fact he is utterly unpolitical at heart, and that is why he is the ideal observer of the two great political forces of the day. This is not to say that Waverley is merely an observer or merely a character over whose neutral shoulder Scott's reader can view the colourful figures of Fergus Mac-Ivor or Bonny Prince Charlie. On the contrary, Waverley's non-political human presence forces the opposed parties to present themselves and their causes in a moderate, sweetly humane light—a light which their actions often enough prove false or only half-true. Edward Waverley is ideally suited (so far as Scott's novel is concerned) to the requirements of this particular historical situation. A different historical situation might, novelistically speaking, require a different sort of hero.

Therefore it would be true to say that what really matters in *Waverley* is not the adventures of Waverley himself but the confrontation of two great socio-political forces, the issue of which is a society quite different in outlook from that which produced the confrontation. Although it is sometimes said that Scott's reason sided with the Hanoverian regime while his emotions sided with the Jacobite cause, this formula does little justice to his artistry and historical awareness. Very roughly speaking, what Scott did in *Waverley* was to show how a comparatively bad cause could win the support of greatly talented and honourable men while a comparatively good cause often depended on the support of selfish, mainly vulgar interests. But even this formula betrays the richness and complexity of Scott's presentation of the two sides. On the one hand, there is the Highland society of the Mac-Ivors, which combines the primitive Gaelic traits of fidelity and personal courage with the civilized Latin qualities of cultural refinement, courtly ambition and duplicity, and Roman Catholic faith. Against this is the Anglo-Teutonic league, chiefly Protestant and mercantile in spirit, but standing for stability, prudence, and—above all—tolerance: tolerance is the great Hanoverian virtue and weapon. It is when a confrontation of this kind occurs in his fiction that Scott is at his best—the polar structure is the essential thing, the relation of the hero to these poles may vary considerably.

Scott himself seems not to have appreciated, at first, how greatly the shape and power of his historical romances depended on his polar structure. In his second novel, *Guy Mannering*, there is indeed a conflict between the Old and New (very much after the fashion of Maria Edgeworth's *Castle Rackrent*, yet lacking its brevity and poignancy); but the New, as represented by the treacherous Lawyer Glossin who gains the ancient Ellangowan estate as a result of the improvidence of its lairds, is too contemptible in everybody's eyes and too generally connived against to be taken seriously as a representative of any powerful social force. Clearly, there can be no question of a 'wavering' hero in this case, because only a complete fool could be taken in by Glossin. On the other hand, Scott does employ one of the procedures of *Waverley* (and Miss Edgeworth's *The Absentee*) by having his hero visit Scotland for the first time and take due notice of the local customs and scenery: it is a good device, but Scott ruins it by having *two*, quite independent, first-time visitors in this novel—presumably on the grounds that two of a good thing must be better than one.

The Antiquary is a much better novel than *Guy Mannering*, containing as it does two of Scott's more memorable characters— Edie Ochiltree and the Antiquary himself. In certain respects, indeed, the old beggar Edie is a prototype of Natty Bumppo: a vigorous old man full of courage and resourcefulness, he is curiously like Cooper's hunter in that his way of life is free of the normal constraints of society, from which he has deliberately opted out. It is for this reason that his imprisonment (like Natty's in *The Pioneers*) is so touching. However, it would be unwise to press this resemblance too far; for there is an element of rascality in Edie's character which is completely alien to that of Cooper's hero. So far as the novel as a whole is concerned, it is, as its title implies, not primarily a book about the past but about the pastness of the past. Here the old parties are neatly represented by a Whiggish Presbyterian laird, a Tory nonjuring baronet, and a Roman Catholic count; but their differences, though sometimes vehement and socially painful, are so academic that they assist each other financially and join together when there is a threat of invasion by the French revolutionaries. Their military commander, the hero of the novel, turns out to be the virtual adopted son of the laird, the prospective son-in-law of the baronet, and the lost heir of the count. *The Antiquary* is rather less schematic in design and pat in conclusion than this brief analysis suggests; but Scott's criticism of life in this novel, as in *Guy Mannering*, is superficial and complacent, on the whole. His social attitudes are insular in a quite literal sense; for the villain of this piece, whose machinations threaten to bankrupt the baronet, is a wicked foreigner vaguely connected with the political enemies of Britain.

Of course such weaknesses are mainly to be attributed to the fact that, as the *Antiquary* 'refers to the last ten years of the eighteenth century', Scott is personally less detached and politically less free in his views than he was when he wrote about the events of '45. Actually, his picture of the Scottish aristocrats of that period is sufficiently damning: feeble-minded and self-indulgent, they seem so decadent that only the threat of invasion could keep them in power. But Scott intended no such subversive criticism when he wrote *The Antiquary*; exactly the contrary. Nor did his Hanoverian myth leave any room for a polar structure in this novel: indeed, had his political preconceptions permitted him to begin to reveal the opposition to the *status quo*, however half-heartedly, the resulting structure of the novel might well have driven him to think more clearly and honestly about his subject. (It is also true, as eighteenth-century couplet-writers sometimes show, that antithetical forms can over-simplify or otherwise falsify the writer's materials, of whatever sort; but I suspect that, at least as often, such forms are an aid to perception, especially in revolutionary era.) However, though we must deplore Scott's complacency in this novel, it is well to bear in mind the point made by Lukacs—Scott's satisfaction with the present helped make him intelligently critical of the past.[4]

In his next major work Scott turned back to the period preceding the Glorious Revolution. The world depicted in *Old Mortality* is altogether less rich, complex, and human than that in *Waverley*. Dominated on the one hand by fanatical Scottish Covenanters, made desperate by royal persecution and an obsessive sense of betrayal, and on the other by scarcely less fanatical Stuart loyalists, it is a world which has no use for the normal desires and occupations of humankind. Though driven temporarily to take the side of the Covenanters, the hero, Henry Morton, finds both sides about equally repugnant: in other words, repulsion rather than, as in *Waverley*, attraction, is the force characterizing the hero's relations with the two poles. Unlike Edward Waverley, Morton is not an especially romantic youth: unpampered, capable, and prudent, he would rather get married and stay out of trouble. Contrasting starkly with him and each other are the old homicide Balfour of Burley, leader of the Covenant forces, and the ruthless Cavalier Claverhouse, who combines Gestapo methods with a naive delight in Waverley's favourite Froissart. In practice, both Claverhouse and Burley operate on the principle that the end justifies the means—any means: it is therefore ironic and appropriate that at the end of the novel, the Glorious Revolution having placed uncovenanted William on the throne, they make a pact. Against them, under William, is Henry Morton.

When the change of polarization comes at the end of *Old Mortality*, it is as formally satisfying as it is politically convincing. Clearly, it was Scott's design to show how ideological extremists, though poles apart at first, must eventually discover that they have more in common with each other than with the rest of mankind—so that a new alignment of forces becomes inevitable. Now a realignment of this kind does not occur in *Waverley*: what happens is that the Scottish Jacobites are unambiguously

[4] Lukacs, *The Historical Novel*, pp. 32-3.

routed and the neutrality of the English Tories (Edward Waverley's party) is confirmed; in a way, the novel is not about an historical action but about an *éclaircissement* of history. To steer between the extremes in this situation is, in effect, to opt out of history: Waverley, as suits his character, retires from public life to the harmlessly anachronistic dreamworld of Waverley Honour. Precisely the opposite is true in *Old Mortality*. By steering between the extremes of Cavalier and Covenanter, Henry Morton finds himself a leader of the governing party and a maker of history.

It is a great pity that Morton is never convincing in this role. Merely by caring for human life and reckoning himself fallible, he is an adequate foil to those ruthless embodiments of secular and spiritual pride, Claverhouse and Burley; but his supposedly great talents are never demonstrated in action, as those of his opponents so memorably are. It is a great pity, because the first thirty-five chapters of *Old Mortality* are perhaps the finest Scott ever wrote. In language, characterization, and general design they probably surpass any section of comparable length in Cooper's fiction. Indeed, had Scott maintained this level of quality to the end, *Old Mortality* would have been one of the greatest novels in the language

In spite of their various defects, however, *Waverley* and *Old Mortality* are clearly novels of a major order, whereas *Guy Mannering*, *The Antiquary*, and Scott's next novel, *Rob Roy*, are not. The failure of *Rob Roy* is the more interesting because in certain obvious ways it represents an effort to develop some of the themes and methods of the two major novels. Perhaps the nature of the failure can be best approached by briefly considering what, on the evidence of *Waverley* and *Old Mortality*, is required for success in an historical novel. They are historical novels of a particular kind: that is, they are primarily concerned with the nationally significant effects of cultural differences and cultural change. Not that Scott neglects the individual human being or underestimates his importance: Balfour of Burley, for example, is as vividly individual a character as one could wish for. But it is true that Scott views such individuals as an able historian would—that is, as they represent cultural differences or as they are the agents and victims of cultural change. Moreover, though literature is ultimately concerned with what is permanent in the changing human condition, the historical novelist can afford to concern himself only with those human traits which are especially expressed or revealed by the particular historical situation he has chosen to depict. Such strict subordination is necessary because Scott's materials are so ample, complex, and shifting. Somehow he must give a faithful, or at least plausible, picture of them and yet also keep his narrative free of clogging detail. His task is formidable; it would be impossible except that during times of cultural crisis and confrontation certain leading features are likely to emerge and thus, in some measure, simplify and shape his materials for him. Essentially, then, the art of the historical novelist is an art of discovery, strict subordination, and presentation.

Such, at any rate, seem the lessons to be drawn from *Old Mortality* and *Waverley*. Scott's literary powers and weaknesses being what they were, I have no doubt that he was at his best as a novelist when his historical interests were most deeply engaged—mainly because then his concern for the true and full significance of a particular national development drove him to be relevant and to make each part subordinate to the whole. *Rob Roy* is an historical novel in which Scott's historical interests appear not to have been fully engaged.

The hero of *Rob Roy* is Frank Osbaldistone, a youth who is superficially like Edward Waverley. Though unshakeably Protestant and Whiggish, Frank is a 'literary type' who openly rebels against his father's plan to bring him into the family business. In fact, Frank's literary interests have made him fastidious rather than romantic: he cannot abide Trade and, when he is rusticated to his uncle's home in the North, he cannot abide the hunting-and-drinking life of a country gentleman. Of course he is responsive to Highland scenery and the romantic presence of Robin Hood Rob Roy: but unlike those of Henry Morton or Edward Waverley, Frank's treasonable impulses only appear to take a political form; if he is a friendly observer of the Jacobites, he is friendly for strictly personal reasons. Neither is he a suitable representative of any politically important social group of that period. Yet on the surface anyway *Rob Roy* is a novel concerned with the Jacobite rising of 1715 and with the cultural differences to which that rising gave political expression. But when we look more closely at rebellious

Frank and Di Vernon, the heroine who is a model of submission to parental authority, and at the various attitudes to various laws exemplified in *Rob Roy*, we may begin to wonder whether this novel is not an essay on Obedience superimposed on an historical subject. It is true of course that the 1715 rising is itself a major example of disobedience or, from a Jacobite point of view, of obedience; but so are all such risings. Perhaps Scott might have written a good novel (though not a good historical novel) if he had been willing to forgo some of the permissible indulgences, or indeed responsibilities, of the historical novelist —such as giving a lengthy account of the emergence of Glasgow as a commercial centre after the Union, or describing the strange customs of a Highland inn. But there is no reason to believe that Scott quite knew what he was doing when he wrote *Rob Roy*: its focus is uncertain, it is full of extraneous characters, and—surest sign of all that Scott was not interested in his ostensible subject—it has a diabolical villain in Rashleigh Osbaldistone whose absurd Machiavellian intrigues are given more prominence than the actual social conditions which precipitated the rising.

Of all Scott's novels, *The Heart of Mid-Lothian* is perhaps the one which least lends itself to brief critical treatment. For the purposes of the present discussion, it seems wisest to direct attention only to Scott's attempt in *The Heart of Mid-Lothian* to create yet another variant of the *Waverley* archetype. From this point of view, the most striking thing about the novel is that its central action, Jeanie Deans's journey to London, exactly reverses Scott's usual procedure (common to all the novels so far written, except *Old Mortality*) whereby an English or Anglicized gentleman travels north without great peril or fatigue to the Scottish border. In this novel a Scottish lower-class woman walks all the way from Edinburgh to London—an action which, in her case, is almost heroic. She is forced to do so because, in *The Heart of Mid-Lothian*, Scott's normally passive hero is reduced to such a state of nervous and physical debility that he is unable to act at all. So feeble indeed is Reuben Butler and yet so like the physically active Waverley, Morton, or Osbaldistone, that one cannot forbear remarking that something feminine in Scott's temperament made him sympathize with essentially weak male protagonists whom the more masculine Cooper

would not have been able to stomach. Reuben Butler's feeble-
ness gives Scott's heroine scope for action; Cooper, to give his
heroines any such scope, had to remove hero and heroine away
from any civilized community, so that the male could be made
captive. However, it would be misleading to suggest that Butler
is not an extreme case of passivity even among Scott's heroes,
since normally they must be physically active and courageous
to be successful as observers of opposed socio-political factions.
In *The Heart of Mid-Lothian* (in spite of the brilliant documentary account of the Porteous riots) Scott was less interested
in creating an historical novel like *Waverley* or *Old Mortality* than
he was in drawing a sympathetic portrait of the Scottish nation.
The function of the feeble hero is to throw the courageous
heroine on the mercy of the community of Scotsmen, thus
enabling them to demonstrate their generosity and solidarity as
they help her on her way. In this patriotic, as distinct from
historical, novel, Scott was again exploring the novelistic
possibilities of the *Waverley* model. Such exploration, in this
novel as in *Old Mortality*, is a form of 'imitation': of course Scott
imitates himself thoughtlessly in other novels, such as *Rob Roy*,
but in his best novels he is himself doing what Cooper or Pushkin
or Manzoni were to do. And great as *The Pioneers*, *The Captain's
Daughter*, or *I Promessi Sposi* undoubtedly are, we may be pardoned if, when we are reading *Old Mortality* or *The Bride of Lammermoor*, we sometimes feel that Scott was his own best imitator.

Another example of this kind of imitation is *The Legend of
Montrose*, a distinctly minor work whose only claim on the
general reader's attention is its principal character, the Falstaffian soldier of fortune Captain Dugald Dalgetty. As a soldier
without political or religious scruples seeking employment in
the civil wars of 1644, Dalgetty might seem an ideal candidate
for the role filled in previous novels by Edward Waverley or
Henry Morton; and doubtless Scott's original plan was to make
him just that. Unfortunately, Dalgetty came to interest Scott
much more than the conflict between the Royalists and the
Parliamentarians—with the result that *The Legend of Montrose*,
though perhaps interesting as a lively essay on Fidelity *vs.*
Ambition, has no interest as an historical novel. However, the
companion-piece of this novel, *The Bride of Lammermoor*, is richly
and intelligently historical.

If *Rob Roy* seems to be a confused rehash of *Waverley*, *The Bride* is in many respects a brilliant refashioning of *Guy Mannering*—which is to say, it is a lineal descendant of Miss Edgeworth's *Castle Rackrent*. Yet at the same time it contains what is certainly Scott's most psychologically profound study of the wavering hero. There are in fact three wavering figures at the centre of *The Bride*, all of whom are destroyed because of the inflexibility of a fourth character. The hero Edgar Ravenswood, dispossessed of his ancestral estate and title by a combination of chicanery and ancestral improvidence, is torn between an obligation to revenge his loss (to act fully in the spirit of his ancestors) and an obligation to accept and even forgive (to act in the law-abiding Christian spirit of the present—immediately post-Union—period). This state of indecision is the more painful because Edgar is by nature a straightforward man of action, simple but strict in his loyalties and affections. Yet this problem might have been resolved somehow had he not fallen in love with the daughter of the usurper. Lucy Ashton is the most interesting of Scott's heroines. By nature she is 'ductile', which means that while she is timid and had far better follow the advice of the song she sings—

> Stop thine ear against the singer,—
> From the red gold keep thy finger,—
> Vacant heart, and hand, and eye,—
> Easy live and quiet die

—she like Edward Waverley, has been early and deeply impressed by the romances she has read, and so is fatally attracted to the lonely, sternly aristocratic figure of Edgar Ravenswood. It is poignantly and ironically true that this daughter of a commercial-political knight of the new order should be in love with the literary chivalric ideal—and then disintegrate when she is put to the test by Edgar and Lady Ashton, two actual survivors from the harsh heroic past. Sir William Ashton, a suave and not wholly unsympathetic version of Lawyer Glossin, is a trimmer of Edinburgh Presbyterian merchant stock who has risen high in the government but has only recently, at the expense of the Jacobitical Ravenswood family, acquired the estate and title commensurate with his wealth and political importance. A man with brains but no character, with genuine affections but no

30

courage, Sir William (for intricate personal, political, and legal reasons) countenances the courtship of Lucy and Edgar without quite admitting to himself or others that this is what he is doing. By a major stroke of irony, the person who prevents this marriage between the Old and New is Sir William's imperious wife, a Douglas whose own unequal marriage has intensified her aristocratic family pride to the point of insanity. In character she is a throw-back to the feudal days when Douglasses and Ravenswoods used Ashtons for footstools—but as she is married to Sir William, she is determined to make upstart Ashton a name to be feared and respected, and, far more vehemently than Sir William does, she is obliged to condemn the religious and political principles of those Scottish nobles who have remained loyal to their ancient Stuart lords. She therefore has reason to despise Edgar and to hate him, too, as one who must know as well as she does how inferior Sir William is. Lucy she regards (with true feudal feeling) as a mere means to the end she has in view, that of making the Ashtons the Douglasses of the non-feudal age.

Unlike *Waverley* and *Old Mortality* and even *The Heart of Mid-Lothian*, *The Bride* is a novel in which the major political events happen off-stage: such events may affect the lives of millions, but in this novel we are concerned only with their effect on the members of two families. But in spite of this narrowing of focus, *The Bride* is still a great historical novel because of the way it registers the shattering psychological effects of cultural confrontation and change; it is a psychological novel in which remarkably little is left to the accidents of personality. What Scott inherited as a story of personal tragedy, he turned into a story of cultural tragedy as well.

Thus the root and trunk of the novel are perfectly sound. But it has rotten appendages, especially in Edgar's old family servant Caleb Balderstone, who is one of the most infuriating 'humours' in Scott's or anybody's fiction. The heavily contrived 'supernatural' element in *The Bride* was generally admired by Scott's contemporaries, and it is at least tolerable today. But a novel so narrowly focused as this one cannot absorb, as *Waverley* or *Old Mortality* could, elements which are thematically relevant but only loosely connected with the main action. Consequently *The Bride* seems more cluttered than any other of Scott's great novels, though its central action is, from start to finish, the most perfect.

The Bride of Lammermoor and *The Legend of Montrose*, both completed in 1819, mark the close of Scott's great creative period as a novelist. A year later Cooper wrote his first novel and then his first imitation of Scott; and although it is known that Cooper was affected by some of Scott's subsequent works (especially *The Pirate*), there is every reason to believe that Scott's decisive influence was made through these earlier novels—before, that is, Cooper's political views diverged too greatly from those of his master. It is possible of course that Scott's transfer to *Ivanhoe* (1820) of the methods used in his Scottish novels may have suggested the possibility of transferring the same methods to the North American scene. But the Scottish novels themselves are so varied that the hint furnished by *Ivanhoe* may well have been superfluous. It is impossible to say how closely Cooper read the Waverley novels before he began writing novels himself; perhaps he read them with mere uncritical enthusiasm. But he could scarcely have failed to sense the spirit of exploration and experimentation at work as, in novel after novel, Scott developed the formal and thematic possibilities of *Waverley* and transferred others from Maria Edgeworth's Ireland to his own Scotland. Like thousands of other readers on both sides of the Atlantic, Cooper waited impatiently for each new work by the 'Great Unknown'. To cater for these profitable demands, Scott wrote far too much at too fast a rate, and sometimes did no more than shufflle around a few stereotypes of his own previous manufacture. Today we are too likely to suppose that Scott as a novelist was never 'serious' and after *Waverley* was only making the most of a financially good thing. But this is to permit an ingenuous literary puritanism to disarm our critical intelligence. Scott's contemporary reviewers generally recognized that he had great faults and that these faults might have a disastrous influence on later writers: they were right; they were right, too, in considering him one of the great inventive novelists in English.

2. *The Spy* AND *Lionel Lincoln*

The Spy is subtitled 'A Tale of the Neutral Ground'; and as 'neutral ground' is a phrase that crops up frequently in the Waverley Novels, Cooper's subtitle can probably be taken as an announcement that he is following in the footsteps of Sir Walter Scott. In any case, *The Spy* certainly is a tale of the neutral ground, i.e. of a particular place (Westchester County in the state of New York) which lay between the camps of the Americans and British during the American Revolutionary War. But it is a strange sort of 'neutral ground'. For it is 'neutral' only in the sense that it is not held unambiguously by either side; so far from being a place of sure security, it is the most lawless and morally equivocal place of all. Appropriately, therefore, the 'wavering hero' of *The Spy*, Mr Wharton, is a coward who tries to be all things to all men. The difference here between Scott and Cooper is striking and significant: weak, corrupt, vacillating Scott's wavering heroes may be at their worst, but they are never, like Mr Wharton, contemptible. Neither, in Scott's usage, does 'neutral ground' carry any suggestion of moral dubiety; on the contrary, 'neutral ground' is to be prized as the place where differences are reconciled or temporarily forgotten, and where masquerade is unnecessary. To Scott the phrase means 'common ground'; to Cooper it means 'No-Man's-Land'. Thus what is frankly an imitation of a Scott novel often seems to be, as well, a sharp critique of Scott's soft centre.

Though secretly a royalist sympathizer, Mr Wharton chooses to live on the Neutral Ground because he hopes to retain the friendship, or anyway escape the hostility, of both sides—thereby ensuring that, whatever the winning side, his extensive possessions will be safe from confiscation. Contrasting sharply with him is his neighbour, the peddler Harvey Birch, who, though generally supposed to be a spy for the British, is in fact a spy for Washington and a patriot who refuses pay for his dangerous services as a double agent. Contrasting with both are those other denizens of the Neutral Ground—the 'Skinners' and 'Cowboys', irregulars in the pay of the Americans and the British, who, under the guise of patriotism or loyalty, loot and murder as they will; for the Neutral Ground lies outside the jurisdiction of either civil or military law. These contrasts and juxtapositions are extremely effective; the more so because this world of disguises, ambushes, and night-raids is, as a whole, contrasted with the daylight world of men in uniform, who fight in the open and act in accordance with military law and the code of honour. The striking thing about this pattern is that it seems to emerge naturally from Cooper's materials: we suspect that the 'neutral ground' of any war would yield such human contrasts—if only the novelist would narrow his focus and wait for the Mr Whartons, the double agents, the Cowboys, and Skinners to reveal themselves, before disappearing again when the hostile battalions march openly onto the stage.[5]

This is not to suggest that Cooper's artistry is not deliberate. In connexion with a similar set of moral contrasts in *The Spy*, James Grossman has noted that

> Cooper does not explicitly connect the two cases or comment on the relative virtues of wild and formal justice. He was a loose, slovenly writer throughout his entire career, but on great occasions, especially in his early work, he kept quiet so well that we can only wonder idly how he learned such restraint, or whether—and this is perhaps the highest form of critical praise—he really knew what he was doing.[6]

I am not sure whether the restraint mentioned by Mr Grossman, which is evident throughout the novel, really was deliberate; but I have no doubt that Cooper *did* know what he was doing when he created the major pattern of moral contrasts discussed above. We can point to other, subordinate, patterns as well. There is, for instance, the series of contrasts based on the different degrees of domestic comfort and companionship enjoyed by Mr Wharton, the American soldiery, and Harvey Birch. Mr Wharton enjoys a life of luxurious self-indulgence and is surrounded by a household of fond female relatives:

---

[5] I regret that when I wrote this analysis of the 'neutral ground' in *The Spy*, I had not yet read the quite similar account given by Donald A. Ringe, *James Fenimore Cooper* (New Haven, 1962), pp. 28–32. It is gratifying to note that we have reached similar readings of this novel despite quite different approaches—Dr Ringe by way of American character and landscape, I by way of Scott's novels. What we have both perceived is the importance of the conflict between appearance and reality in Cooper's fiction. Given this perception, it is not surprising that we also agree in our interpretation of (in spite of different approaches to) *The Bravo*.

[6] Grossman, *James Fenimore Cooper* (New York, 1949), p. 28.

retribution comes when the Skinners burn down his house and his son (a captain in the British army) is very nearly executed as a spy. The camp life of the American soldiers—rude and improvised, yet lively and comradely—is altogether different, as is the life of Harvey Birch. One of the most affecting moments in the novel occurs when Birch discovers how the existence of his hide-out has been betrayed by sunlight reflected from a pane of window-glass:

Birch examined her features as, with open ingenuousness, she related the simple incidents that had made her mistress of his secret; and, as she ended, he sprang upon his feet, and, striking the window with the stick in his hand, demolished it at a blow.

''Tis but little luxury or comfort that I know,' he said, 'but even that little cannot be enjoyed in safety! Miss Wharton,' he added, advancing before Fanny, and speaking with the bitter melancholy that was common to him, 'I am hunted through these hills like a beast of the forest; but whenever, tired with my toils, I can reach this spot, poor and dreary as it is, I can spend my solitary nights in safety.'

The element of self-pity in this and other speeches by Harvey Bird is unfortunate, but the episode is nevertheless moving, especially because we have seen how Mr Wharton and the soldiers live. To suppose that these effects are accidental is, I should say, to be much less sophisticated than Cooper himself.

In fact, Cooper appears at times to be entirely too deliberate. Conveniently for Mr Wharton and for the symmetry of the novel, his two daughters happen to be in love with, respectively, a British officer and an American officer. It is not that such divisions within a single family are necessarily improbable: as Cooper is at pains to show, the American Revolution was in many ways a civil war within the thirteen colonies which inevitably did divide families. Rather, it is the excessive neatness that is objectionable. And the arrangement seems excessively neat because the genteel characters are so stereotyped, so little individualized, that they appear to exist only for the sake of acting out their representative parts in Cooper's didactic scheme. The scheme is not wrong because it is didactic or for any other reason; nor is it a novelist's main business to create 'interesting characters'. But it is his business to make them individual and interesting enough that (although we know better) we regard them, just as we regard actual human beings, as some-how existing for their own sake rather than for some other sake.

This Cooper fails to do in the cases of the Wharton sisters, their lovers, and young Captain Wharton: in so far as their fates seem unimportant to the reader, the main 'story' has only a bare problematic interest. That the novel is the worse for this must be candidly recognized. Yet the novel is none the less consistently absorbing through Chapter XXIV, and is inter-mittently so thereafter. Why is this the case? Most obviously, two of the genteel characters—Mr Wharton and Miss Peyton—are effective, and the non-genteel characters—especially hard-living, hard-fighting Captain Lawton—are generally as vig-orous as they are numerous. More important, however, *The Spy* is what it claims to be, 'A Tale of the Neutral Ground'—a tale, that is, in which the characters exist (though they should not seem to, at first glance) for the sake of a moral landscape. This being the case, it is better that some of the characters be too colourless than that (like Dalgetty in *The Legend of Montrose*) they be too vivid.

As a moral landscape *The Spy* is successful enough to engage its reader's adult attention, and it is a remarkable variant of the *Waverley*-type novel. Unlike Scott's best works, *The Spy* cannot be taken seriously as an historical novel. Cooper simply assumes that the American side was obviously right, a patriotic assump-tion which is revealed most ingenuously in the way George Washington makes his appearance as 'The Father of his Country' in this novel. However, while such an assumption makes this novel much less rich and complex than *Waverley* or *Old Mortality*, Cooper does achieve a limited but genuine success in his treatment of the 'neutral ground'. In this patriotic, as distinct from historical, novel, it is appropriate that the waver-ing hero should be so intellectually, morally, and physically feeble that, for him, there is really never any question of a choice between the American and British causes. He is disqualified as an 'ideal observer'; but then that, in a way, is the point: if he were as intelligent and morally courageous as Edward Waver-ley, he would have to choose the American side and thus remove himself from the Neutral Ground.

After *The Spy*, Cooper turned to new subjects, the frontier in *The Pioneers* (1823) and American Revolutionary War at sea in

The Pilot (1824). Both are imitations of Scott, but neither invites comparison with *The Spy* so much as does Cooper's fifth novel, *Lionel Lincoln, or, The Leaguer of Boston* (1825).

Unlike *The Spy*, *Lionel Lincoln* is a serious and, up to a point, impressive historical novel about the American War of Independence. Lincoln himself is a young British officer of American birth but English education who returns to his native Boston just on the eve of the Revolution. Like the hero of Miss Edgeworth's *The Absentee*, Lincoln is one whose childhood memories incline him to view his fellow-provincials' grievances sympathetically, in spite of the fact that his rank, education, and wealth have placed him among those who, with few exceptions, regard the provincials with condescension or uncomprehending contempt. Given Miss Edgeworth's example, the Irish-American parallel must have been fairly obvious to Cooper; but in other respects—the great national cleavage and clash of political principles—his materials were similar to Scott's. In the event, Cooper achieved a blend of Scott's and Miss Edgeworth's methods which, except for a daring but colossally unsuccessful *dénouement*, might have resulted in an historical novel worthy of comparison with *Old Mortality* or *Waverley*. The ending, however, is so bad as to destroy the novel as a whole, leaving us with what is at best a large memorable fragment.

The chief issue in *Lionel Lincoln* is not political justice as such. Cooper does provide a fairly full account of the events leading up to the crisis of 1775 and examines many of the economic and political issues of the place and time. But his main purpose was to show circumstantially that the fundamental problem was one of imperial prejudice and incomprehension. The following exchange illustrates the problem:

'You have now had some evidence of the spirit that pervades this people,' said Ralph, after a few moments of silence; 'think you still there is no danger that the volcano will explode?'

'Surely everything I have heard and seen to-night confirms such an opinion,' returned Lionel. 'Men on the threshold of rebellion seldom reason so closely, and with such moderation. Why, the very fuel for the combustion, the rabble themselves, discuss their constitutional principles, and keep under the mantle of law, as though they were a club of learned Templars.'

37

'Think you that the fire will burn less steadily because what you call the fuel has been prepared by the seasoning of time?' returned Ralph. 'But this comes from sending a youth into a foreign land for his education! The boy rates his sober and earnest countrymen on a level with the peasants of Europe.'

It is precisely this gap between what the Americans really are and what the British, even Lincoln, suppose them to be, that provides both the main theme and the dramatic form of the novel. The British are convinced that the colonials will not fight and could not if they dared: the Battle of Lexington and Concord, brilliantly described by Cooper, resolves the suspense. Now the British are convinced that, though the Americans may fight, they lack the basic organizational skills to confront a full regular army: the Battle of Bunker Hill, depicted with great clarity and vividness, clears up this misunderstanding. Thus the two major battles described in the novel are made to fulfil an important revelatory dramatic function. These battles are as well rendered as those in *Old Mortality* and are, besides, as integrally related to the main theme of the novel.[7] To make such a comparison is of course to suggest that *Lionel Lincoln* is in some ways a masterpiece of the historical novelist's art. It is that.

Obviously, in a novel concerned especially with the problem of prejudice and incomprehension, the role of the wavering 'ideal observer' is more than usually central. Lincoln is barely adequate in this role, but he is assisted substantially by one of Cooper's best minor characters—that obese epicure Captain Polwarth. The following discussion between Polwarth and Lincoln, occurring after the first shots have been fired at Lexington, reveals how the former provides comic and tragic incomprehension at the same time:

'The thing is a bad thing, Major Lincoln, and, if you will, a wicked thing—but take the assurance of a man who knows the country well, there will be no attempts at vengeance; and as for redress, in a military way, the thing is impossible.'

[7] *Old Mortality* is throughout concerned with the schismatic tendencies of fanatics and, under extreme pressure, their occasional ability to unite in action. The first battle is won by the Covenanting forces joined by the moderate Presbyterians, but the question is whether, even in the face of a common enemy, they can remain so united. They eventually lose the second great battle because of internal dissensions.

'You speak with a confidence, sir, that should find its warranty in an intimate acquaintance with the weakness of the people.'

'I have dwelt two years, Major Lincoln, in the very heart of the country,' said Polwarth, without turning his eyes from the steady gaze he maintained on the long road which lay before him, 'even three hundred miles beyond the uninhabited districts; and I should know the character of the nation, as well as its resources. In respect to the latter, there is no esculent thing within its borders, from a humming-bird to a buffalo, or from an artichoke to a watermelon, that I have not, on some occasion or other, had tossed up, in a certain way—therefore, I can speak with confidence, and do not hesitate to say, that the colonists will never fight; nor, if they had the disposition, do they possess the means to maintain a war.'

'Perhaps sir,' returned Lionel, sharply, 'you have consulted the animals of the country too closely to be acquainted with its spirits?'

'The relation between them is intimate; tell me what food a man diets on, and I will furnish you with his character. 'Tis morally impossible that a people who eat their pudding before the meats after the fashion of these colonists, can ever make good soldiers, because the appetite is appeased before the introduction of the succulent nutriment of the flesh, into——'

'Enough! spare me the remainder,' interrupted Lionel; 'too much has been said already to prove the inferiority of the American to the European animal, and your reasoning in conclusive.'

'Parliament must do something for the families of the sufferers . . . and there I trust the unhappy affair will end. We are now marching on Concord, a place with a most auspicious name, where we shall find repose under its shadows, as well as the food of his home-made parliament, which they have gotten together.'

Little need be said about the irony running through this passage, which here, as elsewhere in Cooper, is unsubtle but effective. Unlike Scott's Falstaffian Dugald Dalgetty, Cooper's Falstaffian Polwarth is always effectively subordinated. It may seem at times that he exists for the sake of what is, as Yvor Winters has observed,[8] a delightful Shakespearian rhetoric—

'Humph!' ejaculated Polwarth; 'The leg is a part of a man for which I see less actual necessity than for any other portion of his frame. I often think there has been a sad mistake in the formation of the animal; as, for instance, one can be a very good waterman, as you see, without legs—a good fiddler, a first-rate tailor, a lawyer, a doctor, a parson, a very tolerable cook, and, in short, anything but

[8] Yvor Winters, *In Defence of Reason* (London, 1960), pp. 194–6.

a dancing-master. I see no use in a leg, unless it be to have the gout; at any rate, a leg of twelve inches is as good as one a mile long, and the saving might be appropriated to the nobler parts of the animal, such as the brain and the stomach.'

'You forget the officer of the light infantry,' said Lionel, laughing.

'You might give him a couple of inches more; though as everything in this wicked world is excellent only by comparison, it would amount to the same thing, and on my system a man would be just as fit for the light infantry without as with legs . . . !'

Much later in the novel, a casualty of the Battle of Bunker Hill, Polwarth has his leg amputated. His painful education complements that of Lincoln; and he emerges slimmed and humanized by his experiences, though no less obsessed with eating, after all. One of the finest moments in the novel occurs near the end when Polwarth discovers that, the town having been long besieged, a poor American family has neither food nor fuel:

'No wood! no provisions!' exclaimed Polwarth, speaking with difficulty; then, dashing his hand across his eyes, he continued to his man, in a voice whose hoarseness he intended should conceal his emotion,—'thou villain, Shearflint, come hither—unstrap my leg!'

The servant looked at him in wonder, but an impatient gesture hasted his compliance.

'Split it onto ten thousand fragments; 't is seasoned and ready for the fire. The best of them,—they of flesh, I mean,—are but useless incumbrances, after all! A cook wants hands, eyes, nose, and palate, but I see no use for a leg!'

There is something touchingly heroic as well as comic about this gesture: for Polwarth has learned perfectly well the 'use of a leg', as he has also learned the new connotations of 'Concord' and the military virtues of 'pudding before the meats'.

Cooper's use of irony is so effective that one is tempted to add Jane Austen to the list of influences apparent in this novel. A more obvious influence is Shakespeare, whose *Henry IV* and *King Lear* affect this novel both for good and ill. (The comparative success with which Scott imitated *Henry IV* in *The Legend of Montrose*, and *Hamlet* and *Macbeth* in *The Bride of Lammermoor*, probably encouraged Cooper to do the same.) All things considered, Polwarth is probably as successful a Falstaffian character as Dalgetty, though, fortunately for the novel, he is a less dominating figure. The influence of *Lear*, indicated by the epigraph on the title page ('First let me talk with this philosopher'), is, however, disastrous. Lincoln's chief contact with the American side is through a wise and mysterious old patriot, Ralph, and the half-wit boy Job Pray; these characters, especially the latter, play their parts well through much of the novel. Alas, as Mr Grossman says, 'At the denouement Cooper by a stroke of melodrama reverses the entire meaning of the story. Ralph is revealed as the father of Lionel and of the illegitimate half-wit. Also, and more amazingly, Ralph, who at the beginning seemed to be the personification of mellow rational wisdom so tolerant that he can find kinship even with the poor half-wit, turns out to be a violent maniac whose love of freedom is embarrassingly literal.'[9] What Cooper thought he was doing is by no means clear; what he certainly did do was to wreck the novel completely. I think we need not suppose that even subconsciously Cooper meant to suggest that there was a serious analogy to be drawn between the American Revolution and a madman's attempt to escape from an asylum. Perhaps Cooper merely intended to show, *à la* Shakespeare, that the words of a madman and a fool might contain profound truth; if so, he badly misjudged the effect which the sudden revelation of Ralph's madness would have, accompanied as it is by violence and death. More important, this personal tragedy forces Lincoln to make a purely personal decision to retire from the war to England: a decision resulting from an accident of personal history, it can have no representative significance. And thus, from the standpoint of the novel as a whole, the conclusion is worse than a reversal of 'the entire meaning of the story' (which might have had some point); the conclusion is meaningless.

Lionel Lincoln might have survived a merely feeble ending, as did *The Spy* or (to take a work of greater scale) *Old Mortality*; but this ending shatters the novel so totally that it cannot be regarded as a complete novel, imperfect but whole. This is not to suggest that the ending was the result of a last-minute inspiration: on the contrary, Cooper seems to have planned the *dénouement* very carefully in advance—and that is why the collapse is so terrific. The loss to American literature is a major one, nothing less than the loss of its only potentially great historical novel about the War of Independence. The language,

[9] Grossman, *James Fenimore Cooper*, p. 42.

the characterization, the circumstantial evocation of place and time, and up to a point the design of the novel—all are ambitious and impressively achieved. Yet when all is said and done, the relatively humble *The Spy* is a much better novel than *Lionel Lincoln*. Though neither is a work of the order of the great Waverley novels, they both show how skilfully Cooper could adapt Scott's methods to an American situation. But the achievement is, after all, a minor one; for the materials are really so like Scott's that it is scarcely surprising that, modified by Cooper no more than Scott himself modified them from novel to novel, his methods worked almost as well in America as they did in Scotland.

III

THE PIONEERS

The Pioneers is Cooper's most impressive imitation of the *Waverley*-type novel. Among the early Leatherstocking tales it occupies a place similar to that of *Guy Mannering* among Scott's earliest novels of Scotland. Like *Guy Mannering*, *The Pioneers* deals with the period 'of our own youth'; *The Last of the Mohicans*, like *Waverley*, embraces 'the age of our fathers'; and *The Prairie*, like *The Antiquary*, brings the action up to a date within two decades of the time of writing.[1] In both sequences we view the gradual fading away of the old order, at the end of which we have the author's assurances that the subject is closed (though of course it is not). To point out this parallel is not to suggest that *Guy Mannering* is at all comparable to *The Pioneers* as a work of art or social observation. Yet both novels are rich in well-remembered scenes of a vanished way of life—primitive, prodigal, egalitarian—and both are centrally concerned with that period of the recent past when the present order achieved a manifest supremacy. If Cooper inherited these fictional preoccupations from Scott, Scott inherited them from Maria Edgeworth, whose *Castle Rackrent* and *The Absentee* furnished the direct models for *Guy Mannering* and *The Bride of Lammermoor*. To this line of succession *The Pioneers* is the heir, and any line that can boast *Castle Rackrent*, *The Bride*, and *The Pioneers* is a brilliant one.

I have already noted that *The Bride* appears to be a refashioning of *Guy Mannering*. And though *The Pioneers* resembles *Guy Mannering* in the ways suggested, in terms of plot and characterization it is more like *The Bride*. Young Oliver Effingham

---

[1] Scott, Preface to *The Antiquary*.

43

believes that he has been defrauded of his ancestral estates by Judge Marmaduke Temple, a man who has risen to eminence because of commercial astuteness and adherence to the American cause during the War of Independence. Like the Ravenswoods, the aristocratic Effinghams—who also belong to the heroic age of their country—have remained loyal to the cause of their old sovereign. And like Edgar Ravenswood, Oliver Effingham falls in love with the daughter of the supposed usurper. Though Judge Temple is in fact innocent of any crime against the Effinghams (it is all a misunderstanding) and though he is by no means so weak a character as Sir William Ashton, none the less he resembles Sir William more than he does any other of Scott's wavering heroes. This is not to ignore the biographical fact that Judge Temple is modelled upon Cooper's own father: the Scott hero most like middle-aged Judge William Cooper is Sir William Ashton.

Critics usually and rightly maintain that this 'main' Effingham–Temple plot is unsatisfactory; indeed, it is but a ghost of the great central tragic action of *The Bride*. As Oliver Effingham and Elizabeth Temple are little better than genteel stereotypes whose personalities are really quite alike, their love has neither the complex interest not the tragic consequences of the love of Edgar Ravenswood and Lucy Ashton. More important, Cooper cannot or does not wish to sustain the parallel between his American Effingham–Temple conflict and the Scottish Ravenswood–Ashton conflict. Since it turns out that the conflict between the Temples and the Effinghams is based on a misunderstanding, Cooper has raised a potentially important historical issue— what if Judge Temple *had* been guilty of such 'patriotic' though unscrupulous conduct?—only to abandon it, filial or patriotic sentiments making a conclusion like that of *The Bride* unthinkable. For the tragic consequences of the conflict between the old and the new orders in North America, we must look elsewhere in *The Pioneers*.

Yet this failure is only marginally important. Though Cooper does not deal effectively with the issues to which the Effingham–Temple relationship gives rise, it is important that he does raise them; for they reinforce and help to define the issues raised by the relationship between Judge Temple, his settlers, and old Leatherstocking. Critics invariably agree that this latter relationship is the moral, imaginative, and thematic centre of the novel; they do not always agree as to what, precisely, the theme of the novel is. I believe that proper attention to the Effingham–Temple plot will help clear up the ambiguities of what is in fact the main plot of *The Pioneers*.

2

Before discussing the Effingham–Temple relationship further, we should try to grasp the essentials of the main Leatherstocking–settlers–Judge Temple relationship. That this is the main relationship is confirmed by the structure of the novel. The action of *The Pioneers* begins on Christmas Eve, just as Judge Temple's daughter returns to her frontier home after several years at a finishing school. It is apparent that Elizabeth's homecoming on this symbolic day marks the beginning of a new era in the settlement: a minister of the Church of England and his genteel daughter have also just arrived, in time to conduct the Christmas services in a community that previously had seen only an occasional itinerant preacher. From this point forward, the major scenes and events are closely related to the changing seasons. The novel ends in the following autumn, just as the natural cycle is coming to its close again, when old Leatherstocking leaves the settlement forever. This symbolic structure is similar in conception to that of *Walden*, in which Thoreau's stay at Walden Pond begins symbolically on the Fourth of July and ends with the rebirth of nature in the spring. Thoreau's theme is the liberation of the individual man; Cooper's general theme is the displacement of the primitive order by civilization. This theme is so built into the structure of the novel that the irrelevancies and absurdities of the Effingham–Temple plot seem and are largely peripheral in the total development.

With one important exception, the main episodes—on which Cooper brings to bear all his artistic and moral intelligence—are those which exemplify man's relationship with nature during the growing year: making maple sugar; massacring pigeons; netting fish from the lake; killing a buck out of season; burning down the forest at the end of a long dry summer. The important exception is the trial and imprisonment of Leatherstocking for resisting an officer of the law, though this too is an indirect result of the old hunter's having killed deer out of season. There are many good reasons for Cooper's having focused his reader's attention more on this relationship between man and nature than on the equally important relationship between man and man. It was Cooper's purpose (as under similar circumstances it was Scott's) to show that something positive was lost, at the same time that something positive was gained, when one order superseded another. And it is precisely in the relationship between man and nature that primitive society, exemplified chiefly by Leatherstocking, is shown to best advantage: Natty Bumppo might be a very ignorant un-natty bumpkin in the drawing-room; but beside the lake when the great flights of pigeons are tumbling mutilated and half-dead out of heaven, he is the only wise man in sight.

Thus we must not suppose that Cooper's principal object was to record a happy time when American settlers lived close to nature, or to recapture the innocent rustic past of his own childhood. That it was mainly happy and rustic, and that Cooper was fond of it, the novel amply reveals; but it was not innocent and the settlers did not live 'close to nature' except in a strictly physical sense. What Cooper plainly saw was that, in any society, relations between man and man or between man and nature must be governed by some kind of law; but that during its transitional phase the American frontier society had no effective laws to govern the relations between man and nature. Templeton in *The Pioneers* is therefore in this respect a 'neutral ground' as much as Westchester County is in *The Spy*. When in order to remedy this evil Judge Temple introduces new game laws, backed up by concrete police powers and the abstract dignity of the Law, they are—after their fashion—wise and effective; but as old Leatherstocking doesn't understand their fashion or believe in the dignity of man-made abstractions, he not only violates the laws but resists the Law. Therefore, although the general theme of the novel is the displacement of an older order by the new civilized order, Cooper focuses special attention on the operations of law in such a transitional community, particularly the law governing man's relations with nature.

Perhaps the episode which best illustrates the chief issues of the novel is the long and vivid account of lake-fishing in Chapters XXIII and XXIV. The settlers use a huge seine to catch the fish, one so huge that a crowd of able-bodied men is necessary to haul it back to shore. Cooper stresses the great effort involved:

But Richard discovered his mistake, when he saw Billy Kirby before him, standing with his feet in the water, at an angle of forty-five degrees, inclining shorewards, and expending his gigantic strength in sustaining himself in that posture. . . .

'I see the "staffs",' shouted Mr Jones; 'gather in, boys, and away with it; to shore with her!—to shore with her!'

At this cheerful sound, Elizabeth strained her eyes and saw the ends of the two sticks on the seine emerging from the darkness, while the men closed near to each other, and formed a deep bag of their net. The exertions of the fishermen sensibly increased, and the voice of Richard was heard encouraging them to make their greatest efforts at the present moment.

Again:

. . . the heavier boat of the seine-drawers approached the spot where the canoe lay, dragging after its toilsome way, the folds of the net, which was already spreading on the water.[2]

Judge Temple disapproves of this kind of wasteful fishing, but he too can be carried away by the profusion of nature and the excitement of the sport:

'Pull heartily boys,' cried Marmaduke, yielding to the excitement of the moment, and laying his hands to the net, with no trifling addition to the force. Edwards had preceded him; for the sight of the immense piles of fish, that were slowly rolling over on the gravelly beach, had impelled him also to leave the ladies, and join the fishermen.

Edwards is young Oliver Effingham in disguise. As the rightful

---

[2] This is the way the passage appears in the 1825 American edition of *The Pioneers*, which is essentially a corrected (rather than substantially revised) version of the original 1823 edition. My quotation is taken from the Holt-Rinehart edition of *The Pioneers*, ed. Leon Howard (New York, 1959), p. 274, which reproduces the 1825 text. In Cooper's later revision of the novel, the passage was amended to read: ' . . . the heavier boat of the seine-drawers approached the spot where the canoe lay, dragging after it the folds of the net'. Clearly, Cooper's revision was made in the interests of improved sentence structure, but without regard for the symbolic contrasts which give these chapters their special distinction and power. It is most probable that in revising a novel he had written almost a decade earlier, Cooper simply overlooked his original intentions and concentrated on the more superficial aspects of style. His revisions to his novels were generally of this kind and, at least in the case of *The Pioneers*, did as much harm as good. The case for reading *The Pioneers* in the Holt-Rinehart edition seems to me a strong one.

owner of the property and the Judge's eventual heir, Oliver is the hope for the future; but here as in other situations he proves himself to have no more self-restraint than the Judge. In one respect, however, the Judge and Oliver are a cut above the rest of the settlers: they have enough understanding to regret what has happened and to try to legislate against its recurrence. The settlers, as Cooper reiterates somewhat tiresomely, believe that the resources of nature are inexhaustible.

Leatherstocking's entrance into this scene is described with a fine visual and symbolic awareness:

Through the obscurity, which prevailed most immediately under the eastern mountain, a small and uncertain light was plainly to be seen, though, as it was occasionally lost to the eye, it seemed struggling for existence. They observed it to move, and sensibly to lower, as if carried down the descent of the bank to the shore. Here, in a very short time, its flame gradually expanded, and grew brighter, until it became of the size of a man's head, when it continued to shine, a steady ball of fire.

Such an object, lighted as it were by magic, under the brow of the mountain, and in that retired and unfrequented place, gave double interest to the beauty and singularity of its appearance. It did not at all resemble the large and unsteady light of their own fire, being much more clear and bright, and retaining its size and shape with perfect uniformity.

As Donald Davie says, 'When the light is finally revealed as the lamp of Leatherstocking's canoe, the straightforward observation of literal fact—that it was clearer and brighter than "the large and unsteady light" of the seine-fishermen's fire—takes on moral reverberations. Yet the literal description is never in danger of thinning out as merely the first level of allegory; on the contrary, as the light approaches, it is observed ever more intently.'[3] Similar moral reverberations are to be found in Cooper's description of Natty handling his canoe:

The light suddenly changed its direction, and a long and slightly-built boat hove up out of the gloom, while the red glare fell on the weather-beaten features of the Leather-Stocking, whose tall person was seen erect in the frail vessel, wielding, with the grace of an experienced boatman, a long fishing-spear, which he held by its centre, first dropping one end and then the other into the water, to

[3] Davie, *The Heyday of Sir Walter Scott*, p. 143.

aid in propelling the little canoe of bark, we will not say through, but over, the water. At the further end of the vessel a form was faintly seen, guiding its motions, and using a paddle with the ease of one who felt there was no necessity for exertion. . . .

The boat glided along the shore until it arrived opposite the fishing-ground, when it again changed its direction, and moved on to the land, with a motion so graceful, and yet so rapid, that it seemed to possess the power of regulating its own progress. The water in front of the canoe was hardly ruffled by its passage, and no sound betrayed the collision when the light fabric shot on the gravelly beach for nearly half its length, Natty receding a step or two from its bow, in order to facilitate the landing.

How beautifully this captures the exact movements and spatial relations! Nor has any writer communicated more effectively how certain men live in such harmony with nature that they seem part of it, not through mystic identification but through long study and practice. No wonder, then, that when Judge Temple invites Leatherstocking to share the booty from the laborious seine-fishing, the old hunter replies:

'No, no, Judge,' . . . 'I eat of no man's wasty ways. I strike my spear into the eels or the trout, when I crave the creatur's; but I wouldn't be helping to such a sinful kind of fishing for the best rifle that was ever brought out from the old countries. If they had fur, like a beaver, or you could tan their hides, like a buck, something might be said in favor of taking them by the thousands with your nets; but as God made them for man's food, and for no other disarnable reason, I call it sinful and wasty to catch more than can be eat.'

'Your reasoning is mine; for once, old hunter, we agree in opinion; and I heartily wish we could make a convert of the Sheriff. A net of half the size of this would supply the whole village with fish for a week at one haul.'

The Leather-Stocking did not relish this alliance in sentiment; and he shook his head doubtingly, as he answered:

'No, no; we are not much of one mind, Judge, or you'd never turn good hunting-grounds into stumpy pastures. And you fish and hunt out of rule; but, to me, the flesh is sweeter where the creatur' has some chance for its life: for that reason, I always use a single ball, even if it be at a bird or a squirrel. Besides, it saves lead; for, when a body knows how to shoot, one piece of lead is enough for all, except hard-lived animals.'

49

Leatherstocking's words express the vision of one whose genius consists in falling into step with nature, never trying to force or much improve her ways. Unfortunately, Natty speaks for a way of life which is now obsolete. The settlers can survive only by turning 'good hunting-grounds into stumpy pastures'; and if they spend their time logging and farming, they have little time to learn how to shoot with 'a single ball'. That they can learn or must be forced not to 'hunt and fish out of rule' is, however, one of the main lessons of the novel. Thus it is old Leatherstocking, the 'lawless squatter' who is later imprisoned for resisting the law, who speaks here as the prosecuting attorney for the old unrecognized law of a now nearly extinct society.

It is important to recognize that Leatherstocking does speak, not for himself, but for an entire society. Shortly after this exchange with Judge Temple, Leatherstocking and his Indian companion John Mohegan (the great Delaware chief Chingachgook, now sadly decayed) spear a single fish for themselves:

'That will do, John,' said Natty, raising his prize by one of his fingers, and exhibiting it before the torch; 'enough is as good as a feast; I shall not strike another blow tonight.'
The Indian again waved his hand, and replied with the simple and energetic monosyllable of—
'Good.'[4]

John's monosyllable has the force of a benediction uttered out of the past by the former lords of primeval North America. Even more than Leatherstocking, old John is a repository of the skills and wisdom of the primitive society which Judge Temple's settlers have displaced. Early in the novel, for instance, he uses a special kind of bark to heal a wound which Judge Temple accidently inflicted on Oliver Effingham. We are left in no doubt that the village doctor in attendance on Oliver is, like the settlers when they fish or hunt, a bungling amateur—though, unlike them, he is anxious to learn. As the doctor himself grudgingly admits,

---

[4] This passage is quoted from the Holt-Rinehart edition, p. 274. The final revised edition omits the saying, 'enough is as good as a feast'. The earlier version is not only more authentic; it exemplifies the way traditions, in the form of common sayings, provide a code for men like Natty who, unlike Judge Temple, lack a trained reasoning faculty. This revision, evidently made for the sake of economy, weakens the force of the original passage considerably.

'It is not to be denied, Judge Temple, but what the savages are knowing in small matters of physic. They hand these things down in their traditions. Now in cancers and hydrophoby, they are quite ingenious. I will just take this bark home and analyze it; for, though it can't be worth sixpence to the young man's shoulder, it may be good for the toothache, or rheumatism, or some of them complaints. A man should never be above learning, even if it be from an Indian.'

Exactly. Unlike the Indians, the settlers either have no traditions or have the wrong ones for coping with their new environment. In spite of his vanity, Dr Todd has the true empirical spirit of his profession, and in time he will become an able practitioner. Judge Temple has the same spirit; like Dr Todd, he is 'never . . . above learning, even if it be from an Indian'.

The case is quite different with Natty and John Mohegan: they are no more adaptable than the settlers. But they have the great advantage of being at home in the wilderness, where their patiently acquired skills and inherited lore are fully relevant and seem like 'second nature' to them. Moreover, Leatherstocking's strict notions about the economy of nature are reinforced by, and are partly an expression of, his craftsman's sense of a proper fitness between means and ends. The unskilled methods of mass destruction used by the settlers imply the crudest kind of *aesthetic* response to nature, quantity rather than quality being the thing that excites them. But Leatherstocking too can be tempted to break the law, not Judge Temple's law (which he refuses to recognize) but the law to which he himself accedes.

We come now to the event which brings about Natty's trial, imprisonment, and eventual departure from Templeton. Natty's dogs, set loose by Squire Hiram Doolittle, begin chasing a buck; the old hunter hears them—

'Laugh if you will, boy,' said Leather-Stocking; 'the hounds be out, and are hunting a deer. No man can deceive me in such a matter. I wouldn't have had the thing happen for a beaver's skin. Not that I care for the law! but the venison is lean now, and the dumb things run the flesh off their own bones for no good. Now do you hear the hounds?'

Natty attempts to stop the chase; for not only is he opposed to hunting 'out of rule', but he is also anxious to avoid trouble with Judge Temple:

... 'the buck has gone by them with the wind, and it has been too much for the poor rogues; but I must break them of these tricks, or they'll give me a deal of trouble.'

But it proves too much for Leatherstocking as well:

As the buck swam by the fishermen, raising his nose high into the air, curling the water before his slim neck like the beak of a galley, the Leather-Stocking began to sit very uneasy in his canoe.

"Tis a noble creatur'!' he exclaimed; 'what a pair of horns! a man might hang up all his garments, on the branches. Let me see— July is the last month, and the flesh must be getting good.' While he was talking, Natty had instinctively employed himself in fastening the inner end of the bark rope, that served him for a cable, to a paddle, and rising suddenly on his legs, he cast this buoy away, and cried, 'Strike out, John! let her go. The creatur's a fool to tempt a man in this way.'

Here we observe the classic sequence of temptation, rationalization, and loss of control. Whether the old hunter is guilty of breaking the law he does recognize, as well as the law of Judge Temple, is left ambiguous: it turns out that the flesh of this buck is good, as Leatherstocking knowledgeably hoped it would be. Nevertheless it is apparent that he too is human in that, given the right circumstances, his passions take charge of his judgment, well informed though it may be. The temptation has its inevitable erotic overtones, but above all it is an aesthetic experience: the buck is a thing of beauty, appreciated as such, and the hunt is a response in kind, barbaric but beautiful:

The dark eye of the old warrior was dancing in his head with a wild animation, and the sluggish repose in which his aged frame had been resting in the canoe was now changed to all the rapid inflections of practised agility. The canoe whirled with each cunning evolution of the chase, like a bubble floating in a whirlpool; and when the direction of the pursuit admitted of a straight course, the little bark skimmed the lake with a velocity that urged the deer to seek its safety in some new turn.

From one point of view, the hunt is a relapse into barbarism, especially in the case of old John. ('Both of the old men now used the language of the Delawares when they spoke.') But at the same time, within a certain sphere, barbarism has a wisdom and refinement superior to that of the 'civilized' community. Even Judge Temple, who shares Natty's dislike of waste, is not motivated by any aesthetic consideration: '. . . it is not as ornaments that I value the noble trees of this country, it is for their usefulness'. Against this utilitarian, i.e. essentially quantitative, standard, rigorously applied, old Leatherstocking and his way of life cannot stand very long.

3

The trial of Leatherstocking is in many ways the central event in the novel, but to understand the issues raised by the trial we should return now to the Temple–Effingham conflict. First, we should consider the somewhat shadowy Effingham family. They represent the old colonial aristocracy of New York at its best:

They were one of the few families then resident in the colonies, who thought it a degradation to its members to descend to the pursuits of commerce; and who never emerged from the privacy of domestic life, unless to preside in the councils of the colony, or to bear arms in her defence. The latter had, from youth, been the only employment of Edward's father. . . . He had served with fidelity and courage, and having been, according to the custom of the provinces, intrusted with commands much superior to those to which he was entitled by rank, with reputation also. When Major Effingham yielded to the claims of age, he retired with dignity, refusing his half-pay or any other compensation for services that he felt he could no longer perform.

The ministry proffered various civil offices, which yielded not only honour but profit; but he declined them all, with the chivalrous independence and loyalty that had marked his character through life.

Major Effingham's son (Oliver's father) became the friend and later the invisible partner of Marmaduke Temple, whose practical sagacity and enterprise were not inhibited by family disapproval of vulgar commerce. Viewed in a national perspective, it is obvious that, useful though the Effinghams may have been during the early years of colonization in North America, the future must lie with men like Temple. Cooper hints broadly at this quite early in *The Pioneers*:

Very soon after the establishment of the independence of the States, by the peace of 1783, the enterprise of their citizens was directed to a development of the natural advantages of their widely extended dominions. Before the war of the Revolution the inhabited parts of the colony of New York were limited to less than a tenth of its possessions. . . . Within the short period we have mentioned, the population has spread itself over five degrees of latitude and seven of longitude, and has swelled to a million and a half. . . .

Our tale begins in 1793, about seven years after the commencement of one of the earliest of those settlements, which have conduced to effect that magical change in the power and condition of the State. . . .

Major Effingham and his family belong to the pre-expansionist phase of American history; indeed, as loyalists, they look rather across the Atlantic than towards the West, with all its unexploited riches.

However, as a soldier during the wars with the French in North America, Major Effingham came to know the wilderness well—much better, in fact, than Marmaduke Temple. The major appears only briefly at the end of the novel, a tattered and senile, yet pathetically dignified and courteous, old man: his present state contrasts poignantly with what we are told of his maturity, when he fought so valiantly that the Delawares named him 'Fire-Eater', made him an honorary member of their tribe, and granted him the land later occupied and developed by Judge Temple. In effect, Major Effingham was the ideal colonial administrator—one who (like Natty Bumppo, at a different level) adapted himself to the ways and customs of the old primitive society of North America, one whose military virtues and bearing made it congruous for him to become the adopted son of the great chief Chingachgook. The virtues of Major Effingham and Leatherstocking, like those of the Indians, were the virtues of a pre-commercial era: faithful, brave, skilled, and even unworldly, such men were; but they lacked the qualities necessary to turn a good hunting-ground into a good pasture.

Judge Temple is a vastly more important and interesting character than Major Effingham. The latter, indeed, is important and interesting only in so far as what is reported about him helps to place the conflict between Leatherstocking and Judge Temple in a larger perspective. But Judge Temple is one of Cooper's finest characters and a most remarkable development of Scott's wavering hero. Personally, Temple is not a man of perfectly upright character like Major Effingham or Leatherstocking. He drinks too much on occasion, he gives important political appointments to his relatives, and, as we have seen, he lacks the self-control which an Indian or an old-fashioned aristocratic training might have given him. Still, he is a man with a benevolent disposition and a good deal of practical intelligence who succeeds where men with greater reserve and scrupulousness might have failed. Cooper plainly regarded him (and regarded his own father) as a legitimate successor of the great statesmen who framed the American Constitution—one who was, in his own right, a Founding Father. For whatever Judge Temple's private weaknesses may be, he is a man of vision as well as enterprise. Cooper rather caricatures the Judge's propensity for laying out carefully ruled avenues in the wilderness; and it is obvious that Cooper is fond of the idiosyncratic and accidental developments which the Judge, as an eighteenth-century city-planner and law-maker, would like to rule ideally out of existence. Yet the behaviour of the settlers offers the strongest possible argument in favour of such planning, perfectly rational and impersonal. The Judge confesses that 'I may possibly look too far ahead, and calculate too deeply'. But it is well he does; for if he lives too much for the future, his settlers live too much for the present, and Leatherstocking too much for the past.

Judge Temple's relation to the Waverley-type hero is fascinating and difficult to define. Though it is possible to discover many traits held in common with the various wavering heroes in Scott's fiction, and even to write as though there were a single 'Hero' of the Waverley Novels,[5] Scott in his prime, like Cooper after him was too much the experimental novelist to be content with repeating Edward Waverley in novel after novel. The archetypal pattern of a hero caught between two opposed forces is of course repeated; but the relationship of the hero to those forces varies considerably, and the hero himself may be as different as Henry Morton is from Dugald Dalgetty, or as Reuben Butler is from Sir William Ashton. Given the pattern, however, all such heroes must be primarily passive characters; Henry

[5] Cf. Alexander Welsh, *The Hero of the Waverley Novels* (New Haven, 1963).

Morton, for example, cannot match the lethally single-minded, active force of Balfour of Burley. The same is true of Mr Wharton in *The Spy* or of Lionel Lincoln. These characters may be given a high rank, but it is difficult to imagine them emerging as genuine leaders (except, perhaps, as in *Old Mortality*, where the factions are so extreme and vicious that there is a strong national reaction in favour of moderation as the greatest good).

But Judge Temple is a leader; and though his realm is a petty one, he stands for a constructive force which has a national significance. Yet he certainly appears to be, and is, a wavering hero. On the one hand, he appreciates the economic wisdom of Leatherstocking and sympathizes with the predicament of the old hunter; but on the other, he is the head of the settlers who had come to change Leatherstocking's beloved hunting-grounds into pastures, and he sometimes impetuously joins the settlers in wasteful sports of which Leatherstocking and his own reason and conscience disapprove. However, it would be wrong to suppose that Judge Temple is torn between the rival attractions of Civilization and Primitivism in the way that Edward Waverley is torn between the attractions of the Jacobite and the Hanoverian causes. Rather, the Judge reflects in microcosm the tensions of the community of which he is the founder—between Reason and the Passions, between the rule of Law and the anarchic impulses of the mob, between a public impersonality and a private personal indulgence. His reason—a staunchly utilitarian reason which smacks of the ledger-book—approves of Natty's resistance to the 'wastey ways' of the settlers. His aim, good businessman that he is, is to make the land yield more than the primitive ways of Leatherstocking or the improvident ways of the settlers make possible. Against the wilderness, against the prodigality of the settlers, against his own unreasonable impulses, the Judge must lay out straight-ruled avenues and frame laws which are like the seine the settlers use to catch fish: mechanical, non-selective, and capacious. Though his real authority is based on his wealth, he is anxious to establish a more permanent authority, of which he will be both creator and instrument—the Law. Given the unsettled, unpredictable nature of this new society, this impersonal abstraction the Law necessarily has far greater dignity and importance than any particular law (e.g. decreeing a closed season on hunting deer), though the latter will resemble the former in making no allowances for exceptional knowledge or circumstances (e.g. deer may not be killed before 1st August, irrespective of Leatherstocking's knowledge and habits). The Judge wishes, good Enlightenment man that he is, to rule and be ruled by Reason and Law. But for good or ill, his strong passions and permissive temperament prevent him from realizing most of his schemes or acting with the strict logic he so much reveres. It is clear that, historically, he will be superseded by the less vigorous but more coherent and refined gentlefolk represented by his own daughter and Oliver Effingham; but he is the Founding Father, the man who tamed both the American mob (so far as that was possible) and the American wilderness.

It is important therefore that Leatherstocking is tried and punished, not for killing a deer out of season, but for resisting the Law itself. A small fine takes care of the deer, and Natty is found not guilty on a charge of assault and battery against Hiram Doolittle when it is shown that the magistrate was acting as a private person in his efforts to search the hunter's cabin. But he is found guilty, and clearly was guilty, of resisting execution of a search-warrant by force of arms. To all appearances, Natty's resistance was an open defiance of the authority and dignity of the Law. But of course the old hunter did not see that Deputy Billy Kirby was a public functionary acting in the course of duty; in his eyes, Billy Kirby was still merely Billy Kirby, a man trying to invade his cabin. And when the Judge finds him guilty, the old man sees him not as Judge Temple but as Marmaduke Temple, a man whose daughter Leatherstocking had himself recently saved from death:

'Talk not to me of law, Marmaduke Temple,' interrupted the hunter. 'Did the beast of the forest mind your laws, when it was thirsty and hungering for the blood of your own child! She was kneeling to her God for a greater favor than I ask, and He heard her; and if you now say no to my prayers, do you think He will be deaf?'
'My private feelings must not enter into——

But this Leatherstocking cannot understand. An oath cannot transform Billy Kirby or the judicial toga transform Marmaduke Temple into different beings—beings somehow invested with an authority which, so far as Leatherstocking is concerned, can only be inherited or earned. This is an occasion when Temple finds the transformation from his private to his public character, from passion to reason, exceedingly difficult; but it is a transformation to which he is accustomed and he succeeds in making it. True to type, Judge Temple later offers privately to pay the large fine he has had to exact in his public capacity: alas, there is no way for the Judge to serve Leatherstocking's prison sentence or to sit in the stocks for him.

I have said that the main theme of the novel is the displacement of the old primitive order of North America by the new civilized order. But the term 'primitive' in this case must primarily mean a society which seeks to adapt itself as far as possible to its environment, while 'civilized' means the reverse. The relation of Leatherstocking and the Effinghams to the Indians is an extension of the same principle. Governed by tradition, by individuals who inherit or earn a personal authority, this primitive society is deeply conservative and conservationalist; it might well be called an 'organic' society. By way of contrast, the community established by Judge Temple takes for granted the plasticity of both nature and man. It is supposed to be ruled by Reason and Law; indeed, in Chapter XXIX there seems to be an allusion to Plato's *Republic*, which may perhaps be taken as a measure of the Judge's ambitions for his little state. Of course the Judge's materials are far less plastic and docile than he requires, and so his achievements sometimes fall ludicrously short of his plans.[6]

4

Henry Nash Smith has shown that 'for at least one section of the reading public . . . Leatherstocking, like Boone, was a symbol of anarchic freedom, an enemy of law and order'. But whatever Cooper's public made of *The Pioneers* and its early sequels, Professor Smith is clearly right to ask, 'Did this interpretation conform to Cooper's intention in drawing the character?'[7]

No less than his readers, Cooper must have been moved by

[6] Cf. *The Pioneers*, Ch. XVI: 'We must run our streets by the compass, coz, and disregard trees, hills, ponds, stumps, or, in fact, anything but posterity. Such is the will of your father. . . .'

[7] Henry Nash Smith, *Virgin Land: The American West as Symbol and Myth* (Vintage ed.: New York, 1957), p. 66.

the ideas then current concerning the nature of savage society. The eloquence of Natty's descriptions of his former idyllic life on the shores of Lake Otsego, before the coming of Judge Temple and his settlers, demonstrates that Cooper himself was indeed 'vividly responsive to the ideas of nature and freedom in the Western forest'.[8] Yet it is surely misleading to say that the narrative in *The Pioneers* 'turns constantly about the central issue of the old forest freedom versus the new needs of a community which must establish the sovereignty of law over the individual'. This is the way the conflict is viewed by the protagonists themselves, but Cooper's own view is a good deal more subtle and complex. What the action of the novel reveals again and again is that Leatherstocking's conduct is governed by a code which is far more strict and demanding than any devised by Judge Temple. Freedom to Natty means, not absence of restraints, but absence of unfamiliar and incomprehensible restraints. On the other hand, the Judge's settlers violate Natty's laws regarding the use of nature simply because, intoxicated by the unfamiliar abundance of good wild things, they see no need for such laws. The Judge and Oliver Effingham do see the need, but, carried away by the excitement of slaughter, they act contrary to their own best intentions. In fact, Templeton is almost as much an anarchic 'neutral ground' as Westchester County is in *The Spy*: in such a transitional community, where neither the old primitive order nor the new civilized order is firmly established, true freedom is impossible—only licence or uncomfortable restraint. To say so, however, is not to endorse Donald Davie's contention that the opposition in *The Pioneers* 'is not between freedom and law, but between freedom and anarchy. For Judge Temple stands for no more than a pious intention, an intention which we are shown clearly can never be fulfilled.'[9] On the contrary, various developments—e.g. the arrival of Elizabeth and Mr Grant—argue that moral progress is being made in Templeton; and it is significant that, Natty's violation excepted, the new game laws are observed.

If Leatherstocking is other and more interesting than a 'symbol of anarchic freedom', this is partly because Leatherstocking's antitype, Judge Temple, is no perfect exemplar of law and order. Cooper's imagination, I have suggested, seems to have

[8] *ibid.*   [9] Davie, *Heyday of Sir Walter Scott*, p. 144.

operated naturally in terms of large antitheses; and it was, after all, that impulsive Federalist squire William Cooper who was, so to speak, 'given'; the surprisingly unimpulsive Leatherstocking, we may suppose, was created as the Judge's antagonist, not the other way around. It is also true, however, that many of the characteristic attitudes of Judge Cooper (and hence of Judge Temple) *were* antithetical to those of the backwoodsman of popular imagination, as described by Henry Nash Smith and Roy Harvey Pearce.[10] The legendary backwoodsman's love of solitude, for instance, contrasts sharply with William Cooper's unromantic response to the unhumanized 'waste' of virgin America:

In 1785 I visited the rough and hilly country of Otsego, where there existed not an inhabitant, nor any trace of a road; I was alone, three hundred miles from home, without bread, meat, or food of any kind; fire and fishing tackle were my only means of subsistence. I caught trout in the brook and roasted them on the ashes. My horse fed on the grass that grew by the edge of the waters. I laid me down to sleep in my watch coat, nothing but the melancholy Wilderness around me.[11]

Judge Cooper's view of the wilderness is almost the same as that of Judge Temple, whose initial reaction to the same scene is a 'mingled feeling of pleasure and desolation'. Oliver Effingham, comparing Otsego as it now is with what it once was, echoes Judge Cooper's language:

'It must have been a sight of melancholy pleasure, indeed,' said Edwards, while his eye roved along the shores and over the hills, where the clearings, groaning with the golden corn, were cheering the forests with the signs of life, 'to have roamed over these mountains, and along this sheet of beautiful water, without a living soul to speak to, or to thwart your humor.'

Leatherstocking has exactly the opposite response:

'Haven't I said it was cheerful?' said Leather-Stocking. 'Yes, yes; when the trees began to be covered with leaves, and the ice was out of the lake, it was a second paradise . . . I can say that I have met but one place that was more to my liking; and that was only to eye-sight, and not for hunting or fishing.'

[10] Pearce, 'The Leatherstocking Tales Re-examined', *South Atlantic Quarterly*, vol. XLVI, pp. 524–36.
[11] William Cooper, *Guide in the Wilderness*, p. 9.

But Natty is not merely a lover of solitude and independence: the economic realities of wilderness and agrarian frontier life, even if expressed in terms of two opposed versions of the Garden of Paradise, are never very far in the background of this novel. The fences erected by Judge Temple's settlers not only thwart Leatherstocking's humour; they thwart him in the act of gaining his livelihood, as he bitterly complains. It is as an economic visionary, after the style of Hamilton or DeWitt Clinton, that Judge Temple shares Judge Cooper's ambition to reclaim 'large and fruitful tracts from the waste of creation'.[12] Thus one major reason why James Cooper's account of the conflict between civilization and non-civilization is both more complex and more truthful than other accounts is that, thanks to his father's example and writings, he had a remarkably accurate knowledge of the economic and psychological facts of frontier life: he at least knew, as few others could, what a Judge Temple would really be like, and he could imagine (with some help from personal observation and reading) what the Judge's ideal opposite might be.

Indeed, Cooper's firm grasp of the circumstantial reality of frontier life is everywhere apparent in *The Pioneers*—so much so that the novel is an irreplaceable document of American social history. It is irreplaceable not merely because it describes the varied activities, scenes, and character types of frontier life with great fidelity, but also because, as Donald Davie has noted,[13] these descriptions amount to something more than the lively genre pictures at which Scott and Maria Edgeworth excelled. One need only compare Cooper's account of lake-fishing in Chapters XXIII and XXIV with Scott's parallel account of salmon-spearing in Chapter XXVI of *Guy Mannering*, to see how far Cooper surpasses his master in this respect:

Often he thought of his friend Dudley, the artist, when he observed the effect produced by the strong red glare on the romantic banks under which the boat glided. Now the light diminished to a distant star that seemed to twinkle on the waters, like those which, according to the legends of the country, the water-kelpy sends for the purpose of indicating the watery grave of his victims. Then it advanced nearer, brightening and enlarging as it again approached, till the broad flickering flame rendered bank, and rock, and tree,

[12] *ibid.*, p. 9. [13] Davie, *Heyday of Sir Walter Scott*, p. 133.

visible as it passed, tinging them with its own red glare of dusky light, and resigning them gradually to darkness, or to pale moonlight, as it receded. By this light also were seen the figures in the boat, now holding high their weapons, now stooping to strike, now standing upright, bronzed, by the same red glare, into a colour which might have befitted the regions of Pandemonium.

Scott's description is charming, a delightful piece of careful observation coloured by Romantic fancy, but it lacks the sensuous immediacy, and symbolic intensity of Cooper's imitation. There are still other respects in which the 'American Scott', because of his inwardness with the rhythms of American life, improves on or goes beyond his great Scottish model.

The powerfully expressive symbolic structure of the novel, though an invention which owes much to *The Seasons*, is profoundly original. Scott had used topography to symbolize and in some measure explain major social and political divisions; but this device did not, as Cooper's use of festivals and seasons did, give an expressive structure to the novel itself. Only slightly less remarkable is Cooper's development of the wavering hero in this novel. In having two such heroes, Judge Temple and young Oliver Effingham, Cooper is but following (with less skill) the example set by Scott in *The Bride*; as in *The Bride*, the result is a less clear, less boldly symmetrical design than we find in *Waverley* or *Lionel Lincoln*. But Judge Temple, though he bears some resemblance to Sir William Ashton, is an entirely new kind of wavering hero. Predominantly active and creative, rather than passive and imitative, Judge Temple is at once of and above the community: through an excess rather than a deficiency of rationality on the one hand, of passion on the other, does he mirror and sometimes actually cause the various conflicts in Templeton. In thus transforming the wavering hero from an indecisive follower to an indecisive, though essentially active and effective, leader, Cooper was in a sense doing no more than striking a compromise between two models—his own father and Scott's Sir William Ashton. But the transformation was effective because appropriate to the dynamic, increasingly democratic pioneering context of the New World after the War of Independence. It was very different from the Old World in which Waverley or Morton found themselves, where ancient factions, powerful and obdurate, left little scope for the individual will; where to be fully and representatively human was to be neutral and retiring.

In some respects, it has to be admitted, *The Pioneers* is a seriously imperfect novel. The Effingham–Temple plot is developed without conviction or inspiration. The action is often jerky and episodic. Though the prose is mainly alert and often beautifully wrought, it falls off badly at times, especially when Cooper is portraying Elizabeth Temple. One or two of his lapses are quite funny:

> 'Come dear Brave; once have you served your Master well; let us see how you can do your duty by his daughter'—the dog wagged his tail, as if he understood her language, walked with a stately gait to her side, where he seated himself, and looked up at her face, with an intelligence but little inferior to that which beamed in her own lovely countenance.

Nevertheless, *The Pioneers* is, as Leon Howard has said, 'the first genuinely original novel in the history of American literature'.[14] And it is more. Like *Huckleberry Finn*, say, or *The Great Gatsby*, it is one of a handful of great novels which deal so profoundly with American experience in the context of American social history that no American literature or history course can be sound without them.

[14] Introduction to the Rinehart edition of *The Pioneers*, p. xviii.

IV

RACE IN THE NEW WORLD

Intreat me not to leave thee, *or* to return from following after thee:
for whither thou goest, I will go; and where thou lodgest, I will
lodge: thy people shall be my people, and thy God my God.

Where thou diest, will I die, and there will I be buried: the
Lord do so to me, and more also, *if ought* but death part thee and
me.

Ruth 1: 16–17

1. *The Last of the Mohicans*

WHEN COOPER COMPLETED *The Pioneers*, he had no plan to
write a sequel to it, much less a series based on Leatherstocking.
His next novel, *The Pilot*, was an open bid to write a better
novel of the sea than Scott's *The Pirate*. Yet after writing a
pseudo-Bluestocking novel of manners, a novel of Revolutionary
War adventure, a 'descriptive tale' of the American frontier,
and then a novel of the sea, Cooper evidently believed that the
time had come when he should dedicate himself to a more
sustained and ambitious effort. Therefore his fifth novel, *Lionel
Lincoln*, was to be the first of a series of historical novels dealing
with the thirteen colonies. The achievements of Hume and
Gibbon and others, translated into fiction by Scott, had made
historical writing in prose (whether fictionalized or not) the
true epic form of the age. Even if he was largely moved by
commercial considerations, it was a sign of Scott's major genius
that he abandoned the long narrative poem in favour of the
historical novel. No less pious and patriotic than Scott, Cooper
was now thinking in terms of a vast national prose epic—such as
Scott's novels of Scotland already constituted, or such as
Shakespeare's history plays had long since achieved for England. But unlike Shakespeare or Scott, Cooper the American

had no ancient national political history to interpret; if he went back before 1775, he encountered thirteen distinct, if inter-related, state histories. Indeed, during and after his own life-time, his nation was still struggling to overcome the formal political divisions of the colonial era—a fact which, in a way, justified any effort to understand the individual character of each of the original thirteen. Yet these historical divisions would surely have prevented his saga, as under the Articles of Confederation they had prevented the nation, from having other than a nominal unity. In any event, *Lionel Lincoln* had only a moderate success, in spite of Cooper's patriotic inten-tions, his patient historical research, and his obviously careful construction and composition; and so the plan to write this series was quietly abandoned.

It is against this background that we must read *The Last of the Mohicans*, the most popular and—for a century after its publi-cation in 1826—internationally famous of American novels. Certainly, when Cooper was writing this sequel to *The Pioneers*, he did not envisage the complete series of Leatherstocking tales we now possess; possibly he did not even envisage its immediate successor, *The Prairie*. But this series was to become the American epic Cooper had thought he was starting with *Lionel Lincoln*. Cooper's great discovery, of which he himself was not perfectly conscious, was that, given the fragmented past and present of the American nation, it was only by moving beyond politics and civilized society (both of them features of the States) that an American writer could come to grips with truly national experience. The wilderness, the frontier, the Westward Movement—these belonged to the nation as a whole in a way that even the Battle of Bunker Hill did not. And not only had each of the colonies experienced these things. As Cooper makes clear in *The Pioneers*, the formation of the American Republic had greatly accelerated the expansion westward. Thus in Cooper's mind American nationhood and the Westward Move-ment—which meant of course the displacement and eventual extermination of the American Indians—were intimately con-nected: each new clearing furnished a sign of the increasing temporal greatness of the nation; and each new clearing also signified, quite palpably, the sacrifice of an ancient and in some ways noble race and way of life. Much as Cooper desired

65

temporal greatness for his country, he never supposed that it alone could justify such a sacrifice. How, if at all, he thought the nation could, or did, atone for the crime is far from apparent; and it may be that, after reading the series, we shall conclude that he never faced the moral issue squarely. Nevertheless, he was the greatest advocate the American Indians ever had precisely because he was a great patriot—one whose love for his country embraced the continent as well as the nation, its past as well as its future.

And yet, so far from being the second book of a deeply serious national epic, *The Last of the Mohicans*, it can be argued, is not an adult work of fiction. For even those critics who express some admiration for this novel—James Grossman, Alexander Cowie, Yvor Winters, Van Wyck Brooks—do not claim that it is much more than a mere adventure story. Donald Davie agrees with them but objects strongly to what he terms the 'moral anarchy' in Cooper himself, evidence for which he discovers in the novel.[1] This, it seems to me, is getting closer to the truth; moreover, Davie is surely right when he maintains that *The Last of the Mohicans* is the least impressive of Cooper's Leatherstocking tales. But is it a mere adventure story?

For a really helpful reading of this novel, I think we must turn to Leslie Fiedler's *Love and Death in the American Novel*.[2] Fiedler's work is an odd blend of frequently irresponsible generalization and over-ingenious, but sometimes really illuminating interpretation of particular works; his treatment of Cooper is no exception. As Fiedler says, 'it is incredible that a book which has moved the world for more than a hundred years should have "no serious concern" with that world'. He goes on to argue that miscegenation is the 'secret theme' of *The Last of the Mohicans*. Further, it is a theme with national, even hemispheric, significance—'the question of the relations between men of different races in the New World'. Yet Cooper's handling of this theme is far from satisfactory: 'Though Cooper's own contemporaries urged him to let Cora and Uncas be joined in marriage, his horror of miscegenation led him to forbid even the not-quite white offspring of one unnatural marriage to enter into another alliance that crossed race lines.' Cooper's

[1] Davie, *The Heyday of Sir Walter Scott*, pp. 109-11.
[2] Fiedler, *Love and Death in the American Novel* (New York, 1960), pp. 197-207.

only solution to the problem of racial relations in the New World is the (ambiguously) sexless companionship of Leatherstocking and Chingachgook. And in the end, the theme of miscegenation in this novel remains 'inert and theoretical, discoverable by scrutiny of the text but not felt in the mere act of reading'.

Now even if we disagree with Fiedler's interpretation, we have to recognize that in *The Last of the Mohicans*—and for the first time in American literature—the close friendship between men of different races becomes a matter of central importance. The friendship between Natty and Chingachgook is one of the immortal friendships of world literature: it has great authenticity and value in its own right, and it has additional literary importance as the prototype of similar friendships in *Moby Dick* and *The Adventures of Huckleberry Finn*—novels which in other respects are certainly vastly superior to *The Last of the Mohicans*. It remains to be seen whether this relationship exists somehow in isolation, without reference to other problems created by a multiracial society.

I agree with Fiedler that miscegenation is the theme of *The Last of the Mohicans*, or, to be more exact, that it is the theme on one level and the vehicle for a more general theme—racial relations in North America—explored here for the first time in American fiction. But I do not think that the theme is 'secret' or wholly 'inert'. It is from D. H. Lawrence's *Studies in Classic American Literature* that Fiedler derives his notions of a 'secret theme' and of Cooper's 'duplicity'.[3] But Lawrence is misleading. Like Scott's, Cooper's characters are usually representatives of a class—national, regional, racial, or social—and therefore their relations with each other are both individual and representative. Such is the case in, for instance, *The Pioneers*, or, more obviously, the first half of *The Spy*. An even better example is *Satanstoe*, a late novel dealing with pre-revolutionary America in which a colonial belle of mixed Dutch and English extraction is courted by a colonial of the same background and by a British officer from 'Home', i.e. England; she eventually chooses to make *her* home with the American. It does not require much cleverness to perceive that Cooper is here exploring the colonial

---

[3] D. H. Lawrence, 'Fenimore Cooper's Leatherstocking Novels', *Studies in Classic American Literature* (New York, 1923).

schizophrenia which had to be healed before a national consciousness, and a nation, could come into being. Cooper almost invariably uses courtship and marriage in this way in his fiction: he doubtless saw his own marriage to Susan De Lancey as representative of the fruitful reconciliation of parties in the new nation. At its best, as in *Satanstoe*, it is a very effective device. An experienced reader of Cooper should therefore guess at once that when mulatto Cora and Indian Uncas are attracted to each other, Cooper is dealing with the relations between the three main races then inhabiting North America, and testing the possibility of their being brought together in an harmonious union. There is nothing secret about this. It is the sort of subject in which Cooper was characteristically interested, and the method he employs is equally characteristic.

When we first meet Cora, she has just caught sight of Magua for the first time:

Though this sudden and startling movement of the Indian produced no sound from the other, in the surprise, her veil also was allowed to open its folds, and betrayed an indescribable look of pity, admiration, and horror, as her dark eye followed the easy motions of the savage. The tresses of this lady were shining and black, like the plumage of the raven. Her complexion was not brown, but it rather appeared charged with the colour of the rich blood that seemed ready to burst its bounds.

In 'tresses . . . like the plumage of the raven' we have an example of the cliché-ridden genteel style of Cooper at his worst, and he is often at his worst in this novel. But there is also subtlety here: Cora's emotions upon first seeing the man who will cause her own death are, almost exactly, those of classical tragedy. The metaphor 'rich blood that seemed ready to burst its bounds' is likewise a premonition, of her love for a man of another race. An image of transgression, it also prefigures one of the few great passages in the work, Natty's description of the falls behind which the party is hiding:

'Ay! there are the falls on two sides of us, and the river above and below. If you had daylight it would be worth your trouble to step up on the height of this rock, and look at the perversity of the water. It falls by no rule at all; sometimes it leaps, sometimes it tumbles; there it skips; here it shoots; in one place 'tis white as snow, and in another 'tis green as grass; hereabouts it pitches into deep hollows, that rumble and quake the "arth" and theraway it ripples and sings like a brook, fashioning whirlpools and gullies in the old stone, as if 'twas no harder than trodden clay. The whole design of the river seems disconcerted. First it runs smoothly, as if meaning to go down the descent as things were ordered; then it angles about and faces the shores; nor are there places wanting where it looks backward, as if unwilling to leave the wilderness, to mingle with the salt! Ay, lady the fine cobweb-looking cloth you wear at your throat, is coarse, and like a fish net, to little spots I can show you, where the river fabricates all sorts of images, as if, having broke loose from order, it would try its hand at everything. And yet what does it amount to? After the water has been suffered to have its will for a time, like a headstrong man, it is gathered together by the hand that made it, and a few rods below, you may see it all, flowing on steadily towards the sea, as was fore-ordained from the first foundation of the "arth".'

While his auditors received a cheering assurance of the security of their place of concealment, from this untutored description of Glenn's, they were much inclined to judge differently from Hawk-eye, of its wild beauties.

Donald Davie has pointed out that Natty is here 'employing an outdated, a pre-Romantic set of standards', also that 'in none of the later (Leatherstocking) novels would Cooper thus permit his genteel characters to condescend to the hunter'. This is true, and it is also true that Natty's beliefs are perfectly consistent throughout this novel. The view of nature expressed here, and ridiculed by Cooper, is the view according to which miscegenation must be condemned and is later condemned by Natty: 'the river fabricates all sorts of images, as if, having broke loose from order, it would try its hand at everything'. This calls to mind a later, equally impressive speech by the villainous Magua, which begins:

'The Spirit that made men, coloured them differently,' commenced the subtle Huron. 'Some are blacker than the sluggish bear. These he said should be slaves, and he ordered them to work forever, like the beaver.'

This is also the view taken by Major Heyward, of course, who as a Southerner cannot think of marrying a woman with the blood of slaves in her veins.

Why does Cooper give his most impressive speeches to

characters with whom, for the moment at least, he is patently
out of sympathy? Is he of the Devil's party without knowing it?
(There are many echoes of *Paradise Lost* in this novel.) And
which is the Devil's party, anyway? Perhaps we have evidence
here of the 'moral anarchy' of which Davie speaks.

Yet it seems to me that Cooper does know what he is doing
and that what we have here is division of sympathies rather
than anarchy. This again is characteristic: much of the power
of *The Pioneers* results from his being about equally sympathetic
with, on the one hand, the North American wilderness and its
inhabitants, and, on the other, with the Westward Movement
and Civilization. Similarly, other works by Cooper show that
he was well able to appreciate both the Romantic beauty which
emerges from Natty's description of the falls and the symmetric-
ally ordered Classical beauty which is alone allowed for by
Natty's view of nature. And I think it is fairly clear that Cooper
believed there was a large element of truth in the arguments
advanced by Natty and Magua concerning the divine origin of
races and their role in the natural order. But it is equally clear
that he understood and was moved by the tragic consequences
of this doctrine. He sympathizes with Cora throughout the
story, and there is no mistaking where his sympathies lie in the
following passage:

'There it was my lot to form a connexion with one who in time
became my wife, and the mother of Cora. She was the daughter
of a gentleman of those isles, by a lady, whose misfortune it was, if
you will', said the old man, proudly, 'to be descended, remotely,
from that unfortunate class, who are so basely enslaved to adminis-
ter to the wants of a luxurious people! Ay, sir, that is a curse en-
tailed on Scotland, by her unnatural union with a foreign and
trading people. But could I find a man among them, who would
dare to reflect her descent on my child, he should feel the weight of a
father's anger. Ha! Major Heyward you are yourself born at the
south, where these unfortunate beings are considered of a race inferior to your own!'

"'Tis most unfortunately true, sir,' said Duncan, unable any
longer to prevent his eyes from sinking to the floor in embarrassment.

'And you cast it on my child as a reproach! You scorn to mingle
the blood of the Heywards with one so degraded—lovely and
virtuous though she be?' fiercely demanded the jealous parent.

'Heaven protect me from a prejudice so unworthy of my reason!' returned Duncan, at the same time conscious of such a feeling, and that as deeply rooted as if it had been engrafted in his nature.

There you have it: prejudice is cruel and irrational—and inevitable wherever different racial or ethnic groups are brought together. Colonel Munro's own strong Scottish prejudice against the English is ironically revealed at the very moment when, with perfect justice, he attacks Major Heyward's prejudice. And how much more than Britain is North America, in reality and in this novel, a battle-ground of races, nationalities, and tribes. French and English are pitted against each other, Indian tribes against each other and themselves, red men against white men and both against black men.

Two things are at issue, then: whether miscegenation is a crime against nature, and, crime or no crime, whether a multi-racial society in North America is possible. To the first question Cooper gives us a deliberately ambiguous answer; he simply doesn't know. At the funeral of Uncas and Cora, the Indian girls speak of the dead:

Clothing their ideas in the most remote and subtle images, they betrayed, that, in the short period of their intercourse, they had discovered, with the intuitive perception of their sex, the truant disposition of his inclinations. The Delaware girls had found no favour in his eyes! He was of a race that had once been lords on the shores of the salt lake, and his wishes had led him back to a people who dwelt about the graves of his fathers. Why should not such a predilection be encouraged? That she was of a blood purer and richer than the rest of her nation, any eye might have seen. That she was equal to the dangers and daring of a life in the woods, her conduct had proved; and, now, they added, the 'wise one of the earth' had transplanted her to a place where she would find congenial spirits, and might be for ever happy.

Natty's reaction is this:

But when they spoke of the future prospects of Cora and Uncas, he shook his head like one who knew the error of their simple creed . . .

Here we clearly have a parallel, or more likely an antithesis, to the passage quoted earlier, where Natty describes the falls and his listeners disagree with his unromantic viewpoint. For I think it is probable from the tone of the later passages that Cooper here inclines to agree with Natty rather than the romantic Indian girls. Still, one cannot conclude simply that, in Cooper's eyes, Natty is wrong about aesthetics and right about morals. When he shakes his head 'like one who knew the error of their simple creed' he is acting so perfectly in character that, to be sure that Cooper also shakes his head, we must be as clairvoyant about Cooper's intentions as Natty supposes himself to be about those of God. And I do not see how the careful paralleling of these passages can be interpreted except as a warning, first, not to confuse morals and aesthetics, but second, not to presume that the individual can so transcend his heredity and environment as to arrive at unbiased judgments in either sphere.

I think this caution reflects genuine uncertainty on Cooper's part. His conclusions about the possibility of a multiracial society are more decisive and grim. Whether Cora and Uncas live or die together, he will be the last of his tribe. The choice, in effect, is between the creation of a new race to inhabit North America or the extermination or total subjection of all races save one. And, to return from the general to the particular, marriage between Uncas and Cora *was* inconceivable—not because of Cooper's 'horror of miscegenation', but because they had nothing to draw or keep them together except sexual desire. And Cooper was right, of course (whatever his contemporaries, Leslie Fiedler, or the Indian maidens might think): the union of Uncas and Cora, the creation of a new race of North Americans, was never more than a forlorn hope. The future lies with Major Heyward and Alice, who will not only 'breed plenty of white children' [4] but will also own plenty of negro slaves. A sense of racial doom is present in this novel as it is in no other Leatherstocking tale. The last words are spoken by the venerable Delaware chief Tamenund, so aged that he had witnessed the first white settlements:

'It is enough!' he said. 'Go, children of the Lenape; the anger of the Manitto is not done. Why, should Tamenund stay? The pale-faces are masters of the earth, and the time of the red-men has not yet come again. My day has been too long. In the morning I saw

---

[4] Lawrence, *op. cit.*

the sons of Unamis happy and strong; and yet before the night has come, have I lived to see the last warrior of the wise race of the Mohicans.'

The three major racial relationships envisaged by Cooper in *The Last of the Mohicans*, then, are those typified by Cora and Uncas, by Alice and Major Heyward, and by Leatherstocking and Chingachgook. We are certainly meant to view them in terms of broad national and historical perspectives—though it is hardly likely that Cooper himself recognized, or dared face, all their implications for the future.[5] Cora and Uncas are both notably adaptable people, though they are at the same time specimens of the best that their respective civilizations can produce: Cora's ability to confront the hardships and dangers of aboriginal North America is frequently stressed; so too is Uncas's freedom from the less noble characteristics of his people, particularly the Indian attitude towards women. What the union of these two promised, then, was a true marriage of the Old and New Worlds—one which would allow North America to retain its essential character and not become so many fake New Yorks, Nova Scotias, New Englands. On the other hand, Alice Munro is utterly helpless in the wilderness, and it is significant that Cooper's Indians take no sexual interest in her. If her type is to survive in the New World, then the New World must be adapted to her; for she cannot adapt herself to it. Luckily for her, Major Heyward glories in his protective role,

---

[5] I perhaps err, as do most contemporary critics, in underestimating Cooper's intellectual courage and awareness. At any rate, an interpreter of *The Last of the Mohicans* and *The Wept of Wish-ton-Wish* must take into account this paragraph from *The American Democrat*, originally published in 1838:
'American slavery is distinguished from that of most other parts of the world, by the circumstance that the slave is a variety of the human species, and is marked by physical peculiarities so different from his master as to render future amalgamation improbable. In ancient Rome, in modern Europe generally, and, in most other countries, the slave not being thus distinguished, on obtaining his freedom, was soon lost in the mass around him; but nature has made a stamp on the American slave that is likely to prevent this consummation, and which menaces much future ill to the country. The time must come when American slavery shall cease, and when that day shall arrive, (unless early and effectual means are devised to obviate it), two races will exist in the same region, whose feelings will be embittered by inextinguishable hatred, and who carry on their faces, the respective stamps of their factions. The struggle that will follow, will necessarily be a war of extermination. The evil day may be delayed, but can scarcely be averted.' (Vintage ed., 1956, p. 173.)

and his racial prejudices assure that North America will be made very safe and easy for Alice and her children. So far as Natty and Chingachgook are concerned, their friendship affords but little hope for the future. For the sad conclusion to be drawn from this relationship seems to be that only such eccentric figures as Natty Bumppo, who opt out of white society, are able to experience the truth that men of different races are brothers. As such relationships are childless, and as men like Natty do not marry, his experience will never be powerfully transmitted, will never become an effective social force. Humanly important as such relationships are, therefore, they do not much affect the destiny of nations or races; they have great personal value but little political import.

On this level, *The Last of the Mohicans* is anything but a frivolous work. Fenimore Cooper was an extremely serious, intelligent, and courageous writer who used his art to explore a great variety of social problems. But as he usually applied his formidable critical intelligence to social rather than literary problems, and as he had a prodigious gift for writing sensational adventure narrative, he was, far more than most great writers, at the mercy of the popular literary conventions of his age. At times he was a great, conscious artist, and even in *The Last of the Mohicans* there is more fully serious, conscious artistry than appears at first sight. But the breathless adventure narrative so dominates this novel that the reader is virtually hypnotized, and if he remains awake he is bound to attend more closely to the absurdities of the plot or the banalities of the diction, than to the serious but scarcely obtrusive theme. Thus, what was merely submerged through Cooper's ineptitude, or, in a way his mis-directed skill, becomes a 'secret theme', presumably unknown to Cooper himself!

Yet surely the passages quoted cannot but have made some impression, however light and brief, on the millions who have read *The Last of the Mohicans*. Moreover, although the feverish, dream-like narrative of adventure does tend to submerge the serious analysis of racial relations, it also provides the relief necessary to give the adventure of the secret cave behind the waterfall great concrete actuality and its attendant symbolism great force. This is the most memorable episode in the novel. Cooper himself could not forget it, and when he later revised

The Pioneers in the light of subsequently written Leatherstocking tales, this episode and the cave itself were noted as having been important in the history of the old hunter. Certainly it was a stroke of genius, the full significance of which Cooper himself doubtless did not understand.

It is only under the pressure of extreme danger, and after their swearing secrecy, that the genteel white characters are permitted to take refuge in the cave; and it is in the cave that Uncas and Cora are first obviously attracted to each other. The sanctuary having been violated by the presence of the uninitiated whites, its discovery by the hostile forces follows swiftly and inexorably. Here Cooper's horror of miscegenation really is unmistakable. But it is not so much the violation of a white girl by a red man that we are made aware of; rather, it is the betrayal of the secret place of the natives by its own custodians, and their consequent loss of power, that is of paramount significance. These meanings, too, are submerged but hardly 'inert'; more than the conscious meanings embodied in the courtship and death of Cora and Uncas, these I am sure do get across to most readers, although in a vague and half-conscious fashion. Perhaps it is mainly because of this episode that *The Last of the Mohicans* has 'moved the world for more than a hundred years', in spite of the fact that it appears to have ' "no serious concern" with that world'.

2. *The Wept of Wish-ton-Wish*

The next Leatherstocking tale, *The Prairie*, is, like *The Pioneers*, more concerned with incompatible ways of life and codes of conduct than with racial relations as such. None the less, *The Prairie* too reveals Cooper's compassionate interest in the tragic racial and cultural consequences of the white man's triumphant march westward. Indeed, for several years racial relations were one of his principal social and fictional preoccupations. In the *Red Rover*, for instance, which was written immediately after *The Prairie*, Cooper seems to have intended at first to deal more than incidentally with the evil social effects of negro slavery. One of the important characters in that novel is a negro seaman named Guinea who for many years has been the loyal but 'inferior' companion of one Dick Fid, a rough yet fundamentally

75

kindly white sailor: when Guinea is at last fatally wounded, Fid's grief breaks down his life-long prejudice:

'Ay, ay, Guinea; put your mind at ease on that point, my hearty, and, for that matter, on all others. You shall have a grave as deep as the sea, and Christian burial, boy, if this here parson will stand by his work. Any small message you may have for your friends shall be logged, and put in the way of coming to their ears. You have had much foul weather in your time, Guinea, and some squalls have whistled about your head that might have been spared, mayhap, had your color been a shade or two lighter. For that matter it may be that I have rode you down a little too close myself, boy, when overheated with the conceit of the skin: for all which may the Lord forgive me as freely as I hope you will do the same thing!'

The negro made a fruitless effort to rise, endeavouring to grasp the hand of the other, as he did so,—

'Misser Fid beg a pardon of a black man! Masser aloft forget he'm all, Misser Richard, he t'ink 'em no more.'

'It will be what I call a d . . . d generous thing, if he does,' returned Richard, whose sorrow and whose conscience had stirred up his uncouth feelings to an extraordinary degree.

No doubt this is not so well done as similar scenes in *Huckleberry Finn*, but it is at least an honourable and humane attempt to break through the crust of racial prejudice and get at the human suffering underneath. But unfortunately, whatever Cooper's original intentions may have been, negro slavery in the New World and its social effects were thrust aside by the rush of the narrative of nautical adventure in the *Red Rover*. Only in connexion with the American Indian could his interest in racial relations be deeply engaged and sustained throughout the length of a novel.

In the *Mohicans* Cooper entertained the possibility that racial prejudices could and should be overcome so far as to permit marriage between members of two races. In no other Leatherstocking tale is this possibility seriously considered. But there is another novel of the American frontier and wilderness which concerns itself with a successfully consummated union between a white girl and an Indian man. *The Wept of Wish-ton-Wish* (1829), written immediately after the *Red Rover* and therefore only a few years after the *Mohicans*, is the most serious and moving of Cooper's studies of the tragic clash between races in

76

the New World. It may also be read as Cooper's contemporary gloss on the meaning of the *Mohicans* and *The Prairie*.

As Leslie Fiedler says, in *The Wept* Cooper 'regresses in time to King Philip's War, to the profoundest roots of American life'. Fiedler's summary of the novel is as follows:

In *The Wept* an Indian boy, Conanchet, captured by whites, is recaptured by an Indian raiding party, who take along with him a girl child of the family which has kept him in captivity. When they are both grown, he makes the white girl, who presumably loves him, his squaw; but when he discovers that her parents are still alive he surrenders her to them, and gives himself up to his Indian enemies, dying by the hand of Uncas, remote ancestor of the handsome young brave of *The Last of the Mohicans*. It is Conanchet, however, who plays the true Uncas role in this novel, being described as 'the last sachem of the broken and dispersed tribes of the Narragansett', whose looks 'bore a close affinity to the Pythian Apollo'. He is, in short, the good Indian, which is to say (for Cooper at least) the vanishing one; but he has stolen a child from her mother, and there is in him, as a red man and a savage, the hint of something revolting to a higher race. Counterbalancing the suggestion of Apollo in his head and face, there is a touch of the Dionysian in his chest: a flabby fullness which indicates 'the animal indulgence of Bacchus'.[6]

Those who have read the novel will realize how misleading this summary is, but for those who haven't the record should be set straight. In the first place, Narra-mattah does not 'presumably' love Conanchet; Cooper stresses her devotion to and affection for him—they are as obviously in love with each other as it is possible to be. Conanchet does not rush out and give himself up to his enemies: he surrenders to them only after every means of escaping and combating them has been exhausted. Nor has he 'stolen a child from her mother'; on the contrary, he has acted in good faith as the sworn protector of the child after the supposed death of all her family. As for 'the hint of something revolting to a higher race', Fiedler suppresses Cooper's elaborate explanation and qualification:

This resemblance, however, to a deity that is little apt to awaken lofty sentiments in the spectator, was not displeasing, since it in some measure relieved the sternness of an eye that penetrated like the glance of an eagle, and that might otherwise have left an impression of too little sympathy with the familiar weaknesses of humanity. Still the young chief was less to be remarked by this peculiar fulness of chest, the fruit of intervals of inaction, constant indulgence of the first wants of nature, and a total exemption from toil, than most of those who either counselled in secret near, or paced the grounds about the building. In him, it was rather a point to be admired than a blemish; for it seemed to say, that notwithstanding the evidences of austerity which custom, and perhaps character, as well as rank, had gathered in his air, there was a heart beneath that might be touched by the charities of humanity.

It is true of course that Cooper can be accused of protesting too much. Perhaps he does. But the knowing critic should at least record what the author seems to think he means, and not merely what the critic knows he *really* means. If we can once get beyond our preconceptions about Cooper's horror of miscegenation and dislike of New Englanders, we shall find that *The Wept* is one of his most intelligent and attractive novels—a much better novel, in fact, than *The Last of the Mohicans*.

Much of its considerable success it owes to a carefully chosen setting. In *The Pioneers* Cooper was to some extent inhibited by the fact that he was writing about Cooperstown: any serious moral question about the white man's possession of the Indian's land had to be headed off. (We are told that the land was deeded to Major Effingham by the Delawares, his adopted tribe. In context this is more than an evasion, since the brotherhood of Chingachgook, the Effinghams, and Leatherstocking is important for other reasons as well.) Yet it is the frontier setting of *The Pioneers*, where the landscape undergoes a visible transformation in the interests of a new civilized economy, rather than the wilderness setting of *The Last of the Mohicans*, which most dramatically confronts the reader with the accomplished fact of usurpation. So long as the Indian's native environment remains intact, it is possible to suppose that he still has a chance, that the land is still his. The clearing brings home how little chance he does have against a completely foreign way of life. On the other hand, a settlement as advanced as Templeton in *The Pioneers* offers but little opportunity for intercourse between whites and Indians, and less reason for the whites to fear the red men: racial relations in Templeton are not an immediate social problem, only a problem of conscience for those few with a long memory.

But the tiny isolated pioneering community in the valley of Wish-ton-Wish is ideally situated to raise the right questions and to afford the white settlers with many unwelcome red visitors. Equally important, the settlers are English Puritans. The Heathcote family, arriving in the valley less than half a century after the first landing at Plymouth, comes armed with a righteous conviction that it is founding a New Jerusalem in the howling wilderness: Cooper may be uneasy about the white man's claim to the red man's land, but the Heathcotes are not. Yet the Heathcotes are also industrious, courageous, and charitable people: and given the age they live in, their background and condition, they act irreproachably—as irreproachably as do the Indians, given theirs. Therefore, although Cooper disliked Puritanism, in this instance it permitted him to concentrate on the cultural and human tragedy of the Westward Movement, personally unembarrassed by the moral dilemma which the Movement inevitably created in his own (so he believed) more humane and enlightened age.

It is important to underscore the fact that—with the single exception of that blatant caricature the Reverend Meek Wolfe —the Puritan characters in this novel are not among the rogues in Cooper's magnificent, unequalled gallery of New Englanders. On the contrary, the Heathcote family inspires a life-long affection and respect in the breast of Conanchet, the sachem of the tribe whose land the Heathcotes now occupy. For this reason he vows to protect the Heathcote children against the vengeance of his own greatly wronged tribe. One of the children he does manage to save from what seems to be the total destruction of the Heathcote family is raised as an Indian girl and eventually becomes his wife. But although Conanchet acts with perfect integrity (entirely apart from any question of love, it is much safer for the girl to be his wife), and although the Heathcote family always try to deal humanely with the Indians, the marriage between Conanchet and Narra-mattah is certainly viewed with horror by her parents—and by Conanchet's Indian associate Metacom as well. Even Conanchet himself doubts the rightness of his marriage, the more so because he is now leagued with Metacom in what is frankly a genocidal war against the whites. In any case, when he discovers that the Heathcotes are still alive in the valley of Wish-ton-Wish, he fulfils his vow to them by returning Narra-mattah to a mother who has long grieved for her missing child.

Narra-mattah is the only person completely convinced that her marriage is right and natural; aside from a dim memory of her mother, she has become, in heart and mind, entirely Indian. She loves Conanchet and is, besides, the mother of his child. The discovery of her half-breed child brings the Puritans' racial prejudice out into the open: her brother Mark is silently indignant; a neighbour suggests that the respected Heathcotes might wish to give away this 'offspring with an Indian cross of blood',[7] and even Narra-mattah's mother cannot disguise her initial prejudiced reaction to the babe:

It would exceed the powers of the unambitious pen we wield, to convey to the reader a just idea of the mixed emotions that struggled for mastery in the countenance of Ruth. The innate and never-dying sentiment of maternal joy was opposed by all those feelings of pride that prejudice could not fail to implant, even in the bosom of one so meek.

Cooper's meaning is not easily mistaken: the prejudice that inspires pride is as contrary to Christianity as it is to Nature ('The innate . . . sentiment of maternal joy'). So far as Nature is concerned, it is all on the side of Conanchet, Narra-mattah, and their child:

A smile on her infant brought the blood back to her heart in a swift and tumultuous current; and Ruth herself soon forgot that she had any reason for regret in the innocent delight with which her own daughter now hastened to display the physical excellence of the boy. From this scene of natural feeling . . .

Or earlier in the novel:

The eye of the warrior, as he looked upon the ingenuous and

---

[7] We should note that *The Wept* is dedicated to 'the Rev. J. R. C.'. Cooper thus addresses him: 'You have every reason to exalt in your descent, for, surely, if any man may claim to be a citizen and a proprietor in the Union, it is one that, like yourself, can point to a line of ancestors whose origin is lost in the obscurity of time. You are truly an American. In your eyes, we of a brief century or two must appear as little more than denizens quite recently admitted to the privilege of a residence.' No doubt this dedication was partly designed to make Cooper's own position on miscegenation unequivocally clear: perhaps he wished to dissociate himself from the views expressed by Leatherstocking in the *Mohicans*.

confiding face of the speaker, was kind to fondness. The firmness had passed away, and in its place was left the winning softness of affection, which, as it belongs to nature, is seen, at times, in the expression of an Indian's eye, as strongly as it is ever known to sweeten the intercourse of a more polished condition of life.

Yet innocent and natural though the love of Narra-mattah and Conanchet is, it cannot survive. In the end, Conanchet, knowing that he has to die, tells her that she must stay with her white parents and forget him and her Indian past:

'Let thy mind be like a wide clearing. Let all its shadows be next the woods; let it forget the dream it dreamt among the trees. 'Tis the will of the Manitou.'

'Conanchet asketh much of his wife. Her soul is only the soul of a woman!'

'A woman of the pale-faces; now let her seek her tribe. Narra-mattah, thy people speak strange traditions. They say one just man died for all colors. . . . If this be true, he will look for his woman and boy in the happy hunting-grounds, and they will come to him. . . . Let Narra-mattah forget her chief till that time, and then, when she calls him by name, let her speak strong; for he will be very glad to hear her voice again.'

But whatever the colour of her skin may be, the shock of this red man's death kills her as well. Thus a terrible irony hangs over all Conanchet's theories that, in spite of her Indian up-bringing, she will be better off among 'her own people'. Here too we must bear in mind that Narra-mattah, like her mother, was christened Ruth: like Hawthorne after him, Cooper took advantage of the Puritans' practice of naming their children after Old Testament figures. He rightly expected his readers to draw the obvious parallel between this Ruth and the Ruth who said, 'Intreat me not to leave thee . . . thy people shall be my people. . . .'

Perhaps in no other novel does Cooper so strongly affirm the determining power of environment—a power which his stoical Indians and his Calvinistic white characters interpret as the inscrutable will of God. Another ironic expression of the view that environment is fate is the way Conanchet is captured by a hostile tribe: he might easily have escaped but for his noble effort to save a white man who lacked the skill and agility necessary for flight from Indian pursuers. This episode hardly proves

that white and red men should not mix in friendship; it does
help to confirm what in fact emerges as the main theme of the
novel—that race, if not quite neutral (since Cooper leaves open
the possibility that each race may have certain peculiar 'gifts'),
does not matter in the eye of God and would not matter in the
eye of man either if racial lines were not identical with cultural
lines.

And such is the meaning of the remarkable conclusion of *The
Wept of Wish-ton-Wish*. The shock of Conanchet's death leaves
Narra-mattah half-conscious, but suddenly she regains her white
childhood; the 'dream . . . dreamt among the trees' is lost and
once again she has her childish fear of the forests and Indians:

The full and sweet organs next rolled from face to face, recognition
and pleasure accompanying each change. On Whittal they became
perplexed and doubtful, but when they met the fixed, frowning, and
still commanding eye of the dead chief, their wandering ceased
forever. There was a minute, during which fear, doubt, wildness,
and early recollections, struggled for the mastery. The hands of
Narra-mattah trembled, and she clung convulsively to the robe of
Ruth.

'Mother! mother!' whispered the agitated victim of so many
conflicting emotions, 'I will pray again,—an evil spirit besets me.'

Ruth felt the force of her grasp, and heard the breathing of a few
words of petition; after which the voice was mute, and the hands
relaxed their hold. When the face of the nearly insensible parent was
withdrawn, to the others the dead appeared to gaze at each other
with a mysterious and unearthly intelligence.

It is 'an evil spirit besets me' that does the work here: Conanchet has been her very best spirit, and Cooper does not allow
us to forget that she 'had . . . long lived in his kindness'. The
irony is as illuminating as it is painful; for it would scarcely be
possible to confront the reader with more startling evidence of
the effects of environment on a youthful mind. As Yvor Winters
observed some thirty years ago, Cooper's conception here
'deserved a more successful rendering, but . . . is rendered
with sufficient success to merit more appreciation than it has
received'.[8]

I do not suggest that Cooper was himself entirely free from
the racial prejudices he attributes to the Heathcotes. In this

---

[8] Winters, *In Defence of Reason*, p. 192.

connexion it is significant that Cooper quite clearly admires and approves of the Heathcotes on the whole; to him it is neither surprising nor very repugnant that they regard 'the heathen' as an inferior race. And in this he shows more historical awareness than some of his own critics have shown. Cooper's deliberate verdict was that racial prejudice, given man's fallen nature, was inevitable so long as different races existed: and I am afraid that he was right. But he also rightly believed that it was worth trying to understand the problem and to communicate that understanding to others. In turn, he has himself been misunderstood, misrepresented, and condemned. It is of course easy to misunderstand *The Last of the Mohicans*. But only careless reading, coupled with rigid preconceptions, can account for the usual misinterpretations of *The Wept of Wish-ton-Wish*.

V

THE PRAIRIE

THE LEATHERSTOCKING IS inescapably one of the great characters of world literature. Not excepting Dostoievsky's Myshkin, there is no greater 'secular saint' than Natty Bumppo. Like all such characters, from Don Quixote to Dostoievsky's saintly fools, Natty is essentially a tragi-comic figure, modelled ultimately on Christ. It is obvious that when a divine or saintly figure is thrust, comparatively helpless, into a worldly milieu, the possibilities are comic or tragic or both. Even in the case of Christ the humorous aspects of his predicament (though of the most grim and tragic sort) are brought home when he is paraded as King of the Jews. Indeed, so obvious are the comic potentialities that when we encounter a character like Parson Adams or Pickwick, in whom little else is realized, we rightly feel that Fielding's or Dickens' moral intelligence is inferior to that of Cervantes or Dostoievsky. Perhaps the best statement of the problem of the secular saint (or the real saint even) is to be found, not in Christian literature, but in Plato's parable of the cave:

'Nor will you think it strange that anyone who descends from contemplation of the divine to the imperfections of human life should blunder and make a fool of himself, if, while still blinded and unaccustomed to the surrounding darkness, he's forcibly put on trial in the law-courts or elsewhere about the images of justice or their shadows, and made to dispute about the conceptions of justice held by men who have never seen absolute justice.'

'There's nothing strange in that.'

'But anyone with any sense . . . will remember that the eyes may be unsighted in two ways, by a transition from light to darkness or from darkness to light, and that the same distinction applies to the mind. So when he sees a mind confused and unable to see clearly he will not laugh without thinking, but will ask himself whether it has come from a clearer world and is confused by the unaccustomed darkness, or whether it is dazzled by the stronger light of the clearer world to which it has escaped from its previous ignorance.'

(Republic, VII, 517–18)[1]

At the same time, reminding us of Socrates' fate, Plato has Socrates observe that the prisoners in the cave, '. . . if anyone tried to release them and lead them up . . . would kill him if they could lay hands on him'. Such was also the fate of Christ, such virtually the fate of Prince Myshkin.

Don Quixote, on the other hand, is lucky enough to die with his boots off, though he too has intruded with his reforming zeal where neither he nor it was welcome. It would be monstrous, rather than tragic, for him to be executed by an offended society, since he is, after all, really daft, and since his subversive chivalric ideals present no credible threat to the existing order. To some extent, of course, his adventures parody the descent of the wise man into the cave, because he brings his chimeras with him and because his behaviour seems to prove the rightness of Plato's warning against uncensored reading. None the less, the final problem of the reader of Cervantes' novel is to ask himself whether the Don has emerged from the light or from the cave, and whether we live in the cave or, as we suppose, in the light. The laugh may be on us.

The name 'Natty Bumppo' is a sufficient indication of the comic potentialities of Cooper's character, but nowhere in the series does he become a figure of fun or truly live up to the name he inherited from his parents. To be sure, the element of broad caricature shows through occasionally, and in his first appearance in *The Pioneers* his manners are certainly bumpkinish:

'No—no—Judge,' returned the hunter, with an inward chuckle, and with that look of exultation, that indicates a consciousness of superior skill; 'you burnt your powder, only to warm your nose this cold evening . . . if you're for a buck, or a little bear's meat, Judge, you'll have to take the long rifle, with a greased wadding, or you'll waste more powder than you'll fill stomachs, I'm thinking.'

---

[1] My quotations from the *Republic* are taken from H. D. P. Lee's translation (Harmondsworth, 1955).

As the speaker concluded, he drew his bare hand across the bottom of his nose, and again opened his enormous mouth with a kind of inward laugh.

But even at this moment, he is also the man of skill, acting knowledgeably in his own milieu. Judge Temple may wield a handkerchief more dexterously and often, but his incompetence with a gun has just caused him to miss a buck and wound Oliver Effingham. In this way Cooper prevents the old hunter from being made a victim of satire, at the same time that he underlines how out of place the hunter would be in society. For it is quite true that, translated into polite society, Leatherstocking would cut as absurd a figure as Don Quixote on the highways of Spain. But unlike other secular saints in literature, he never intrudes his presence where it would appear ungainly or subversive. (Almost alone among the characters in *The Pioneers*, Leatherstocking never sets foot in the Judge's mansion.) Exactly the opposite is true: an ungainly and subversive society intrudes itself upon him.

The upshot of this intrusion is that Leatherstocking is dragged into a court of law where his ignorance of legal decorum and issues does lead him to behave in the most clownish fashion— or what might have been the most clownish fashion, had Cooper wished to depict it so. Of course Leatherstocking is no Socrates on trial; neither can it be supposed that Judge Temple's justice is the justice of the Cave, while that of the old hunter is the absolute justice outside. Nevertheless, the blinding transition from lightness to darkness, or vice versa, is an appropriate simile for what happens to characters who cross cultural frontiers in the Leatherstocking saga. And in the case of Leatherstocking's trial in *The Pioneers*, if we except the final qualifying clause, it would be true to say that 'he's forcibly put on trial in the lawcourts . . . about the images of justice or their shadows, and made to dispute about the conceptions of justice held by men who have never seen absolute justice'. For the trial is very much about the images of justice or their shadows and not about the violation of any particular law. So far as Natty is concerned, the shadow without the substance, the sign without intrinsic worth, possess no authority and perhaps no reality. So long as Judge Temple seems to him an essentially unjust man, Sheriff Jones and Deputy Kirby lawless men, and Magistrate Doolittle a self-seeking intruder, no badge or title can give them authority in his eyes. Apart from the name he was born with, his own titles—Hawkeye, for instance, in *The Pioneers*—do accurately reflect the qualities of the man. The simple integrity of this viewpoint is not of course to be confused with the philosopher's sophisticated distrust of the world of appearance. At times, as when Oliver Effingham offers him paper money at the end of the novel, the old man is extremely naive:

> The old man took the notes, and examined them with a curious eye, when he said—
> 'This, then, is some of the new fashioned money that they've been making at Albany, out of paper! It can't be worth much to they that hasn't larning! No, no, lad—take back the stuff; it will do me no sarvice.'

His 'out of paper!' well expresses his incredulity that the banknotes could have any real value anywhere, let alone in the wilderness—though he seems to allow that the words on the notes might be worth something to those who are literate! Yet it is, after all, a simplicity which guards him against corruption; and the simplicity which refuses to recognize the authority of men like Jones and Doolittle is rather like the simplicity of the child who saw that the emperor wore no clothes. For they, not Hawkeye, are the clowns when they appear in roles for which they are suited neither by aptitude, character, nor experience. But every word and gesture of the old hunter proclaims him to be exactly what he pretends to be, neither more nor less.

But civilization, at any rate in a frontier community, is driven to makeshifts. The energetic virtuoso, willing to undertake anything, may prove more useful than the modest specialist. Such a virtuoso is Sheriff Richard Jones, amateur architect, doctor of hogs and humans, prospector, etc. He is one of the most brilliant of Cooper's minor characters, the human equivalent of the country store. But though his kinsman Judge Temple patronizes him, the Judge also understands the shortcomings of his type:

> . . . 'You are of opinion, Judge Temple, that a man is qualified by nature and education to do only one thing well, whereas I know that genius will supply the place of learning, and that a certain sort of man can do anything and everything.'

'Like yourself, I suppose,' said Marmaduke, smiling.

'I scorn personalities, sir,' returned the Sheriff; 'I say nothing of myself; but there are three men on your patent, of the kind that I should term talented by nature for her general purposes, though acting under the influence of different situations.'

'We are better off then, than I had supposed,' said Marmaduke. 'Who are they?'

'Why, sir, one is Hiram Doolittle; he is a carpenter by trade, as you know, and I need only point to the village to exhibit its merits. Then he is a magistrate, and might shame many a man in the distribution of justice, who has had better opportunities than himself.'

'Well, he is one,' said Marmaduke, with the air of a man who was determined not to dispute the point.

'Yes, sir, and Jotham Riddle is another.'

'Who!' exclaimed the Judge.

'Jotham Riddel.'

'What, that dissatisfied, shiftless, lazy, speculating fellow! he who changes his county every three years, his farm every six months, and his occupation every season! an agriculturist yesterday, a shoemaker today, and a schoolmaster to-morrow! that epitome of all the unsteady and profitless propensities of the settlers without one of their good qualities to counterbalance the evil! Nay, Richard, this is too bad or even—but who is the third?'

'As the third is not used to hearing such comments on his character, Judge Temple, I shall not name him,' said the indignant Sheriff.

The character of Jotham Riddel is not unlike Dryden's Zimri ('all Mankind's Epitome'), but it is more like Plato's character of the Democratic man:

'In fact,' I said, 'he lives for the pleasure of the moment. One day it's wine, women, and song, the next bread and water; one day it's hard physical training, the next indolence and ease, and then a period of philosophic study. Next he takes to politics and is always on his feet saying or doing whatever comes into his head. Sometimes all his ambitions are military, sometimes they are all directed to success in business. There's no order or restraint in his life, and he reckons his way of living is pleasant, free, and happy.'

(*Republic*, VIII, 561)

Riddel's impoverished New England origins gave him no taste for the sensual indulgences of Plato's Democratic man; but in other respects the trio of Jones, Riddel, and Doolittle is a fair likeness of what Plato disliked in democracy. On the positive side, they have the energy and cock-sureness necessary (in the absence of specialists) to get any job done; on the negative side, they invariably botch the job, more or less seriously. As the founder of a new community, Judge Temple would prefer to follow Plato's plan to make each of his citizens a specialist; certainly his opinion 'that a man is qualified by nature and education to do only one thing well' is exactly the same as Plato's. But aside from such queer ducks as Lawyer Van der School (queer but honest), the only specialist in sight is Leatherstocking.

If we continue to use Plato as our guide, it follows that Leatherstocking is the only just man in sight:

> 'And further, we have often heard and often said that justice consists in minding your business and not interfering with other people.'
>
> *(Republic,* IV, 433)

How unlike busy, snooping Squire Doolittle, Sheriff Jones, and Jotham Riddel! And how well the following expresses Leatherstocking's values:

> 'And won't [the just rulers] try to follow the principle that men should not take other people's belongings or be deprived of their own? . . . So we reach again by another route the conclusion that justice is keeping to what belongs to one and doing one's own job.'
>
> *(Republic,* IV, 433)

By a strange transmutation the values of the *Republic* become the values of the American frontiersman. Cooper understood that the boastfulness of the hunter might disguise the essential humility of the man who accepted his own limitations and made the most of his talents; that the hunter's dislike of interference and respect for privacy might be an expression, not merely of the 'habits of his secluded life' (the explanation given in *The Prairie*), but of a specialist's sense that each man should have his own job and the freedom to get on with it; and that the simple integrity of such a man, in the conformity between what he is and what he professes, may be the true measure of the just man. Is it for the sake of a Platonistic ethical contrast, or is it merely an accidental fact of Otsego county history, that the criminals who are supposed to be tried at the same session with Natty are counterfeiters?[2]

The Leatherstocking's saintly humility takes many forms. For instance, though he is called a 'lawless squatter' and is supposed to have no respect for higher authority, he is in truth the most obedient man in the settlement. Cooper drives this point home ironically just at the moment that the Judge is about to sentence Leatherstocking:

'Nathaniel Bumppo,' commenced the Judge, making the customary pause.
The old hunter, who had been musing again, with his head on the bar, raised himself and cried, with prompt military tone—
'Here.'

The same spirit of Christian humility causes him vehemently to reject Mahtoree's atheistic materialism and the natural scientist's evolutionary theory that man might eventually become as perfect as his Creator.

Another aspect of his humility (as I have suggested earlier) is revealed in his view of nature. So far as he is concerned, the North American wilderness is little less than a new Garden of Eden which it is the worst kind of pride and folly for men to try to alter or improve:

'Thou sayest well, Leather-stocking,' cried Marmaduke, 'and I begin to think it time to put an end to this work of destruction.'
'Put an end, Judge, to your clearings. An't the woods His work as well as the pigeons? Use, but don't waste. Wasn't the woods made for the beasts and birds to harbour in? and when men wanted their flesh, their skins, or their feathers, there's the place to seek them.'

Such a strict interpretation of the lawful relationship between man and nature humbles and limits man to the condition of

[2] If there is any positive evidence that Cooper had read *The Republic*, I have overlooked it. Incidents or attitudes in *The Pioneers* which might seem to indicate a debt to Plato can in every case be shown to have a factual basis in Otsego County history, though these facts, as recorded in Judge Cooper's *Guide* and James Cooper's *Chronicles of Cooperstown* (Cooperstown, 1838), seem to have furnished little more than hints which Cooper elaborated and wove into a pattern. My contention is not that Cooper superimposed the theses of *The Republic* on his raw materials, but that a moral pattern does exist in *The Pioneers* which can be elucidated by reference to Plato. It is at least likely that, while a student at Yale, he may have come in contact with Plato's works; his much-admired tutor was the distinguished classical scholar James Luce Kingsley.

the Indian—no bad thing, in the eyes of Leatherstocking. But if it is a philosophy which civilized man cannot afford to accept, it is one which is based on, and which in turn inculcates, humility in the face of God and God's nature. It is therefore appropriate when Nature conspires with Cooper to express the moral grandeur of the old trapper in the great scene at the beginning of *The Prairie*:

> The sun had fallen below the crest of the nearest wave of the prairie, leaving the usual rich and glowing train in its trace. In the centre of this flood of fiery light a human form appeared, drawn against the gilded background as distinctly, and seemingly as palpable, as though it would come within the grasp of any extended hand. The figure was colossal; the attitude musing and melancholy; and the situation directly in the route of the travelers.

An interesting optical phenomenon, Dr Obed Bat would have said, had he been present when Ishmael Bush and his family witnessed this sight with superstitious awe. Leatherstocking's reverent attitude, based on intimate knowledge of nature, lies not between but in a different sphere from the superstitious ignorance of the Bush family and Dr Bat's arrogant belief that he has mastered nature when he has (inaccurately) classified natural phenomena.

In all the Leatherstocking tales, but especially in *The Pioneers* and *The Prairie*, Cooper is careful to point out that frontiersmen like Natty Bumppo are usually among the most disreputable of men. Rather than combining the best traits of both races, they normally combine the worst. Why Natty should be an exception is, finally, inexplicable—though no more puzzling than the actual emergence in contemporary society of gentle, honest men out of a milieu (a Chicago slum, let us say) which characteristically produces criminals. But the character of Cooper's saintly scout is perfectly coherent and, contrary to most critical opinion, remarkably well developed from the beginning. It is true that his manners are purified, that he strikes attitudes at once more humble and more heroic, and that he is given more opportunity to show off his aesthetic response to nature, in the novels written after *The Last of the Mohicans*. On the whole, however, these developments do little more than highlight features already present in the original portrait in

The Pioneers. That portrait is of a just man in a society which seems to him, and which in many ways is, unjust. Behind the snaggle-toothed, buckskinned exterior, the old solitary is, paradoxically, the ideal citizen of an ideal republic which never did and never will exist on the face of the earth—in spite of the ambitions of men like Judge Temple. Since he lacks, almost entirely, the missionary spirit of, for instance, Socrates or Don Quixote, Leatherstocking abandons the settlements to their own fate; and by retiring to a sphere in which he is incongruously at home, he ceases practically to be a potentially comic figure. A tragic figure, however, though no martyr, he certainly is. His tragedy lies in his awareness that everything he has loved best is swiftly disappearing from North America and that, as a white man, he is deeply implicated in the process of destruction. Though this tragedy is more than merely implicit in *The Pioneers*, the full tragedy is revealed only in *The Prairie*, where the Leatherstocking finds that not even the seemingly illimitable vastness of a great continent can afford him refuge from the sound of the axes.

2. THE WAVERING HERO AND THE HERO OF THE LEATHERSTOCKING TALES

Leatherstocking's lack of a missionary spirit is one of the most interesting and important things about him. We can readily see that this characteristic is closely related to his specialist's feeling that each man should mind his own business. Equally important, Natty Bumppo is a humble man who 'knows his place'—in more ways than one, including some which do not appeal to twentieth-century critics. His place, as he tells would-be benefactors in *The Pioneers* and *The Prairie*, is in the wilderness among the Indians. A strange place for a white man and a Christian, it may be; but it is precisely because of his long association with both races that he has come to appreciate the virtues of both, each in its own place, with the aptitudes and customs adapted to its circumstances. The inevitable corollary of this view is that each has its limitations and that therefore each works out its own salvation best by sticking to the things it knows and does best. To Christian missionary activities among the Indians (in spite of his own personal debt to the

Moravians), to the white settlement of North America generally (in spite of his own colour), this attitude is fundamentally hostile. It also makes his own position anomalous. But as chance has thrown him among the Indians and long practice revealed and matured a remarkable aptitude for their way of life, both he and the Indians recognize his right to dwell among them. This relationship with the Indians is itself a most humble one: he idolizes the Delawares and invariably defers to the chief Chingachgook. True, he tends to think of himself as a 'civilized' man, and he shares his author's feeling that genteel white ladies and gentlemen are altogether more precious than the rest of humanity. But his admiration for the 'gifts' and acquired skills of the red men is none the less profound. He may excel them in some of the things they do best, but he never forgets that they are his tutors and the rightful owners of the ground he walks on. Who is he to reprove them for taking a scalp? Cooper's Indians, it should be added, always advocate the same 'leave-alone' policy.

This chasm between the two races and their respective ways of life is one which, in some ways, the Leatherstocking is uniquely equipped to bridge. He can act as interpreter, he can serve as an example to both races of the good qualities of both. Indeed, he is living proof that the Indians and the white Christians are fundamentally more like than unlike. Yet from the start Cooper's Leatherstocking tales are based on a recognition that cultural differences which appear minor and peripheral to, say, Dr Johnson's philosopher Imlac, appear all-important to an old man who is asked to learn new tricks. This is no more than Scott, or Maria Edgeworth before him, had recognized. But the nature of Cooper's North American materials forced him to acknowledge a greater cultural cleavage than any that existed in Ireland or Scotland. And this meant that he would have to abandon the 'wavering' hero of Scott. For Scott's wavering hero reveals, not only that there are two more or less opposed sides between which to waver, but also that the two sides have so much in common that neither appears repulsively alien or subhuman to a neutral observer. This is not to imply that Scott or his Edward Waverley viewed the Highlanders as a mere lump of Common Humanity picturesquely decorated; on the contrary, the main body of the Highlanders are viewed as a strange, barbaric, and frightening lot. They really are uncomfortably different. But Scott was aware that the polar structure which British society had assumed during periods of crisis was a simplification—a murderous simplification—of social reality. British society was basically more like a spectrum, with many intermediate hues between the infra-red of the wild Highlanders and the ultra-violet of the pusillanimous merchant classes of the Lowlands. Yet this simile is misleading in so far as it suggests that Scott was concerned with the entire human spectrum; far from it, he was concerned with only a wide section of it. Thus, between the body of the Highlanders and Fergus Mac-Ivor stands Evan Maccombich, between Fergus and Sir Everard Waverley stands the Baron Bradwardine, and so on; but even those who are farthest apart are white men, Christians, and monarchists. When the extremes are yet farther apart, as in *Old Mortality*, Scott's wavering hero rejects both. In the long run—so Scott's interpretation of recent British history goes—the common interest will triumph over the self-interest of extremists, and such differences as remain will amount to little more than picturesque variations within an undivided realm.

Cooper envisaged no such reconciliation of parties in North America; a war of extermination was being fought out in the West while he was writing these novels. For although a few intermediate types like Leatherstocking, the bee-hunter Paul Hover, or the squatter Ishmael Bush might be discerned, the polar structure which British society assumed during times of crisis was the normal condition of North America and would remain so until the frontier reached the Pacific. So long as the representative of the old primitive order in North America was a white Christian who had served with the British army at one time, so long as the opposing party of settlers was composed largely of ignorant and crude levellers, a Judge Temple might be found to waver between them. But between Indians and white men and their respective ways of life, the differences really were enormous. And as the poles were so far apart to begin with, a man's sympathies were likely to be fixed permanently by the accident of birth and upbringing. The reversion of Chingachgook from a drunken, basket-weaving Christian to a noble savage is a case in point. So there could be no representative wavering hero, no Edward Waverley to be strongly attracted, no Henry Morton to be strongly repelled, by both sides.

In the absence of a hero who experiences such conflicts of allegiance and identity, Cooper lacked the organizing centre necessary to create a novelistic structure based on true balance and antithesis. The Leatherstocking, after all, has the surest sense of identity, and his sympathies with the two sides do not conflict. What is more, the Leatherstocking's determination to stick to his own terrain prevents the action from taking place on 'neutral ground', where the two sides might act more or less freely and representatively. Consequently, though the opposition between white and red men is fierce enough in *The Prairie* and *The Last of the Mohicans*, these novels lack the powerful polar structure of *The Pioneers* and Scott's greatest novels. In both, the Indians, abetted by Leatherstocking, make a magnificent plea on behalf of their race and way of life, and against the invading white European race; but on the other hand, the few helpless white characters are not free to speak and act representatively—all they dare ask is to be allowed to do what the Indians would like all the white invaders to do, i.e. go back where they came from. The result is not that our sympathies are divided between two opposed ways of life, two cultures and races, but that the claims of an entire way of life on our moral sympathies are countered by the claims of a few individuals who, though types themselves, dare not behave towards the Indians as white men typically do. Actually, the case made out for the Indians and their way of life produces much the stronger impression, and so these novels avoid being inconsistent and morally incoherent. But it can scarcely be maintained that the action in these novels is so suitable a vehicle for the theme or that the structure is so formally satisfying as in the best work of Scott. This is not to suggest that Cooper was wrong to abandon his previous model; it is to say that, apart from *The Pioneers*, the virtues of the Leatherstocking tales are not the virtues of the Waverley Novels.

By abandoning Scott's wavering hero in favour of the Leatherstocking figure, Cooper gained not only a fuller development of that figure but also a more sympathetic and inward-seeming portrait of the American Indians than would otherwise have been possible. Excellent as some of Scott's characters are—Jeanie Deans and John Balfour of Burley, for example—none has the legendary stature and imaginative reality which the five Leatherstocking tales give to Natty Bumppo. And excellent as Scott's portraits of unfamiliar peoples usually are, he does often lapse into what strikes the reader as mere antiquarianism, or connoisseurship of the exotic. Cooper does better in this respect in spite of the fact that his materials were much less familiar (to himself as well as to his readers) than were Scott's. To explain this achievement we have to refer to a point made in connexion with Leatherstocking's trial in *The Pioneers*—namely, that the blinding transition from lightness to darkness, or vice versa, is an appropriate simile for what happens to characters who cross cultural frontiers in the Leatherstocking saga. It is true that characters like Waverley and Frank Osbaldistone are also dazzled, confused, and misled by the change they encounter once they reach the Highlands; but not so far that they lose their dignity, not so much that the reader will suppose them gulled when they gaze awe-struck at picturesque Flora Mac-Ivor and her romantic Highland minstrelsy or Helen MacGregor striking a pseudo-sublime pose. In a Leatherstocking novel the white characters other than Natty are helpless and often undignified. Especially in *The Prairie* the bewilderment of the white characters is played off against the experienced eye of the old trapper, who coolly anticipates each move by the Indian enemies. The effect of this contrast is to focus attention, not on the oddness of the red men, but on the ignorance of the white beholders. For good measure, in the *Mohicans* and *The Prairie* the strange figures of David Gamut and Dr Obed Bat make their appearance. Neither is wholly successful; indeed, Bat is nearly as trying as Scott's Caleb Balderstone. But in a crude and obvious way they drive home the point that those who are out of place, i.e. the whites, are the absurd, incredible figures in this landscape. Their presence here violates decorum. Of course Bat and Gamut would be odd ducks anywhere, but to say so is merely to remind us that white civilization itself produces stranger birds than the Indians.

By stressing the blinding effect of crossing cultural frontiers, Cooper not only escapes the false exotic note that frequently creeps even into Scott's best work; he also seeks to inculcate a salutary humility in his reader. Throughout the series, Cooper's view of man is essentially pessimistic, i.e. Christian, in its emphasis on the limitations of human understanding and the vanity of most human aspirations. For this general moral theme the hero and characteristic action of the Leatherstocking tales serve as a most powerful vehicle. Again and again the novels show that the skill and wisdom of man are a result of his observing limits and that the minute he crosses them he is lost in a wilderness. So far from accepting the tenets of primitivism or exalting the Noble Savage, Cooper employed the materials of primitivism to present the opposed Christian view of man. Yet Leatherstocking has been called a 'Faust in buck-skins'.[3]

3. *The Prairie*

It is in *The Prairie* that Leatherstocking attains his sainthood and that the very different materials of *The Pioneers* and the *Mohicans* are—however improbably—yoked together. *The Pioneers* is a novel of manners and social analysis, whereas the *Mohicans* is a tale in which a narrative of adventure is used as a vehicle for social analysis. Though the latter is not so intellectually contemptible as has often been supposed, the former is one of Cooper's most thoughtful and richly intellectual works. *The Prairie* is nearly as adventurous as the *Mohicans*; it is in some ways a novel of manners; and it is a good deal more intellectually pretentious than *The Pioneers*. This sounds like an unlikely mixture, and to my knowledge nobody has ever claimed that *The Prairie* was a perfectly homogeneous work. Yet it has been claimed that *The Prairie* 'has more inner coherence and unity of tone than the other books in the [Leatherstocking] series'.[4] Is this so?

It is true, as Richard Chase says, that 'the prairie itself lends unity to this novel'.[5] Viewed against this 'bleak and solitary' landscape, even the gigantic figures of the Bush family are dwarfed. Here in 'God's clearing' only the moral stature of the Leatherstocking (so memorably captured in the vision of

[3] Leslie Fiedler, *Love and Death in the American Novel*, p. 189.
[4] Richard Chase, *The American Novel and its Tradition* (London, 1958—originally published in New York, 1957), pp. 56–7.
[5] *ibid.*, p. 57.

Chapter I) seems both human and great. The open vistas of the prairies and the approach of the 'great change' encourage Cooper to attempt the pictorial and the human sublime more often than in any other Leatherstocking tale: he is often successful. In none of the other tales, except possibly *The Pathfinder*, are his individual images more arresting:

> The moon broke from behind a mass of clouds, and the eye of the woman was enabled to follow the finger of Ishmael. It pointed to a human form swinging in the wind, beneath the ragged and shining arm of the willow. Esther bent her head and veiled her eyes from the sight. But Ishmael drew nigher, and long contemplated his work in awe, though not in compunction. The leaves of the sacred book were scattered on the ground, and even a fragment of the shelf had been displaced by the kidnapper in his agony. But all was now in the stillness of death. The grim and convulsed countenance of the victim was at times brought full into the light of the moon, and again as the wind lulled, the fatal rope drew a dark line across its bright disk. The squatter raised his rifle with extreme care, and fired. The cord was cut and the body came lumbering to the earth, a heavy and insensible mass.

Exceptionally in this novel, the language of this passage is comparatively simple and direct: it does not get between the reader and the scene described. Yet in spite of Cooper's fustian in other descriptive passages ('the hour of their voracious dominion had not yet fully arrived'), they are often pictorially effective in their own right and lend a baroque, though not specious, grandeur to personages and events which might otherwise seem plebeian, commonplace.[6]

The question, however, is not whether *The Prairie* contains magnificent scenes and passages, but whether these are so related to the rest of the work and each other that the novel has 'more inner coherence and unity of tone' than, for instance, *The Pioneers*. Certainly at an elementary structural level there is such a relationship, as Henry Nash Smith has pointed out.[7]

---

[6] Cooper's descriptions of the prairie are not, of course, based on first-hand observation; and vivid though his images are, it could hardly be maintained that the presence of the prairie is felt in this novel as it is in, say, *A Son of the Middle Border* or *My Antonia*. But the relationship between character and landscape, even if it is not an authentic or strictly realistic one, is nevertheless firmly established.

[7] Henry Nash Smith, Introduction to *The Prairie* (Rinehart ed., New York, 1950).

Richard Chase accepts Professor Smith's analysis and elaborates it as follows:

As always there are passages of vivid action—a buffalo stampede, a prairie fire, and an Indian battle, which alternate with the stately pictorial passages. And even this elementary narrative structure—the alteration of the active and the static—takes on a more than usual significance in *The Prairie* because the imminence of the hero's death, as well as his own reflections upon it, leads us to be mindful of the mysteries of time and eternity.[8]

There is such a pattern of alternating repose and frenetic activity—and a great improvement it is on the narrative pattern of the *Mohicans*, in which the action seems unrelenting over quite long stretches. But Professor Chase's discovery of a general thematic significance in this pattern does not accord with my experience of the novel. Doubtless the pattern helps to bring out the extraordinary soundness and vigour of the tireless old trapper, whose physical state is a manifestation of his moral and spiritual condition. In this way it prepares us for the conclusion of the novel, when Leatherstocking is about to die:

His vigor in a manner endured to the very last. Decay, when it did occur, was rapid, but free from pain. . . . A sympathizing weakness took possession of all his faculties. . . .

Yet life lingers on, 'reluctant to depart from a shell that had so long given it an honest and honorable shelter'. When the end does come at last, it is accompanied by a sudden, dramatic access of physical strength when the old soldier rises to his feet to answer the call of his Maker. To this extent the pattern of repose and activity may be said to contribute to the thematic development of the novel.

There is, however, a distinction to be made between moments of human relaxation from action and moments when the author switches from narration of human action to 'sharp visual images conceived as if they were paintings lacking the dimension of time'.[9] Both interrupt the action, but the latter linger in the memory more or less vividly and independently as images 'lacking the dimension of time'. When we are reading, however, the

[8] Chase, *op. cit.*, p. 57.
[9] Smith, Introduction to *The Prairie*, p. ix.

medium does not permit us to experience these descriptive passages as moments of stasis:

> Ishmael chose a spring that broke out of the base of a rock some forty or fifty feet in elevation, as a place well suited to the wants of his herds. The water moistened a small swale that lay beneath the spot, which yielded, in return for the fecund gift, a scanty growth of grass. A solitary willow had taken root in the alluvion, and profiting by its exclusive possession of the soil, the tree had sent up its stem far above the crest of the adjacent rock, whose peaked summit had once been shadowed by its branches. But its loveliness had gone with the mysterious principle of life. As if in mockery of the meagre show of verdure that the spot exhibited, it remained a noble and solemn monument of former fertility. The larger, ragged, and fantastic branches still obtruded themselves abroad, while the white and hoary trunk stood naked and tempest-riven. Not a leaf nor sign of vegetation was to be seen about it. In all things it proclaimed the frailty of existence, and the fulfillment of time.

Here the subject is stasis itself, the passage might almost be a skilful description of a particular painting. Yet Cooper's skill consists in treating the subject as a development in time, moving swiftly from the signs of present fertility backwards to a period of greater fertility and then gradually forward until, in the last phrase, he reaches 'the fulfillment of time'. A similar development is to be found in most of the other great descriptive passages in this work, e.g. of the birds in Chapter XII. Only in retrospect do these passages acquire a static character, though of course they begin to assume this character as soon as we have finished reading them. But that the division into 'static' and 'active' is misleading is a less important point than that these images do stick in the memory long after most of the action of the novel has faded into an indistinct blur. They are solemn, vivid, imposing—sublime. But though they are important in their own right and affect other parts of the narrative, they are not (as memory would have it) the novel.

By common consent, the action in which the Bush family appears is much the best part of the novel, and the best descriptive passages are closely associated with this action and these characters. With a few exceptions, such as the battle between Hard-Heart and Mahtoree, the remainder of the novel (which amounts to about half its pages) contains what is perhaps the feeblest and most mechanical narrative in the entire Leatherstocking series. The improbability that any of the white characters, except Leatherstocking, would have travelled into this region might be overlooked by the charitable reader; but the arbitrary way Cooper deposits them in the middle of the prairie wilderness makes the contrasts between their behaviour and that of Leatherstocking, who is at home there, seem crudely contrived. Compare, for instance, Paul Hover with Billy Kirby of *The Pioneers*. After his own fashion, Kirby is as much a hero as Leatherstocking, who was the Achilles of the preceding heroic age and ethos. When we read *The Pioneers* we realize that Kirby's age, too, is passing; a legendary aura already surrounds him. Kirby and Leatherstocking are opposed, and yet they honour and admire each other: the contrast between them is as moving as it is historically instructive. Hover the bee-hunter, in his own proper context, also might have offered an instructive contrast with the slayer of men and deer; in this context he is merely ridiculous. The Bush family at least know how to take care of themselves and have a kind of dignity. In their company Leatherstocking too has dignity. But in the company of the other white characters, whose gaucherie and ignorance is designed to exhibit his superior wisdom and skill, the Leatherstocking's character degenerates and the action becomes mechanical and repetitious. Since Cooper obligingly provides him with witless and headstrong greenhorn companions, old Natty need hardly exert himself to seem exceptionally clever. Not satisfied with this advantage, however, the old trapper usually refuses to explain in advance why he advocates certain tactics which invariably seem foolish to his foolish companions, e.g.:

'Come lads, come; 'tis time to be doing now, and to cease talking; for yonder curling flame is truly coming on like a trotting moose. Put hands upon this short and withered grass where we stand, and lay bare the 'arth.'

'Would you think to deprive the fire of its victims in this childish manner?' exclaimed Middleton.

A faint but solemn smile passed over the features of the old man, as he answered—

'Your gran'ther would have said, that when the enemy was nigh, a soldier could do no better than to obey.'

The captain felt the reproof, and instantly began to imitate the

industry of Paul, who was tearing the decayed herbage from the ground in a sort of desperate compliance with the trapper's directions. Even Ellen lent her hands to the labour, nor was it long before Inez was seen similarly employed, though none amongst them knew why or wherefore.

Cooper adds, 'When life is thought to be the reward of labor, men are wont to be industrious.' The comment is only slightly more banal than the formula Cooper uses to create suspense and admiration. When Leatherstocking uses a back-fire to stop the fire that is rushing towards the party, his companions, finding themselves saved, think the feat miraculous. 'It will do—it will do', says Leatherstocking modestly. The device is usually less obtrusive than this, but under any circumstances it is a cheap one. By using it so often Cooper very nearly fritters away the reader's respect for his hero.

When we take into account the cumulative effect of such episodes, especially those which involve Dr Obed Bat, it seems remarkable that *The Prairie* has acquired a critical reputation second only to *The Deerslayer* among the Leatherstocking tales. It is true that the parts of the novel concerned with the Bush family are as good as anything Cooper ever wrote. But the superior 'inner coherence and unity of tone' Professor Chase describes is a critical mirage which I can account for only by supposing that he trusted his memory of a book he had not read at all recently. Then indeed the great sombre descriptive passages, hanging unchanging in the memory, might seem to dominate the novel and give it unity of tone. But let the reader come afresh to Chapter X or any extensive part of Chapters XIV through XXX, and he might well wonder whether his memory was not of a different book. This is not to deny that it is the total impact of the novel that matters most. Obviously the powerful opening and concluding chapters are well placed to achieve their maximum effect. But the long stretches of bad prose and worse foolery, masquerading as wit and wisdom, also achieve their appalling impact. Effective though his use of the season of autumn is at times to darken the mood and remind us of the hero's approaching end, Cooper did better with the seasons in *The Pioneers*, where they organize his materials, control the mood, and enforce his analysis with the authority of traditional symbolism. Thus what was complex and in some ways original in *The Pioneers* becomes relatively simple and well-worn in *The Prairie*. The Bush family is a great and original creation. But too often *The Prairie* seems to be a synthetic and self-conscious work which does what was done better in *The Pioneers* or even, at times, the *Mohicans*. Here, when he could no longer imitate Scott to any advantage, he tried to imitate himself—sometimes to the extent of self-parody.

VI

AN AMERICAN GENTLEMAN
IN EUROPE

IN 1822, after a quarrel with the De Lanceys and after the sensational success of *The Spy*, Cooper moved to New York City, where his regular associates were no longer the landed gentry but were, rather, other authors and artists, newspaper editors, lawyers, publishers, and other professional men. It was not until 1836, when he and his family occupied a renovated Otsego Hall, that Cooper was again in frequent and familiar contact with the society in which he had grown up. This fourteen-year period of dislocation may, I think, be defined as the period when Cooper was, or was becoming, a political liberal. This is not to suggest that he was a simple-minded Federalist before 1822, or that upon recrossing the threshold of Otsego Hall he suddenly abandoned all his liberal views. Such, clearly, was not the case. Nevertheless, there is much evidence to suggest that his political attitudes were shaped, quite as much by his immediate human environment and his own role in it, as by large political issues and events. Cooper the itinerant gentleman—whose claims to consideration were his genius, information, and manners—was a very different person from Cooper the master of Otsego Hall. So was a provincial young squire in Westchester County different from an American gentleman in Europe, and those Fenimore Coopers different from the Europeanized celebrity who had the honest façade of Otsego Hall gothicized before he would move in.

Otsego Hall had just received its new façade when, in 1836, Cooper wrote:

Although never illiberal, I trust, I do not pretend that my own

notions have not undergone changes, since, by being removed from
the pressure of the society in which I was born, my position, perhaps, enables me to look around, less influenced by personal considerations than is usual; but one of the strongest feelings created by
an absence of so many years from home, is the conviction that no
American can justly lay claim to be, what might be and ought to
be the most exalted of human beings, the milder graces of the
Christian character excepted, an American gentleman, without this
liberality entering thoroughly into the whole composition of his
mind. By liberal sentiments, however, I do not mean any of the
fraudulent cant that is used, in order to delude the credulous; but
the generous, manly determination to let all enjoy equal political
rights, and to bring those to whom authority is necessarily confided,
as far as practicable, under the control of the community they serve.[1]

According to this definition, Cooper was neither a liberal nor
an *American* gentleman in 1821; for in that year he expressed
his full sympathy with the reactionary Federalist representatives who, at the state Constitutional Convention, tried to deny
'equal political rights' to all.[2] When he moved to New York
City next year, he did not of course forsake all of his old Federalist friends. Chancellor James Kent and Peter Augustus Jay,
in particular, became even closer friends and were prominent
members of the luncheon club Cooper founded, the Bread and
Cheese. But the political complexion of the Bread and Cheese
(and therefore of Cooper's friends during 1822-6) may be
judged by the fact that two of its leading members were the
editors Charles King and William Cullen Bryant. King, later
to attack Cooper for his Jacksonianism, was one of the most
conservative editors of the day; Bryant, in whose *Evening Post*
Cooper later counterattacked the Whigs, was one of the most
progressive. If we are to judge from these associates and from
such novels as *Lionel Lincoln*, the Cooper of this period was
studiously non-sectional and non-partisan. His aim was to be
America's novelist and an American. When he sailed for
Europe in 1826, Clinton was Governor of New York and John
Quincy Adams was President: it may have seemed that, after a
long nightmare of factions, the nation was returning to those

---

[1] *A Residence in France; with an Excursion up the Rhine, and a Second Visit to Switzerland* (Paris, 1836), p. 238.
[2] Letter to Governor John Jay (6 Sept. 1821), *Letters*, vol. I, p. 70.

halcyon days when John Adams, Washington, and Jefferson worked together for the commonweal.

One of Cooper's first callers after he arrived in Paris was Marie Joseph Paul Yves Roch Gilbert du Motier, Marquis de Lafayette—the companion-in-arms of Washington, the respected friend of Jay, Adams, and Jefferson. Cooper had first met the Marquis briefly during the latter's triumphal visit to the United States in 1824. Himself one of the youngest veterans of the American Revolution, Lafayette returned in time to visit the ancient venerables Jefferson, Adams, and Madison, all of whom had long since retired from the political scene and forgiven each other. No American had anything to forgive Lafayette: he had been the friend and defender of American liberty twenty years before Federalism and Republicanism were hatched; as the boy general who chased Cornwallis to Yorktown and who was loved and esteemed by Washington, he was by far the most glamorous figure of the American Revolution. His tour of the United States had, therefore, an electrifying national effect—and on none of its citizens more than on James Fenimore Cooper. As a boy, Cooper had been stirred by stories about Lafayette;[3] as an adult, he was able to help supervise a great *fête* in New York in Lafayette's honour.[4] Of all the men in Europe, Lafayette was probably the one Cooper most wished to know.

Lafayette was almost always accessible to Americans; indeed, America was so often in his mouth and American visitors in his company that by his own more conservative countrymen he was commonly regarded as a bad Frenchman. Certainly he had a very genuine affection for America, and equally certainly he was flattered by the veneration of Americans. But he had another reason for praising Cooper's country. Lafayette had some claim to being the leading European liberal of his age. After his participation in the American Revolution, he was destined to take a prominent part in the early stages of the French Revolution and in the resistance to Bonaparte. Later he was in close touch with the revolutionists in Latin America, Greece, and Poland. In France, when Cooper knew him, after

---

[3] Letter to F. A. de Syon (23 Sept. 1825), *Letters*, vol. I, p. 126.
[4] Cf. Cooper's description of it in his letter to the *New York American* (15 Sept. 1824), *Letters*, vol. I, pp. 114–19.

a lifetime of warfare against despotism, he was a popular idol and his character for liberalism was deeply respected even by those who questioned his capacities as an effective revolutionary leader. That they were right to question them was unhappily demonstrated during Cooper's stay in Europe. As Commander of the National Guard during the July Revolution of 1830, Lafayette had it in his power to declare either a republic or a constitutional monarchy. Acting partly on the advice of the U.S. Minister to France, W. C. Rives, he chose to recognize Louis Philippe as King—only to be gradually deprived of his power, as the right-wing tendencies of the 'Citizen King' became more open.[5] It was a bitter personal defeat as well as yet another demoralizing frustration of the popular will in Europe. Nevertheless, as he had done for half a century, Lafayette continued to act as a fearless propagandist for the liberal ideal— always citing the United States as the polar star by which Europeans should be guided.

It was rather as a European liberal than as an adopted son of the United States that Lafayette sought to publicize American institutions and to circulate accurate information about the Americans' way of life. Frenchmen as well as Americans were called upon to assist him in this good cause: one of them, Alexis de Tocqueville, was probably helped on his way by letters of introduction furnished by Cooper at the request of Lafayette.[6] But Cooper was able to write more than letters of introduction. He was already the first novelist to describe familiar American manners in concrete detail, and his sympathy with American political institutions was evident in his every page. Here indeed was the great publicist Lafayette had been looking for, who might correct the misimpressions of America created, consciously or unconsciously, by European travellers and carefully nurtured by Lafayette's political enemies. Unfortunately, Lafayette was not content that Cooper should write American

---

[5] Brand Whitlock, *La Fayette* (New York, 1929), vol. II, p. 33. My impression of Lafayette is based largely on Whitlock and on Lafayette's *Mémoires* (Paris, 1837–8), 6 vols. For information about his relations with Cooper, the chief primary source is Cooper's *Letters*, vols. I and II, though this must be supplemented by *Notions of the Americans, passim*, and by *A Residence in France, op. cit.*, pp. 1–25.

[6] Stuart W. Jackson, ed., 'Lafayette Letters and Documents in the Yale Cooper Collection', *Yale University Library Gazette*, vol. VIII (April 1934), pp. 113–46. Cf. Lafayette's note to Cooper (Spring, 1831), pp. 126–7 in Jackson.

novels; it was at his suggestion that Cooper embarked upon *Notions of the Americans*, a book of travels in America written in epistolary form by an imaginary European nobleman with liberal views. Later, in order to refute Government claims that a monarchy was a cheaper form of government than a republic, Lafayette asked Cooper to publish a comparative analysis of the costs of government in America and France. Neither of these efforts did Cooper or European liberalism much good. In the *Notions*, though his facts were sufficiently accurate, his constructions were so uniformly and uncritically favourable to America that no European (save Lafayette, perhaps) and only a minority of Americans could have accepted them. His participation in the finance controversy of 1831–2 made him the target not only of the *Juste Milieu* in France but of conservative editors in America, who disliked his new democratic principles generally and who charged him, in particular, with meddling in another nation's internal affairs.[7]

Clearly, one of the effects of his contact with Lafayette was to confirm Cooper's hostility to American party and sectional interests. Lafayette himself, as a hero of the American Revolution, was both above and before such interests. In the *Notions*, written in 1827, Cooper has a kind word for Jefferson as well as Jay, for John Quincy Adams as well as Andrew Jackson, for Calhoun as well as Clay. This is to be so studiously impartial as to be vapid. None the less, from the lofty perspective of Lafayette and his new disciple, it was American principles rather than American persons or parties that truly mattered. Lafayette had staked his life and fortune on the conviction that these principles were as valid for Europe as for America. So far as Cooper was concerned, the moral for an American novelist was clear:

> The literature of the United States is a subject of the highest interest to the civilized world; for when it does begin to be felt, it will be felt with a force, a directness, and a common sense in its application, that has never yet been known. If there were no other points of difference between this country and other nations, those of its political and religious freedom, alone, would give a colour of

[7] For a detailed study of Cooper's role in the finance controversy, cf. Robert E. Spiller, 'Fenimore Cooper and Lafayette: The Finance Controversy of 1831–1832', *American Literature*, vol. III (1931–2), pp. 28–44.

the highest importance to the writings of a people so thoroughly imbued with their distinctive principles, and so keenly alive to their advantages. The example of America has been silently operating on Europe for half a century; but its doctrines and its experience, exhibited with the understanding of those familiar with both, have never yet been pressed on our attention. I think the time for the experiment is getting near.[8]

And arguing that, from the novelist's point of view, democracy made for an impoverishing uniformity of manners, Cooper concludes that it is the proper business of the American novelist, not merely or necessarily to depict American scenes and manners, but to promulgate distinctively American political opinions.[9] This was his aim, not only in the three 'European novels' (*The Bravo, The Heidenmauer,* and *The Headsman*) which he published between 1831 and 1833, but also in the two sea romances which he wrote immediately after the *Notions*. Both *The Red Rover* (1828) and *The Water-Witch* (1830) are novels in which Cooper tries to trace the development of distinctively American political opinions before the formation of the American republic.

It was easy enough for Cooper to be non-partisan in his American political views so long as he remained in Europe; but he should have remembered that the differences between Federalists and Republicans had been real, and that both parties had quite sincerely claimed to represent the true, distinctively American political position. Their differences were not, of course, so great as those which separated Lafayette from Casimir Périer, leader of the reactionary Doctrinaires. But they were taken seriously by that 'heated politician' Judge William Cooper, and his son was made of no less combustible stuff. In any case, it was true that for the time being the nation as a whole had accepted Jeffersonian Republicanism and that (by 1827) Cooper had gone along with it. This was enough to place him far to the left of most of the governing powers of Europe. The longer he stayed in Europe and the more he learned about the corrupt oligarchies in France and England and the oppressive despotisms in Austria and Poland, the farther left he moved.

One way of following the movement of Cooper's political

---

[8] *Notions of the Americans,* vol. II, p. 122.   [9] *ibid.,* pp. 100–1, 108–12.

position is to examine his changing attitude to Thomas Jefferson. As late as 1823, he was able to write:

> You know my antipathies, as you please to call them, to Mr Jefferson. I was brought up in that school where his image seldom appeared, unless it was clad in red breeches, and where it was always associated with the idea of infidelity and political heresy. Consequently I would have gone twice as far to see the picture of almost any other man. . . . But you will smile when I tell you its effect on myself. There was a dignity, a repose, I will go further, and say a loveliness, about this painting, that I never have seen in any other portrait. . . . In short I saw nothing but Jefferson, standing before me, not in red breeches and slovenly attire, but a gentleman, appearing in all republican simplicity, with a grace and ease on the canvas, that to me seemed unrivalled. It has really shaken my opinion of Jefferson as a man, if not as a politician; and when his image occurs to me now, it is in the simple robes of Sully, sans red breeches, or even without any of the repulsive accompaniments of a political 'sans culotte'.[10]

Were it not for Cooper's affiliations with the most entrenched New York Federalists, this partial change of heart would seem remarkably belated; for by 1823 Jefferson was already a national myth. In 1827, Cooper went so far as to call him 'that distinguished statesman'.[11] But after the publication of Thomas Jefferson Randolph's *Memoir, Correspondence, and Miscellanies, from the Papers of Thomas Jefferson* in 1829, Cooper had an opportunity to study Jefferson closely. Now he was ready to admit his error: 'Have we not had a false idea of that man? I own he begins to appear to me, to be the greatest man, we ever had.'[12] As might be expected, both his praise and his censure of Jefferson are intimately related to the history of his own political views. Commending Jefferson, he writes, 'His knowledge of Europe was of immense service to him. Without it, no American is fit to speak of the institutions of his own Country. . . .'[13] But writing in defence of Hamilton, the enemy of Jefferson but the ally of William Cooper and John Jay, he comments as follows:

> I have no doubt that Hamilton was, at heart, a monarchist. This is no imputation on his talents, for all the theories of the day had that

---

[10] Letter to Charles Kitchel Gardner (24 April–17 June? 1823), *Letters*, vol. I, pp. 95–6.   [11] *Notions of the Americans*, vol. II, p. 169.
[12] Letter to Charles Wilkes (9 April 1830), *Letters*, vol. I, p. 411.
[13] *ibid.*, p. 411.

tendency. It is not probable that Hampden carried his ideas of liberty as far as a moderate Tory of our time is disposed to concede. Had Hamilton been sent to Europe, and had he taken a near view of those institutions, and that state of society, which he so much admired at a distance, his sagacity would at once have enabled him to separate the ore from the dross, and to have found how little there is of the former. But as a theory, his creative mind only aided in lending it plausibility and force; whereas, had he been able to correct his premises by actual observation, the deductions would have been very different.[14]

Clearly, though never a monarchist himself, Cooper is here reasoning from his own experience. Personal observation of European conditions, supported by the information and interpretations of Lafayette, had prepared him for the acceptance of Jeffersonian doctrines.

Soon he was at work on *The Bravo*, the one novel he wrote which might justly be considered revolutionary propaganda. Inspired by the temporary success of the July Revolution and also probably by his conversations with the exiled national poet of Poland, Adam Mickiewicz, he anticipated and indeed longed for popular risings throughout Europe. In fact, it was while he was writing *The Bravo*, during the winter of 1830-1, that the Poles rose against the Czar. Lafayette had been one of the instigators of the revolt and, now that it had taken place, he tried to organize assistance for the Poles. One of his acts was to get Cooper to form an American Polish Committee in Paris in order to gain financial and moral support for the revolutionaries. Meetings were held at Cooper's house and he took charge of publicity for the Committee. There can be no doubt that his sympathy and support, though they could not influence the outcome of the insurrection, did at any rate ease the lot of those patriots who managed afterwards to escape to Western Europe and America. It was especially during this period that with his pen, his purse, and his counsel, Cooper tried to do for Europe what Lafayette had done for America with his sword.[15]

---

[14] Entry in Journal (24 Sept. 1830), *Letters*, vol. II, p. 32.

[15] For a more detailed account of the conduct of Lafayette and Cooper in connexion with the Polish insurrection, cf. Robert E. Spiller, 'Fenimore Cooper and Lafayette: Friends of Polish Freedom', *American Literature*, vol. VII (1935-6), pp. 56-76. The same author's *Fenimore Cooper: Critic of His Times* (New York, 1931), pp. 99-189, is the standard account of Cooper's European years.

In many ways Cooper the expatriate, author of *The Bravo* and generous supporter of the Polish revolutionaries, is the most attractive Cooper of all. Yet it is also true that 'removed from the pressure of the society in which [he] was born', he could easily afford to shift his political ground. The shift might not have been so easy had he, in the first place, supposed that American and European parties were divided along the same lines, i.e. along class lines. On the contrary, as a propagandist for distinctively American political opinions, he had persuaded himself that no such division existed in America—the ideal republic of Cooper's friend Lafayette, friend of Thomas Jefferson:

Our gentry put themselves in opposition to the mass, after the revolution, simply because, being in the habit of receiving their ideas from the most aristocratic nation of our time, they fancied there were irreconcilable interests to separate the rich man from the poor man, and that they had nothing to expect from the latter class should it get into the ascendant. They consequently supported theories adverse to the amalgamation, and as a matter of course, the instinct of the multitude warned them against trusting men opposed to their rights. The error has been discovered, and although individuals among those who were prominent in supporting exclusive doctrines are necessarily proscribed by opinion, the nation shows all proper deference to education and character; when these are united to money and discreetly used they are of necessity still more certain of notice. Jefferson was the man to whom we owe the high lesson that the *natural* privileges of a social aristocracy are in truth no more than their *natural* privileges. With us, all questions of personal rights, except in the case of the poor slaves, are effectually settled, and yet every valuable interest is as secure as it is anywhere else.[16]

Even allowing for the fact that this is a letter to the English poet Samuel Rogers, written in support of the Reform Bill, it seems to be a fairly accurate reflection of his view of America in early 1832. Nothing seemed more natural to him than that an intelligent aristocrat should also be, like Jefferson or Lafayette, an ardent democrat. When conservative American newspapers attacked him for his authorship of *The Bravo* and for his participation in the Finance Controversy, he first became aware of the very real conflict of interests which had been going on during his absence. When he returned, he would have to make a choice of parties, as under Jackson every American did.

[16] Letter to Samuel Rogers (19 Jan. 1832), *Letters*, vol. II, p. 180.

VII

BUCCANEERS OF THE LAND
AND SEA

1. THE EARLY SEA ROMANCES

THROUGHOUT THE nineteenth century the United States had
two major frontiers: one the agrarian frontier to the west, the
other the maritime frontier of the Atlantic and, eventually, the
Pacific Oceans. So far as national wealth and defence were
concerned, the maritime frontier was by far the more important
during the first half of the century—largely because British
imperial policy had favoured agrarian development in the
American colonies but had inhibited the growth of an effective
colonial merchant marine. Good historian that he was, and
former naval officer too, Cooper could not but recognize—he
was in fact eager to assert—that national greatness depended
less on such pioneering ventures as Cooperstown than on the
emergence of a powerful navy and merchant fleet. It was therefore nearly inevitable that the patriotic author of *The Spy* should
sooner or later try his hand at sea fiction, and equally inevitable
that this fiction should express an ardent maritime nationalism.
Indeed, so bound up with each other were the sea and American nationhood in Cooper's mind that his three earliest sea
romances form a distinct trilogy 'depicting', as Thomas Philbrick has argued, 'the growth of the separation between
America and England and the slow awakening of an American
national consciousness'.[1]

The first of these romances, *The Pilot* (1823), seems at first

[1] *James Fenimore Cooper and the Development of American Sea Fiction* (Cambridge,
Mass., 1961), p. 58. My discussion of *The Pilot*, *The Red Rover*, and *The Water
Witch* is heavily indebted to this admirable work.

113

sight to be not much more than an amphibious version of *The Spy*: the mysterious commanding figure in disguise is John Paul Jones rather than George Washington, the two politically opposed heroines of *The Spy* are increased to three (the first pro-American, the second virtually neutral, the third pro-British), and the scene is the English coast, which, given the presence of non-combatants and the American navy, is the closest thing possible to a nautical 'neutral ground'. Here the wavering figure of Mr Wharton is exchanged for his exact opposite—stiff-necked, unshakeably Tory Colonel Howard, who has abandoned his American possessions out of loyalty to his King and his 'home', i.e. England. *The Pilot* does, in short, exhibit some invention, though of the most mechanical sort. It has one brilliant caricature in the New England sailor Tom Coffin and one interesting minor character in John Paul Jones's abandoned fiancée Alice Dunscombe. But taken as a whole, *The Pilot* is a schoolboyish novel, vitiated especially by an ingenuous and rather unsavoury patriotism. The only sections of it which can be read with any pleasure today are the nautical sections, which form only a minor part of the action. It was enormously popular in its day, however, and its pictures of American naval skill and daring doubtless diverted many young men from West Point to Annapolis.

Yet this is not quite fair to Cooper or *The Pilot*. Cooper himself regarded *The Pilot* as one of his most courageous innovations, and so, up to a point, it was. We know that Cooper wrote it in response to Scott's lubberly but well-received *The Pirate*. Cooper admitted that Scott had achieved *vraisemblance* in his depiction of nautical matters, and he was enough of a literary theorist to acknowledge that this was the chief thing. Yet, as Aristotle had maintained, it was best to be at fault in nothing whatever: Cooper's ambition was to match Scott in *vraisemblance* and to surpass him in accuracy; indeed, to write in such a way as to command the respect of sea-faring men. At the same time, as a maritime nationalist, he wished to win respect *for* those men. His achievement in a few passages of *The Pilot* was to combine vivid descriptive prose and technical nautical language so artfully that the latter, not baffling the lay reader too much, actually enhanced the realistic effect of the former. Employed in this fashion, it also helped make his seamen seem a separate race who possessed a body of arcane knowledge and skill which the landsman must view with respect or even with awe. Even in this first experimental sea romance, Cooper's powers as a depictor of maritime adventure were remarkable; in his subsequent sea tales he revealed powers scarcely inferior to those of Melville or Conrad, both of whom were his conscious debtors. For the sea-faring characters he invented to participate in these stirring scenes, alas, not so much can be claimed. Yet Cooper's American sailors serve their purpose: skilful, daring, they obey their outlandish code with the same strictness that Natty Bumppo obeys his; and their contempt for the landsman's customs and conventions makes them credible rebels against British rule, whether before or during the American War of Independence.

Cooper's second sea romance, *The Red Rover*, was as popular as its predecessor, and deserved to be much more so. As a tale of maritime adventure it is probably Cooper's best: in particular, the chase of the *Caroline* by the Red Rover's pirate ship is, as sheer narrative of physical adventure, among Cooper's most brilliant performances. But the narrative of adventure does not exist merely for its own sake. The human part of the action (the sea being the greatest actor of all) does of course reveal something about the character of the human actors. Both captains are superlative seamen—brave, skilful—and Wilder of the *Caroline* is chivalrous and loyal as well. The pirate captain is a more complex character, after the style of Byron's heroes: indeed, *The Red Rover* is very heavily indebted to *The Corsair* and *Don Juan* (especially the former) for its descriptions of the ocean and maritime action, as well as for the more obvious Byronism of the Rover. An American colonial by birth, the Rover has taken to piracy as a result of having been insulted and wronged by the British; at present a man without a country (the date of the action is 1759), the Rover dreams of a day when Americans will be independent and he will exchange his blood-red flag for one never yet seen on land or sea. Unfortunately, the character and traits of the Rover are too derivative for comfort, and the unravelling of the plot is as melodramatic as it is improbable. Yet the most damaging criticism of the novel is that its theme and action are not well integrated. In the first, the twenty-first, and the last chapter Cooper deals more or less explicitly with the historical situation in which the characters find themselves: ironically, it is in 1759, just a few years before the War of Independence, that American loyalty to Britain is at its highest; ironically, too, the outlaw Rover is the only character in sight who perceives that American commercial and civic well-being can be obtained only through independence. This is a theme with which much might have been done, but it cannot be done if the author forgets his theme for many chapters at a time and indulges himself and his readers in an exciting narrative of adventure. So true is this that a single chapter (XXI) provides most of the evidence that allows one to pronounce *The Red Rover* something more than a mere tale of maritime adventure.

In some ways *The Water Witch* (1830) is a fairly close imitation of *The Red Rover*. Tom Tiller ('the Skimmer of the Seas') is a smuggler rather than a pirate; like the Rover, the Skimmer delights in disguises and deceptions; on the contraband ship as on the pirate ship there is a woman disguised as a young man. Most important, perhaps, both the Rover and Skimmer are natives of America who defy the authority of the British king long before their land-bound kinsmen do. At the same time, since Cooper cannot afford to suggest that American seamen are invariably rebellious against government, in both novels he opposes to these outlaw captains American-born, but strictly loyal, officers of the British navy.

In at least one respect *The Red Rover* is certainly superior to *The Water Witch*: the chase of the *Caroline* is more exciting than anything in the later book, mainly, I think, because in the case of *The Water Witch* we the readers are following the (unsuccessful) hunters rather than, as in *The Red Rover*, the desperate hunted. Moreover, *The Water Witch* is less of a sea romance in that, like *The Pilot*, much of its action takes place on land. And yet, regarded as part of a trilogy concerned with 'the growth of the separation between America and England and the slow awakening of an American national consciousness', *The Water Witch* gains much and loses little by being closely associated with the scenes and interests of the land and land-bound inhabitants of America. Though the action of *The Water Witch* takes place during the reign of Queen Anne, this novel reveals much more about the issues underlying the American independence movement than do the other members of this trilogy, in spite of the fact that their actions take place during or shortly before the War of Independence. Neither *The Pilot* nor *The Red Rover* give more than a hint that the principal cause of colonial disaffection was a commercial one. Nor do they intimate that, because many of the colonials were of non-English origin while many others were refugees from political wars in England, a sense of separateness from the mother country had long existed in America. But in *The Water Witch* these two factors are ever present in the person of Alderman Van Beverout, the New York (New Amsterdam) merchant who deals with smugglers in defiance of the customs regulations imposed by Parliament in the interests of British industry and commerce. His greedy and seditious, though not altogether unattractive, presence assures that the action will never turn into mere maritime adventure divorced from the main theme of the novel.

For Cooper's purposes as a novelist and propagandist, smuggling is the best possible activity to bring seamen and landsmen together and to contrast their passions, interests, and skills. Compared with piracy, smuggling is so innocuous an activity that Cooper can afford to treat the Skimmer indulgently; yet, precisely because it is not so flagrant a crime, it is the more corrupting—involving not merely the seditious Dutch merchant but the noble English governor of the colony, who regards his governorship as a splendid opportunity to improve his private fortune. In turn, the connexion between Governor Cornbury and the Skimmer gives Cooper an opportunity to exhibit another source of American hostility to England: to the manly, classless Skimmer there is nothing out of the way in his shaking hands with an English lord to seal a bargain of great consequence; but the action alarms the effeminate Cornbury:

. . . finding himself freed from the presence of a man who had treated him with so little ceremony, the ex-governor shook his head, like one accustomed to submit to evils he could not obviate, and assumed the ease and insolent superiority he was accustomed to maintain in the presence of the obsequious grocer.

'This may be a coral or a pearl, or any other precious gem of the ocean . . .,' he said, unconscious himself that he was in a manner endeavoring to cleanse his violated hand from the touch it had endured, by the use of his handkerchief, 'but it is one on which the salt water hath left its crust.'

This is not to suggest that *The Water Witch* is an historical novel like *Lionel Lincoln* or *The Pioneers*, both of which give us a richly circumstantial picture of a particular time and place. On the contrary, *The Water Witch* is one of Cooper's most fanciful works; he himself described it as 'probably the most imaginative book ever written by the author'. Yet the imagination at work in this novel is anything but aerial or vague: the images, incidents, and characters are indeed exaggerated and brought into an ideal rather than probable juxtaposition; but they owe their vividness and sensuous immediacy to Cooper's powerful grasp of the concrete objective world of old New York and the Atlantic Ocean, of ships and seamen, and, above all, of the language and mental processes of sailors and merchants. For this reason it is a far more instructive work than either *The Pilot* or *The Red Rover*, and, since it effectively demonstrates American commercial dependence on an enlightened maritime policy, it is the more adult expression of American maritime nationalism. But it was a comparative failure with the American reading public, who, though they revelled in the naive patriotism and novelty of the two previous sea romances, evidently were only baffled by the mature and delicate art of *The Water Witch*.

2. *The Water Witch*

And yet the American reading public perhaps sensed that treasonable impulses were present in this queer baroque romance of the land and sea. Cooper began work on *The Water Witch* when he was living in Florence, a regular guest of the expatriate English nobility residing there and a close observer of the political developments then taking place in Europe. There was no period of his life when he was a more ardent American or a more severe critic of the despotic and oligarchic institutions of the Old World. England in particular seemed to him the enemy, not only of American independence and freedom, but of European freedom as well. England epitomized the rule of thoroughly corrupt and selfish materialistic interests which would do anything to maintain their economic and political ascendancy at home or abroad.[2] This view of England,

[2] Cf. Cooper's letter to Horatio Greenough (15 Sept. 1829), *Letters*, vol. I, pp. 389–91, in which he asks, 'Have you seen Cobbetts creed, on the subject of

somewhat softened, is present throughout *The Water Witch* and does in fact govern Cooper's analysis of the relationship between England and her North American colonies. To this extent the novel is a genuine expression of American maritime nationalism. Indeed, its indebtedness to *The Red Rover* strongly suggests that Cooper at first intended it to be no more than an extension and refinement of that popular celebration of the Americanism of American seamen.

However, other experience supervened and, so it appears, shifted the focus of the novel quite remarkably. After writing five chapters of the novel in Florence, Cooper moved to Sorrento, where, in a delightful villa overlooking the Bay of Naples, he nearly completed the work. All the biographical evidence argues that Sorrento was one of the high points of his European experience. Writing to Horatio Greenough, he described the twenty miles around Naples as 'rich beyond an equal, including natural objects'.[3] And the long, almost rhapsodic description of Naples in *The Water Witch* is no less emphatic:

I have visited many lands, and seen nature in nearly every clime; but no spot has yet presented, in a single view, so pleasant a combination of natural objects, mingled with mighty recollections, as that lovely abode on the Sorrentine cliffs!

The speaker is Seadrift, a lovely girl disguised as a man and companion of the Skimmer of the Seas, but it might well be Cooper himself, writing as he gazes out the window on the magnificent Bay of Naples. The description is much too long to be quoted in full, but it is so enthusiastic that Seadrift's consolatory praise of New York harbour seems empty:

Of the bays, each seems to have been appropriated to that for which nature most intended it—the one is poetic, indolent, and full of

[3] Letter to Horatio Greenough (5 Nov. 1829), *Letters*, vol. 1, p. 396.

---

what England ought to do, in order to maintain her trade and maritime ascendancy? Now this is exactly the unrighteous principle on which that Government has acted these four hundred years, and yet it is always preaching morals!' Cooper was then writing the 'middle chapter' of *The Water Witch*. Cobbett had just said it was the duty of an English minister to oppose any movement abroad, whether just or unjust, which might lessen the power and influence of England. The English sailor Trysail's reasoning in *The Water Witch* is similar to Cobbett's. Cf. Cobbett, *Political Register*, 22 Aug. 1829.

graceful but glorious beauty; more pregnant of enjoyment than of usefulness. The other will, one day, be the mart of the world!

And:

Speak of the many rivers, the double outlets, the numberless basins, and the unrivalled facilities of your Manhattan harbor; for in time they will come to render all the beauties of the unrivalled Bay of Naples vain. . . .

Seadrift, or, rather, James Fenimore Cooper, tries hard here to be an honest philistine, but even his syntax betrays him: though the *facilities* of Manhattan are unrivalled, the *Bay* of Naples remains 'unrivalled' even when Cooper tries to say that, somehow, it is eclipsed by its American rival. By the standards of Alderman Van Beverout it would of course be eclipsed, but Seadrift is opposed to these standards, as is Cooper himself.

Though many of his countrymen might have thought otherwise, there was nothing unpatriotic in the view that the beauty of Naples was a more precious thing than all the future wealth of 'the mart of the world'. None the less, it was a view which, if it did not exactly subvert, certainly did not support the case of the American maritime nationalists. And this is only the most striking example of the opposition Cooper sets up between Trade and Art, prose and poetry, land and sea, and security and adventure, in *The Water Witch*. As Donald Davie has perceived,[4] at the imaginative centre of the novel is a contrast between the values of Northern European bourgeois protestantism and the values of Mediterranean (especially Neapolitan) civilization. New York the future 'mart of the world', is explicitly associated with London, Venice, and Amsterdam; its chief commercial representative, Amsterdam-reared Van Beverout, is modelled after Shakespeare's Jew of Venice. It is in the light of these associations that we must read Seadrift's verdict on Naples and New York, and his (her) brief but evocative description of Venice:

. . . commerce is like the favour which attends the rich, and the queen of the Adriatic is already far on the decline. That which causes the increase of the husbandman occasions the downfall of a

---

[4] *The Hey-day of Sir Walter Scott*, pp. 162–5. This is the best critical discussion of *The Water Witch*, though both Davie and I are heavily indebted to Yvor Winter's brilliant pioneer appreciation of the novel.

city. The lagoons are filling with fat soil, and the keel of the trader is less frequent there than of old. Ages hence, the plough may trace furrows where the Bucentaur has floated! The outer India passage has changed the current of prosperity, which ever rushes in the widest and newest track. Nations might learn a moral, by studying the sleepy canals and instructive magnificence of that fallen town; but pride fattens on its own lazy recollections to the last!

This passage was written before Cooper had studied Venice and her history carefully, and therefore we must not suppose that the vain Venice of *The Water Witch* is the sinister Venice of *The Bravo*. All the same, the decadent vanity and declining power of Venice (once the mart of the world) is no good omen for the future of New York and an American policy of maritime nationalism.

The truth is that *The Water Witch* is the most profoundly Romantic of Cooper's novels, the least 'socially responsible'. Seadrift, in whose mouth is placed the praise of Naples and the judgment of Venice, is the assistant to the redoubtable Skimmer of the Seas, whom she has been taught to regard as her brother. Her father (unknown to himself) is Alderman Van Beverout, who is also the uncle of the other heroine of the novel, Alida. In the end, both Seadrift and Alida are offered a choice between the land and the sea: Alida may wed either heroic Captain Ludlow of H.M.S. *Coquette* or wealthy Oloff Van Staats, the Patroon of Kinderhook; Seadrift also has the choice of settling down with stolid Van Staats, blessed and dowered by her father, or of running away with the romantic Skimmer, 'with a ship for a dwelling—the tempestuous ocean for a world!' Not improbably (but somewhat surprisingly, in a book by Cooper), the unfortunate Van Staats is rejected by both women. The nature of the choice they have to make is summed up well by Seadrift, addressing Van Staats and Ludlow when both are rivals for the hand of Alida:

The officer of the queen thinks a glance of the eye, from a wilful fair, means admiration of broad lands and rich meadows; and the lord of the manor distrusts the romance of warlike service, and the power of imagination which roams the sea.

Actually, Ludlow is neither romantic nor imaginative, except possibly in the eyes of Alida; and she sacrifices little in the way of wealth or station when she prefers him to the Patroon of Kinderhook (who *is* romantic enough to fall in love with Seadrift). Seadrift it is who makes the authentically romantic gesture: she rejects wealth, respectability, stability—everything a good bourgeois life can offer—in favour of a life of adventure, beauty, and imagination with the lawless Skimmer on his lovely brigantine *The Water Witch*.

What is so striking about the exposition of these views and values is that Cooper, usually the most didactic of writers, here tends to rely on allusions (especially to Shakespeare) and sometimes subtly nuanced irony. In Chapter VIII, for instance, Alida (who has lately read *The History of the American Buccaneers*) is sitting in her room alone late in the evening, somewhat worried about the appearance of a ship in the bay near her uncle's house:

. . . then, ashamed of terrors that she was fain to hope savored more of woman's weakness than of truth, she endeavored to believe the whole some ordinary movement of a coaster, who, familiar with his situation, could not possibly be either in want of aid, or an object of alarm. Just as this natural and consoling conclusion crossed her mind, she very audibly heard a step in her pavilion. It seemed near the door of the room she occupied. Breathless, more with the excitement of her imagination, than with any actual fear created by this new cause of alarm, the maiden quitted the balcony, and stood motionless to listen. The door, in truth, was opened with singular caution, and, for an instant, Alida saw nothing but a confused area, in the centre of which appeared the figure of a menacing and rapacious freebooter.

'Northern lights and moonshine!' growled Alderman Van Beverout, for it was no other than the uncle of the heiress, whose untimely and unexpected visit had caused her so much alarm.

A 'menacing and rapacious freebooter' Uncle Van Beverout certainly is: it is a moment of recognition which has more truth than falsity in it. But Cooper does not labour the point, his touch here is unexpectedly deft and humorous. At other points in the novel the touch is less light but equally effective. For example, the Alderman's villa is named 'Lust-in-Rust', doubtless a pleasant jingley name in his ears but one which well sums up the gross materialistic character of its owner. The honorific

titles of European potentates furnish Seadrift, on another
occasion, with a motive for Swiftian invective:

'I believe there is a mandate of sufficient antiquity, which bids us
to render unto Caesar the things which are Caesar's.'
'A mandate which our modern Caesars have most liberally construed! I am a poor casuist, sir; nor do I think the loyal commander
of the *Coquette* would wish to uphold all that sophistry can invent
on such a subject. If we begin with potentates, for instance, we shall
find the Most Christian King bent on appropriating as many of his
neighbors' goods to his own use, as ambition, under the name of
glory, can covet; the Most Catholic, covering with the mantle of his
catholicity a greater multitude of enormities on this very continent,
than even charity itself could conceal; and our own gracious
sovereign, whose virtues and whose mildness are celebrated in verse
and prose, causing rivers of blood to run, in order that the little
island over which she rules may swell out, like the frog in the fable,
to dimensions that nature has denied, and which will one day inflict
the unfortunate death that befell the ambitious inhabitant of the
pool. . . .'

It is appropriate indeed that this tale set in the age of Queen
Anne should remind us at times of Swift, at other times (especially in the many passages devoted to feminine luxury) of the
gorgeous fancy of *The Rape of the Lock*.

But it is rather to Shakespeare than to Pope, to *The Merchant
of Venice* and *The Tempest* than to *The Rape of the Lock*, that
Cooper is most indebted.[5] Remarkably indulgent though his
criticisms of Alderman Van Beverout are, Cooper shows how
the alderman's love of money has perverted his human nature,
just as Shakespeare had shown in the case of Shylock. When
Van Beverout learns that his niece has left his house mysteri-
ously, it happens that he learns at the same time that a prized

[5] Cf. E. P. Vandiver, 'James Fenimore Cooper and Shakespeare', *Shakespeare
Association Bulletin*, vol. XV (1940), pp. 110–17, and W. B. Gates, 'Cooper's
Indebtedness to Shakespeare', *P.M.L.A.*, vol. LXVII (1952), pp. 716–31. *The
Merchant of Venice* had in fact proven to be particularly relevant to Cooper's main
fictional-social interests during the first decade of his career. From *The Last of the
Mohicans* (1826) to *The Wept of Wish-ton-Wish* (1829) one of Cooper's predomina-
ting interests was in racial relations and particularly in racial or tribal revenge.
Quotations from *The Merchant of Venice* are used as chapter epigraphs in all of
these novels, especially in connexion with Magua in the *Mohicans* and Uncas and
Meek Wolfe in *The Wept*. And *The Merchant of Venice* was, of course, no less relevant
when, in *The Water Witch*, Cooper began his fictional exploration of the evils of
commercial interests.

gelding has been ridden to death by one of his slaves: the dia-
logue which follows the discovery is modelled, though not
closely, on Shylock's 'My daughter!—O my ducats!'—

'She was a pleasant and coaxing minx, Patroon,' said the burgher,
pacing the room they occupied, with a quick and heavy step, and
speaking unconsciously of his niece, as of one already beyond the
interests of life; 'and as wilful and headstrong as an unbroken colt.
Thou hard-riding imp! I shall never find a match for the poor,
disconsolate survivor. But the girl had a thousand agreeable and
delightful ways with her. . . .'

And should there be any doubt in our minds that the Alderman
is a modern Shylock, Cooper uses passages from *The Merchant
of Venice* as epigraph-commentaries on the action in Chapters
VIII–XII. In the end, like Shakespeare's Jew, the Alderman
loses his own daughter as a punishment for his greed. For
Eudora ('Seadrift') cannot bring herself to abandon the gay,
beautiful world of *Tempest*-like invention represented by the
Skimmer and his brigantine.

When the Skimmer and Seadrift leave the New World, never
to return, they take with them certain qualities which, so the
novel implies, an American can rediscover only in Italy and the
plays of Shakespeare. And yet the novel itself is a re-embodi-
ment of those very qualities, it is the marvellous *Water Witch*
returned. The language especially is marvellous, alive in this
novel as it is in no other American book before *Moby Dick*. One
example must suffice:

'Foul tongues and calumnies! Master Seadrift, this unlawful
manner of playing round business, after accounts are settled and
receipts passed, may lead to other loss besides that of character. The
commander of the *Coquette* is not more than half satisfied of my
ignorance of your mis-doings on behalf of the customs, already; and
these jokes are like so many punches into a smouldering fire on
a dark night. They only give light, and cause people to see the
clearer—though, heaven knows, no man has less reason to dread an
inquiry into his affairs than myself! I challenge the best accountant
in the colonies to detect a false footing, or a doubtful entry, in any
book I have, from the memorandum to the ledger.'
'The Proverbs are not more sententious, nor the Psalms half as
poetical, as your library. But why this secret parley? The brigantine
has a swept hold.'

'Swept! Brooms and Van Tromp! Thou hast swept the pavilion of my niece of its mistress, no less than my purse of its Johannes. This is carrying a little innocent barter into a most forbidden commerce, and I hope the joke is to end before the affair gets to be sweetening to the tea of the province gossips. Such a tale would affect the autumn importation of sugars!'

Archaic and highly artificial this language obviously is; and its paraphrasable content does not amount to much. The purpose of this elaborate, imagery-loaded prose is twofold: to sustain a tone approximating that of Shakespearian comedy, and to reproduce as it were the medium in which each of the chief characters swims. Van Beverout's language is laden with commercial and material images; the Skimmer's with the sea and wind and elegant ships; Seadrift's with feminine finery, gorgeous landscapes, and political morality. The result is an extraordinarily rich texture, in which the real and unreal are brilliantly interwoven. It need hardly be added that the imagery associated with each character helps to express his moral state and to articulate the various conflicts (land and sea, trade and art, etc.) which govern the meaning of the novel.

As Yvor Winters has observed, *The Water Witch* is imperfect in relatively minor ways. The haughty Ludlow, though apparently meant to be somewhat absurd, is surely much more absurd than Cooper intended him to be. Alida's valet is a feeble character. The Skimmer's assisting the *Coquette* against her French attackers tends to blur the moral issues of the novel by showing that, after his fashion, the Skimmer is a patriot, that 'the heart could never be outlawed'. Worst of all, the magical tricks indulged in by the Skimmer and Seadrift, while amusing and thematically relevant at the level of sleights-of-hand, become slightly embarrassing whenever Cooper seems to suggest that they have a genuinely supernatural character. But Winters may well be right when he maintains that, 'questions of scope aside, it is probably Cooper's ablest piece of work, as it is certainly one of the most brilliant, if scarcely one of the most profound, masterpieces of American prose'.[6] Why 'scarcely . . . profound'? It is true that the far less perfect *The Pioneers* is a more complex and searching treatment of human experience and consequently a greater novel. And yet this first important

[6] *In Defence of Reason*, p. 197.

extended fictional account of the rival claims of materialism and culture in America—no slight theme, after all—is both sophisticated and deeply serious. The inability of the public to appreciate the originality and poetic quality of this minor classic of American literature foreshadows already the catastrophic reception of *Moby Dick* and *The Confidence Man*.

VIII

THE EUROPEAN NOVELS

1. *The Bravo*

THE WHILE HE was writing *The Water Witch*, Cooper, the recent convert to political liberalism, was surveying the art treasures of Florence, Naples, and Rome. As the novel reveals, the natural and artificial beauty of the Mediterranean world cast quite as potent a spell over his mind as did Lafayette's call to political action. It is not surprising then to find that in *The Water Witch* the representative of democratic manners, the Skimmer, is allied with the representative of cultural refinement, Seadrift. Neither is it surprising to find that the merchant Van Beverout is allied with the degenerate aristocrat, Cornbury: already Cooper was beginning to explore, in fictional terms, the nature of the political, economic, and artistic relationships between America and Europe. If America was to give the world democracy, what would she take in return from Europe: the commercial skills of Northern Europe, or the artistic accomplishments of the South? The implied verdict of *The Water Witch* is that neither art nor democracy could flourish in America so long as she was dominated by mercantilism, the natural political expression of which was oligarchy. Regarded in this light, *The Water Witch* is the point of departure for almost all the novels he wrote during the 1830's. Yet it is clearly a transitional novel which belongs at least as much to Cooper's early as to his middle period. *The Bravo* (1831) is likewise a transitional novel. On the one hand, it is the first and best of a series of novels written in response to, and as commentary on, immediately contemporary socio-political developments in Europe or America. On the other, it belongs to the fictional genre—the 'romance'—which dominated his early period, but which was displaced by other genres

—the novel of manners, the family chronicle novel, the allegorical satire—as he became more and more directly involved in contemporary politics, and as he became more self-consciously a social historian.

I shall make no attempt here to define the terms 'romance' and 'novel'. Suffice it to say that, as nearly all Cooper's fictional narratives are composed of the same ingredients—disguises, improbable rescues, circumstantial details from social history, actions motivated by a desire for revenge or by economic necessity—he wrote no work which could be classified as 'pure novel' or 'pure romance'. None the less, certain stock devices from traditional romances are used so lavishly in works like the *Mohicans* and *The Spy* that we cannot but describe them as romances; whereas in a work like *The Pioneers*, though the same devices are used, they are used sparingly and the centre of interest lies elsewhere.

The favourite devices of the old romancers, and Cooper's favourites too, are those which involve some form (often crude and improbable) of deception. Disguises, transformations, ruses —these are the stock-in-trade of *The Pilot*, the *Mohicans*, and the *Red Rover*, as they are of the old romances Cooper loved to read when he was a boy. But he differed from most other writers of romance in that his almost childish addiction to these devices was countered by a no less strong attachment to frankness, truth, 'simplicity'. If with one part of his being he revelled in the intricate dissemblings of Shakespeare's comedies—and Shakespeare was certainly the romancer who most influenced him— with another part he stood allied with Cordelia and Kent against a world of duplicity, error, and illusion. I suspect that these ambivalent feelings extended even to his own occupation as a fictionalist. At any rate, this alternating attraction to, and repulsion from, deception, is especially manifested in his depiction of the 'neutral ground' in *The Spy*. However badly damaged in other respects by a merely juvenile indulgence in 'make-believe', *The Spy* in its 'neutral ground' section represents a limited but impressive success which demonstrates that Cooper's ambivalent attitude to deception could lead to exceptional moral complexity and dramatic tension.

Both *The Water Witch* and *The Bravo* are characterized by an atmosphere of extreme unreality. Disguises, secret interviews, ruses of all kinds are so frequent that, at first glance, these two works seem among the most self-indulgent of his productions. In fact, however, they reveal a profoundly moral preoccupation with the nature of deception. In *The Water Witch* there are two realms of deception: that represented on the land by Van Beverout and Lord Cornbury, that on the sea by the Skimmer and Seadrift. Little further need be said about the sordid political and commercial duplicity practised by the Governor and the Alderman, but it is remarkable that Cooper, so little the aesthete, should have countered it with the ideal of deception as exquisite invention, deception as play. It is true that, as is usual in Cooper's fiction, the deviousness of the two land-rogues is also countered by the frankness and simplicity of the sailors. But one of these sailors, the unimaginative Ludlow, is made the butt of numerous practical jokes by the crew of the *Water Witch*; and the Skimmer, though fundamentally open and truthful, is nearly as cunning an artificer as Seadrift. And Seadrift—the 'hapless and playful' Seadrift, the 'agent of so many pleasant masquerades'—she is the moral heroine of the romance. As her rejection of all the advantages offered by the Alderman and the Patroon goes to prove, the forms of deception of which she is past-mistress are not only comparatively innocent themselves, but they also encourage the development of disinterested, unworldly values.

In *The Bravo*, however, Cooper found nothing to say in favour of deception. For several years he had been a close student of the devious manœuvres of European governments, and by the time he began *The Bravo* he was in Paris, an intimate friend of Lafayette during the July Monarchy, when the 'Liberals' were seeking to install a *de facto* aristocratic government under the guise of a constitutional monarchy. Writing after the fall of Lafayette and the completion of *The Bravo*, Cooper commented as follows on the government of England:

You make a difference between the peers and the Commons which does not exist. There is no Commons in England, strictly speaking. It is the kin, the friend, the nominee of the Lord who sits—The exceptions are too immaterial to affect the system except as a *check*, by public opinion etc., but not as an estate. What the reform may do remains to be seen. Fear has driven them into it, and if they do all they promise, why the government will become exactly what

129

Lafayette wished to make France—a nominal monarchy but virtually a republic. That England will come to this in less than fifty
years I believe, though the prestige of their detestable aristocracy will
for a long time linger in the slavish minds of their people. . . .
Now this is all I mean, except it is to say that all fictions are dangerous in their nature, and that which can be obtained directly
ought not to be sought indirectly.

There is at this moment a deep conspiracy, among the higher
classes, to cheat the lower out of their natural rights. Public opinion
requires that it should be done with great art, and I am thoroughly
convinced that the whole secret of the present amity between England and France is owing to a settled plan between the aristocrats
to support each other. Without being on the spot, it is impossible
to know how cowardly these people are whenever there is the least
cause of fear, or how insolent they become the moment they think
the danger is over.[1]

Venice had been a nominal republic but virtually an aristocracy; and Cooper, with his strong republican convictions and
his view that 'all fictions are dangerous in their nature', must
inevitably have regarded its government as supremely sinister
and detestable. Indeed, all Cooper's strictures on Britain and
France apply with still greater force to Venice as he portrayed it
in *The Bravo*.

Early eighteenth-century Venice was in fact an ideal subject
for Cooper. The traditional Venetian use of masks must have
made a particularly strong impact on a mind so fascinated by,
and suspicious of, all forms of deception. Even Venetian architecture seemed to him based on vain and meretricious principles. The condition of its society was an epitome of what, in
his darker moods, he regarded as the human condition generally. Thus *The Bravo* begins and ends with descriptions of the
evening entertainments of Venice—the endless round of dis-
tractions which keep men's minds off such tragedies as those
enacted in this book:

At the usual hour the sun fell below the mountains of the Tyrol,
and the moon re-appeared above the Lido. The narrow streets of
Venice again poured out their thousands upon the squares. The
mild light fell athwart the quaint architecture and the giddy tower,
throwing a deceptive glory on the city of the islands.

The porticoes became brilliant with lamps, the gay laughed, the

[1] Letter to Mrs Peter Augustus Jay (16 June 1831), *Letters*, vol. II, pp. 106-7.

130

reckless trifled, the masker pursued his hidden purpose, the canta-
trice and the grotesque acted their parts, and the million existed in
that vacant enjoyment which distinguishes the pleasures of the
thoughtless and the idle. Each lived for himself, while the state of
Venice held its vicious sway, corrupting alike the ruler and the
ruled, by its mockery of those sacred principles which are alone
founded in truth and natural justice.

Cooper saw the state of Venice as a soulless 'monied corpora-
tion' of aristocrats which, to retain its power, must pretend
always to rule in the interests of the populace and at the same
time employ a network of spies and secret police planted everywhere, even among the aristocrats themselves. Since the ultimate power of the state is entrusted to a secret Council of Three,
which acts strictly in the interests of the state, governmental
actions have no visible source; they come from 'above', as the
people put it. By many such hints Cooper identifies the state of
Venice with the Kingdom of Darkness, Kingdom of the Father
of Lies. Built as it is, and maintained, by deception, Venice is a
place where appearances are so untrustworthy that the law of
probability is suspended within its precincts: here the child
betrays its parents, the trusted servant is a spy, the infamous
hired assassin is an innocent man! Here deception itself is under-
cut by deception until all action seems to acquire a totally
random quality. And yet, so absolute is the secret intelligence
and police power of the Council of Three that its decrees seem
to be the decrees of fate. Much of the power of the novel is a
result of this conflict between chance and necessity in the lives of
characters whose powers of individual decision and action have,
for the most part, been cancelled.

We can scarcely doubt that Cooper welcomed a fictional
situation which permitted him almost unlimited indulgence in
the pleasures of coincidence and deception. But *The Bravo* is
anything but a work of escapist literature: there is no happy
ending: on the contrary, the story is one of almost intolerable
tragedy in which the innocent perish or go mad and the guilty
prosper, secure in fortune and conscience.

As an imperialist state, Venice is dependent on a strong navy,
which must of course be manned by the lower classes. It is this
which provokes the enmity between old fisherman Antonio and
the Council of Three:

'Thou art acquainted, doubtless with his opinions concerning the
recent necessity of the state to command the services of all the youths
on the Lagunes in her fleets?'

'I know that the press has taken from him the boy who toiled
in his company.'

'To toil honourably, and perhaps gainfully, in behalf of the
Republic!'

'Signore, perhaps!'

'Thou art brief in thy speech tonight, Jacopo! But if thou knowest
the fisherman, give him counsel of discretion. St Mark will not
tolerate such free opinions of his wisdom. This is the third occasion
in which there has been need to repress that fisherman's speech; for
the paternal care of the Senate cannot see discontent planted in the
bosom of a class it is their duty and pleasure to render happy.'

Such is the language of deception and self-deception practised
by the rulers of Venice. We see through it easily enough, but it is
credible that in a city controlled by merchant aristocrats and
money-lenders who speak like Shylock ('It is wonderful to contemplate how great a value may lie concealed in so small a
compass') such transparent equivocations are spoken without
self-consciousness. In the twisty reasoning of the Venetian senators we have the decadent contemporary (early eighteenth-
century) counterpart of the vigorous mercantile fantasies of
Alderman Van Beverout.

To a large extent, though by no means exclusively, *The Bravo*
is a tale of class conflict. Cooper is careful to show that all
classes are wronged and corrupted by the Venetian state: the
aristocratic Donna Violetta and Don Camillo are opposed by
the state in their wish to be married; and Jacopo (the 'bravo' of
the title), whose father had been a respectable minor functionary of the state, is forced by the Council of Three to assume
the role of a hired assassin. But the old peasant fisherman
Antonio, who lives outside the city on the lagune, is the real
hero of the novel. The unschooled spokesman for the most ex-
ploited class, he is a proletarian hero such as could not fail to
please the most Marxist of critics. Against the total duplicity of
the capitalistic Venetian state, he stands, a figure of simple spontaneous truthfulness and direct action; he is the Leatherstocking
of the Lagunes. But Antonio is an entirely convincing and moving character, and, though Cooper can perhaps be charged

with drawing his contrasts too starkly, the old man is a worthy, though hopelessly outmatched, opponent of the powers of darkness. It is no accident that in the course of the novel his lagune— open to the sky and sea breezes—becomes the symbol of refuge from the dark labyrinthine canals and overhanging palaces of the evil city.

Aside from a few passages in *The Sea Lions*, Cooper never succeeded elsewhere in evoking the dark places of the human mind and spirit as he did in *The Bravo*. Casual remarks are pregnant with sinister innuendo:

'Men like you, father, merit the esteem they crave. Are you long of Venice?'

'Since the last conclave. I came into the Republic as confessor to the late minister from Florence.'

'An honourable trust. You have been with us then long enough to know that the Republic never forgets a servitor, nor forgives an affront.'

"Tis an ancient state, and one whose influence still reaches far and near.'

'Have a care of the step. These marbles are treacherous to an uncertain foot.'

'Mine is too practised in the descent to be unsteady. I hope I do not now descend these stairs for the last time?'

Doubtless this is rather melodramatic, as in fact the entire novel is. Oddly, the tone and even the symbolism are closer to Webster than to Shakespeare:

There is a lonely spot on the Lido di Palestrina where Catholic exclusion has decreed that the remains of all who die in Venice, without the pale of the Church of Rome, shall moulder into their kindred dust. Though it is not distant from the ordinary landing and the few buildings which line the shore, it is a place that, in itself, is no bad emblem of a hopeless lot. Solitary, exposed equally to the hot airs of the south and the bleak blasts of the Alps, frequently covered with the spray of the Adriatic, and based on barren sands, the utmost that human art, aided by a soil which has been fattened by human remains, can do, has been to create around the modest graves a meagre vegetation, that is in slight contrast to the sterility of most of the bank.

But it is rather with the novels of a more recent student of the evil combinations of greed, self-deception, and politics—Cooper's great admirer Joseph Conrad—that *The Bravo* must be compared. As socio-political melodramas, both *The Secret Agent* and *Under Western Eyes* are far more polished works than Cooper's novel; among other things, Conrad knows better than to risk so much overt didacticism as we encounter in *The Bravo*, which sometimes reads like a tract. And yet, such is the sombre intellectual authority of its expository passages and such the moral impact of its main scenes (especially the gondola race, the murder of Antonio, and the execution of Jacopo), that this comparatively unsophisticated work survives the comparison quite well. Like its companion-piece and peer, *The Water Witch*, it lacks the wealth of circumstantial reality, the variety of human personalities and aspirations, of *The Pioneers*. But it is one of the most impressive romances Cooper ever wrote; it is one of the works, by virtue of its unflinching regard for truth, which must be taken into account in any comparison of the achievements of Cooper with those of his predecessors and contemporaries.

2. *The Heidenmauer* AND *The Headsman*

The Bravo was a great success in Europe, though it was of course attacked by Tory and Doctrinaire reviewers. What was disconcerting, however, was that its reception in America—home of democratic principles—was decidedly luke-warm. Not only did it fail to find readers;[2] it was attacked by the conservative American press, led by Cooper's old friends William Leete Stone and Charles King. The most offensive review was written by the son of Cooper's old friend Chancellor James Kent. Judging from his letters of this period (1831–3), Cooper was taken completely by surprise; not until after he had written the novels did he discover that the European conflicts of interest described in *The Bravo* and *The Heidenmauer* might have their contemporary American parallels. His demoralization was swift and deep; *The Headsman*, he vowed, would be his last novel. Had he been less obsessed with internal European politics and American foreign policy, he would have known that Jackson's war with the Bank of the United States had again polarized American politics and that his own attacks on the wealthy classes

[2] Cf. Letter to Cary and Lea (30 Dec. 1831), *Letters*, vol. II, pp. 169–70.

of Europe would appear to have a strong Jacksonian party bias.[3]

The Heidenmauer was written while Cooper still enjoyed good relations with his American public and before he came to believe that distinctively American political principles were as little appreciated in America as in benighted Europe. It is much the best novel he wrote between *The Bravo* and, almost a decade later, *The Pathfinder*. The long autobiographical introduction of this novel takes the form of a travelogue which begins in Paris, and sweeps through several of the countries of Europe—now on the eve of general revolution:

Quitting Cologne, its exquisite but incomplete cathedral, with the crane that has been poised on its unfinished towers, five hundred years, its recollections of Rubens and its royal patroness, we travelled up the stream so leisurely as to examine all that offered, and yet so fast as to avoid the hazard of satiety. Here we met Prussian soldiers, preparing by mimic service, for the more serious duties of their calling. Lancers were galloping in bodies across the open fields; videttes were posted, the cocked pistol in hand, at every hay-stack; while couriers rode, under the spur, from point to point, as if the great strife, which is so menacingly preparing, and which sooner or later must come, had actually commenced. As Europe is now a camp, these hackneyed sights scarce drew a look aside. We were in quest of the interest which nature, in her happier humours, bestows.

Eventually the party reaches the town of Deurckheim on the Palatinate, where the ruins of a Roman encampment, of a medieval abbey and baronial castle provoke reflections on the slow yet certain progress of civilization—and particularly on one of the major developments in that progress, the Protestant Reformation. The vast perspectives of time and place opened up in the introduction effectively 'place' the action of the main narrative: on the face of it, the action is no more than a local incident of the early sixteenth century—the destruction of the

---

[3] Bewley, *The Eccentric Design*, p. 64. In *A Letter to His Countrymen* (New York, 1834), pp. 11–12, Cooper claims that when he wrote *The Bravo* he had a 'painful conviction' that many Americans preferred aristocracy to democracy. Obviously he knew this to be a fact, since some of his old Federalist friends were quite openly hostile to democracy. But there is no evidence to suggest that, in 1830, Cooper regarded these men as a dangerous political force; whiggery, which began as an anti-Jackson coalition of Clay, Webster, and Calhoun forces, had not yet been hatched.

local Benedictine abbey by the local baron leagued with the local burghers; but Cooper's point is that general revolutionary movements have a local base and that they are part of an historical process. Ostensibly, the baron and burghers destroy the abbey because they deplore monastic corruption; though they are not converts to Luther, they take advantage of his preachments against the church and of the general unrest in Germany caused by the adoption of his doctrines elsewhere. Thus, though he never appears, Luther is in a way the chief character of the novel. But in another way he is completely outside the action:

It has been seen that Emich [the local baron], though much disposed to throw off the dominion of the church, so far clung to his ancient prejudices as secretly to distrust the very power he was about to defy, and to entertain grave scruples, not only of the policy, but of the lawfulness of the step his ambition had urged him to adopt. In this manner does man become the instrument of the various passions and motives that beset him, now yielding, or now struggling to resist, as a stronger inducement is presented to his mind; always professing to be governed by reason and constrained by principles, while, in truth, he rarely consents to consult the one, or to respect the other, until both are offered through the direct medium of some engrossing interest that requires an immediate and active attention. Then, indeed, his faculties become suddenly enlightened, and he eagerly presses into his service every argument that offers, the plausible as well as the sound; and thus it happens that we frequently see whole communities making a moral pirouette in a breath, adopting this year a set of principles that are quite in opposition to all they had ever before professed. Fortunately, all that is thus gained on sound principles is apt to continue, since whatever may be the waywardness of those who profess them, principles themselves are immutable, and when once fairly admitted, are not easily dispossessed by the bastard doctrines of expediency and error. These changes are gradual as respect those avant-couriers of thought, who prepare the way for the advance of nations, but who, in general, so far precede their contemporaries, as to be utterly out of view at the effectual moment of the reformation, or revolution, or by whatever names these sudden summersets are styled; but as respects the mass, they often occur by *coup-de-main*; an entire people awakening, as it were, by magic, to the virtues of a new set of maxims, such as the eye turns from the view of one scenic representation to that of its successor.

Our object in this tale is to represent society, under its ordinary faces, in the act of passing from the influence of one set of governing principles to that of another.

The 'engrossing interest' of the burghers of Deurckheim is to be free of the feudal exactions of the abbey: the 'engrossing interest' of Count Emich is to eliminate the abbey as a rival seigneurial power. The upshot is that the burghers exchange an ecclesiastical master for a secular one:

Deurckheim, as is commonly the case with the secondary actors in most great changes, shared the fate of the frogs in the fable; it got rid of the Benedictines for a new master. . . .

None the less, a revolution has taken place. The temporal power of the Church in this part of Germany has been destroyed; the principle of reformation, or purification, of the Church has been advanced, irrespective of the real motives of those who attacked her in this particular locality. At the same time, the ground for future revolutions has been prepared; for we cannot believe that the burghers of Europe will always accept the rule of the aristocrats. And so we come back to the scene described in the introduction to *The Heidenmauer*, of Europe again on the verge of general revolution.

One of the defects of the novel is that the sole informed and intelligent exponent of Lutheranism, Berchtold, is never given a chance to say anything in its behalf. And all the other devout and unworldly characters—Father Arnolphe, Lottchen, Meta, Ulrike, and Odo von Ritterstein—are firm in their loyalty to the Church, though none are blind to its faults. The result is that Cooper appears to have less sympathy for the cause of reform than he actually did have. It is true, of course, that he had no wish to *argue* the case for reform:

Had our efforts been confined to the workings of a single and a master mind, the picture, however true as regards the individual, would have been false in reference to a community; since such a study would have been no more than following out the deductions of philosophy and reason—something the worse, perhaps, for its connection with humanity; whereas, he that would represent the world, must draw the passions and the more vulgar interests in the boldest colors, and be content with portraying the intellectual part in a very subdued background.

Nevertheless, by removing Luther entirely from the scene and making Berchthold no more than a shadow, Cooper wrote a novel which, today, reads very much like the work of a highly intelligent and critical Roman Catholic controversialist! Not entirely, of course; but *The Heidenmauer* is so little a work of Protestant propaganda that Marius Bewley is right to repudiate Professor Spiller's contention that it shows 'the effect of Lutheranism in liberating the mind of man from superstition, and the social order from corruption and hypocrisy'.[4] But neither is Mr Bewley correct in supposing that the novel implies nothing more encouraging for civilization than a regression during the sixteenth century 'from the world of the imagination to the world of profit'.[5] Cooper's interpretation of human progress and the nature of revolutions was far more subtle and complicated than either of these readings allow for.

Enormously rewarding at the level of socio-political history and analysis, *The Heidenmauer* fails somehow to be a distinguished novel. For one thing, the prose is more than usually prolix and involuted. More important, Cooper's moral sympathies were not deeply engaged by the controversy between the Benedictines and their secular opponents: of neither side could he approve or greatly disapprove, and the few characters with whom he did sympathize were not much affected by the outcome of the conflict. The result is that *The Heidenmauer* as a whole is a moralistic novel without the moral passion which informs and invigorates *The Bravo*.

Cooper's next essay in the historical novel, *The Headsman* (1833), lacks the moral intensity of *The Bravo* and the complex socio-political interest of *The Heidenmauer*. Perhaps no other novel by Cooper is so single- and simple-mindedly devoted to illustrating a thesis:

Of all the cruelties inflicted by society, there is none so unrighteous in its nature as the stigma it entails in the succession of crime or misfortune; of all its favors, none can find so little justification, in right and reason, as the privileges accorded to the accident of descent.

To drive home this democratic thesis, Cooper relates the tale of

[4] Spiller, *Fenimore Cooper: Critic of his Times*, p. 220.
[5] Bewley, *The Eccentric Design* (London, 1959), p. 56.

a family who have inherited from the dark ages the post of state executioner (headsman) of Berne: despised for being headsmen and yet unable to free themselves from the hereditary obligation, they do surely engage the sympathy of the reader. But Cooper betrays his thesis and his characters by having his hero, supposedly the only son of the headsman, turn out to be the long-lost son of the Doge of Genoa—not the heir of a curse, but of fabulous wealth and honours. The discovery that Sigismund is the son of the Doge clears up another mystery—how the headsman (in spite of some excellent qualities) could have such a 'noble' son: presumably he has inherited his qualities from his noble ancestry! In this way, despite the author's good intentions, *The Headsman* turns into an argument in favour of hereditary aristocracy. Another unhappy feature of the novel is that a good third of its pages are given over to mere travelogue, to descriptions of Swiss scenery and customs that contribute little to the development of the comparatively serious theme. As usual, Cooper is effective in describing physical adventure: the dangers of crossing Lake Geneva and the Pass of St Bernard late in the autumn are made as vivid and concrete as one could wish. But these are minor achievements, after all. They cannot compensate for the intellectual and moral muddle or what looks like the padding-out of the novel by pages of irrelevant description. There is an alarming slackness about *The Headsman* which makes one appreciate why some of Cooper's contemporaries believed that, at last, he was written out.

Cooper himself admitted as much in his private correspondence: 'I never did anything with the disgust and reluctance that I felt while at work on the *Headsman,* and I cannot conceive of a consideration that would induce me to tax my feelings in the same way again.' [6] In fact the wind was taken out of his sails when, in 1832, he discovered that America was not entirely with him. To make things even more demoralizing, the official American government representatives in Paris, Minister William Cabell Rives and Attaché Leavitt Harris, were worse than useless to him during the Finance Controversy; Rives was silent and equivocal, while Harris openly maintained that American democracy was costlier than French monarchy. Angered by their conduct at the time, Cooper felt

[6] Letter to John Whipple (14 Jan. 1834), *Letters*, vol. III, p. 28.

publicly humiliated when the U.S. Government saw fit to promote Harris:

I am the object of constant attacks in the American papers, and chiefly I believe because I have defended American principles and their action, in foreign countries. They who undervalue them are rewarded with office. Mr Harris, he who so ably, God save the mark!—defended the French government in the late Finance question, has just been appointed Chargé d'Affaires to this Court!!! Truly, we have fallen upon evil times. . . . Verily we are immeasurably contemptible and that, as the French say, *pour cause*![7]

It was in this mood that he returned to America in the autumn of 1833.

[7] Letter to Horatio Greenough (13 June 1833), *Letters*, vol. II, p. 383.

IX

HOME AS FOUND

And have you heard the news from Maine,
And what old Maine can do?
She went hell-bent for Governor Kent,
And Tippecanoe and Tyler too,
And Tippecanoe and Tyler too.
—*Whig Campaign Song*, 1840

I. THE OLD HERO

WHEN COOPER RETURNED to America in 1833, he discovered, among many symptoms of social and political decline, a re-emergence of the party strife which, in 1828, he had hopefully regarded as cured once and for all.[1] Throughout his career he had deplored the evils of party politics, and during the last twenty years of his life he consistently denied that he belonged to either of the great national parties of that era.[2] Yet it can be shown that he endorsed most of Jackson and Van Buren's policies, that he gave his constant support to Democratic party candidates for state and national office, and that he was vilified by the Whig press precisely because he was generally regarded as a leading spokesman for the Democrats.[3] Why did Cooper maintain this fiction, which seems to have fooled nobody but himself?

[1] Cf. *Notions of the Americans*, vol. II, p. 170.

[2] Cooper's most trenchant criticism of parties is to be found in *The American Democrat*, pp. 176–80, where, among other harsh judgments, he remarks that 'It is a very different thing to be a democrat, and to be a member of what is called the democratic party; for the first insists on his independence and an entire freedom of opinion, while the last is incompatible with either.'

[3] Cf. Dorothy Waples, *The Whig Myth of James Fenimore Cooper* (New Haven, 1938), *passim*, and Arthur M. Schlesinger, Jr, *The Age of Jackson* (London, 1946), pp. 375–80.

A partial answer is that, however much he hated the Whigs, he could not love the Democrats—he would support them but not join them. But a more fundamental reason for his aversion to political parties was that the Founding Fathers—Washington, Jay, and Jefferson among them—had denounced parties as one of the evils which the Republic had particularly to fear. Cooper was by no means the diehard believer in Constitutional immutability that he has sometimes been made out to be,[4] but he was convinced that the political maxims of the Founders had the marrow of truth in them and that the nation ignored them at its peril. Indeed, what had gone wrong with the nation during his absence—so Cooper quickly came to believe—was that its affluent classes had lost faith in the principles of the old Republic and had become increasingly infected by European, especially English, opinions and practices. In particular, the urban commercial class which formed the backbone of the Whig party had all the oligarchical interests and aspirations of the European Doctrinaires: the difference between the American and European Doctrinaires was that the former was out of, the latter in, power; thus, in a sense, the Doctrinaires (i.e. the hard-core of Whiggery) were the revolutionary party in America, whilst 'the democrat . . . [was] the conservative, and, thank God, he . . . [had] something worth preserving'. This was Cooper's diagnosis in 1834;[5] his prescription was a return to first principles and thorough exposé of the American oligarchical party.

Such also were the diagnosis and prescription of Andrew Jackson, who more than any other man was responsible for the re-emergence of violent party politics in America. There can be little doubt that Jackson's words and actions helped Cooper to formulate his own position, and moreover that Jackson's executive policies channelled, though they did not dictate, Cooper's subsequent political thinking during the 'thirties. But if Cooper usually agreed with the policies of the Jackson administration, he sometimes disagreed with them too. On the vital question of

[4] As, for instance, in George J. Becker's 'James Fenimore Cooper and American Democracy', *College English*, vol. XVII, No. 6 (March 1956), pp. 325–34.

[5] This diagnosis is to be found scattered throughout Cooper's letters between 1833 and 1838; the first important public statement of it is in *A Letter to His Countrymen* (New York, 1834), from which I have taken Cooper's remark that in America the 'democrat is the conservative'.

foreign policy, for instance, Cooper concluded in the end that Jackson's predecessor John Quincy Adams, now a sort of Whig, had been by far the more enlightened President.[6] As for Cooper's interest in the Bank issue—which for Jacksonians was *the* issue —it was not the Bank Monster, but the unconstitutional efforts of Whig Senators to prevent Jackson from removing government deposits from the Bank, that excited his indignation: the Bank itself, in a modified form, might be desirable or even necessary as a regulatory force in the national economy;[7] but legislative usurpation, undertaken in the interests of the monied classes, was a subversion of the American form of government designed to bring it more in line with the British Parliamentary system—it was a conspiracy to create an oligarchy![8] Cooper's point is not the main Jacksonian point, but his tone is thoroughly Jacksonian. More important than Cooper's agreement with specific points and emphases of Jacksonian policy was his faith in the courage and integrity of General Jackson, once the Defender of New Orleans, now the Defender of the Old Republic as defined by Thomas Jefferson. To account for the attractions of this symbolic crusader figure, we shall have to consider two Jacksons—first, Jackson the General; second, Jackson the Jeffersonian.

A nationalist, an historian of naval and military heroes, Cooper could not but admire a man who was one of the most celebrated Indian fighters of the day and who, at New Orleans, had gained the most brilliant American victory of the War of 1812. Discussing Jackson as a candidate for the Presidency in

---

[6] *Gleanings in Europe: England*, vol. II, ed. R. E. Spiller (New York, 1930), p. 374.

[7] Cooper did not entirely approve of the Second Bank of the United States, but especially after the depression of 1837 he recognized the need for a national financial institution similar to the Bank: cf. Letters to James De Peyster Ogden (6 June 1840 and 31 Jan. 1841), *Letters*, vol. IV, pp. 43 and 113–14. Cooper also enjoyed cordial social relations with the (by Jackson party-liners) hated President of the Bank, Nicolas Biddle.

[8] Cf. Letter to William C. Bryant and William Leggett, for the *Evening Post* (8 Jan. 1835), *Letters*, vol. III, pp. 83–4: 'It is meet that we distinguish between the principles of our own system, and the senseless cry of those who bow to Baal. We must protect the President in the exercise of his duties, or it is plain they will, sooner or later, be wrested from him, by that most formidable of all the evils under which we labour, legislative innovations.' Clearly 'Baal' stands for England. For similar references, cf. the letters written by Cooper, under the pseudonym of A.B.C., to Bryant's *Evening Post* in vol. III of the *Letters*, especially p. 120.

1824, Cooper scorned the suggestion that Jackson's military background should count against him:

His political honesty is unquestionable, and his patriotism without a blot. Still his want of experience in matters of state, and even his military habits, were strongly urged against him. The former may be a solid objection, but, it is more than absurd, it is wicked to urge the military character of a citizen, who meritoriously leaves his retirement in the hour of danger to carry those qualities with which nature has endowed him, into the most perilous, and commonly the least requited service of his country, as an argument against his filling any station whatever.[9]

The image of Jackson leaving his retirement in the hour of danger is a conscious or unconscious allusion to Cincinnatus and thereby to Washington, who was the 'Cincinnatus of the West'. Cooper knew that Jackson lacked the alabaster perfection of Washington; what is more, at the time he wrote this passage he believed that the nation had no need of a Cincinnatus to rescue its political fortunes. But should bad times come, here was a leader of whom Cooper could write, 'If the decision of this extraordinary man was so brilliantly manifested in the moment of need, his subsequent prudence is worthy of the highest commendation.' [10] An image of Jackson as the incorruptible fighter, a sort of homespun, hot-tempered Washington, clearly moved Cooper deeply, as it moved so many other Americans. Admiring references to Jackson in Cooper's private and public utterances show that he thought of him in terms of a man strenuously engaged with an opponent: 'hickory will prove to be stronger than gold'; 'a plain and manly statement of the facts'; 'the old man is very firm, and will not yield an inch'.[11] Like Jackson himself, Cooper tended to see the struggle against the Whigs as a struggle for the very survival of the Republic. So far as foreign affairs were concerned, Cooper believed that the quickest way to gain the respect of Europeans was to present a firm and, if need be, aggressive front: his greatest disappointment with Jackson was that the Old Hero wasn't always aggressive enough.[12]

[9] *Notions of the Americans*, vol. II, p. 175.
[10] *ibid.*, pp. 173–4.
[11] Quotations from *Letters*, vol. III, pp. 21, 112, and 143.
[12] Cf. Letter to Louis McLane (17 April 1831), *Letters*, vol. II, p. 70: 'Almost the only advantage the country had to gain by the late change at home, was in the

It is no accident that Cooper announced his conversion to Jefferson and to Jackson in the same breath:

I think you must own Mr Jackson has sent a very good message to Congress. I do assure you it has done, both him and us credit, all over Europe. I deem it sound, constitutional, democratic and intelligible. I am much inclined to believe, we did well, in changing. What do you think of Jefferson's letters? Have we not had a false idea of that man? I own he begins to appear to me, to be the greatest man, we ever had.[13]

This message, which Cooper elsewhere describes as 'a capital one—sound from beginning to end' [14]—is a thoroughly Jeffersonian document, evidence of Jackson's firm intentions of returning to the plain first principles of the Old Republic. It is an interesting document in its own right, and, given Cooper's wholesale endorsement of it, we shall scarcely do better than to examine it with some care. One of its leading Jeffersonian points is the need for strict construction of the Constitution:

I regard an appeal to the source of power, in cases of real doubt [concerning constitutionality], and where its exercise is deemed indispensable to the general welfare, as among the most sacred of all our obligations. Upon this country, more than any other, has, in the providence of God, been cast the special guardianship of the great principle of adherence to written constitutions. If it fail here, all hope in regard to it will be extinguished. That this was intended to be a government of limited and specific, and not general powers, must be admitted by all; and it is our duty to preserve for it the character intended by its framers.[15]

It is on grounds of dubious constitutionality that Jackson condemns, in the same message, the Bank of the United States and Federal subvention of internal improvements. This is in the

[13] Letter to Charles Wilkes (9 April 1830), *Letters*, vol. I, p. 411.

[14] Letter to Horatio Greenough (28 Jan. 1830), *Letters*, vol. I, 402.

[15] Message to Congress communicated 8 Dec. 1829. This and subsequent quotations from this message are taken from Andrew Jackson, *Annual Messages, Veto Messages, etc.* (Washington, 1835), pp. 5–24.

supposed character of the new incumbent for decision, and this he has taken effectual means to defeat, by preaching an extraordinary love of harmony, whenever he has opened his mouth. Is it possible that his advisers thought it necessary to purge him of a warlike reputation, in this drenching manner?' One of the striking things about this passage, written to a major figure in the Jackson administration, is that it shows how little Cooper was then interested in the domestic issues which, supposedly, led one to favour either Adams or Jackson.

Jeffersonian tradition, as is Jackson's plea for frugal government:

> In connexion with this subject, I invite the attention of congress to a general and minute inquiry into the condition of government; with a view to ascertain what offices can be dispensed with, what expenses retrenched, and what improvements may be made in the organization of its various parts, to secure the proper responsibility of public agents, and promote efficiency and justice in all its operations.

But much as Jackson shares Jefferson's desire to reduce Federal government activities to a minimum and to leave things to 'individual enterprise'—Jackson in his first message to Congress is verbally echoing Jefferson's first message—still a moderate tariff will be necessary:

> . . . and it may be regretted that the complicated restrictions which now embarrass the intercourse of nations, could not by common consent be abolished, and commerce allowed to flow in those channels to which individual enterprise—always its surest guide— might direct it. But we must ever expect selfish legislation in other nations; and are therefore compelled to adapt our own to their regulations, in the manner best calculated to avoid serious injury, and to harmonize the conflicting interests of our agriculture, our commerce, and our manufactures.

But although the interests of agriculture, commerce, and manufactures are to be harmonized, Jackson is as clear as was Jefferson that commerce and manufactures are no more than the handmaids of agriculture:

> The agricultural interest of our country is so essentially connected with every other, and so superior in importance to them all, that it is scarcely necessary to invite it to your particular attention. It is principally as manufactures and commerce tend to increase the value of agricultural productions, and to extend their application to the wants and comforts of society, that they deserve the fostering care of government.

Jefferson's agrarian democracy then is to be preserved, and Jackson shows himself even more responsive to the wishes of 'the people'. He favours direct election of the President because it is 'the first principle of our system—THAT THE MAJORITY IS TO GOVERN'. And an efficient postal system is necessary because

It is to the body politic what the veins and arteries are to the natural—conveying rapidly and regularly, to the remotest parts of the system, correct information of the operations of the government and bringing back to it the wishes and feelings of the people.

Such were the Jeffersonian principles as restated by Jackson and enthusiastically endorsed by Cooper. Jackson's language abounds in figures taken from medical science. Like Cooper, he believed that his task was to restore the body politic to Jeffersonian health and vigour. This was in many ways a conservative, or even reactionary, aim; and, as Marvin Meyers has convincingly argued,[16] much of the appeal of Jacksonianism, especially for Cooper, lay in its nostalgia for a simple natural commonweal which, even in Jefferson's time, belonged to the golden past.

Jackson's nostalgia takes yet another intriguing turn in this message. Jefferson in his *Notes on Virginia* and in his first message to Congress had been an unusually sympathetic and informed commentator on the problems of the American Indians. Jackson had a glamorous, but bloody, reputation as an Indian fighter. But nothing, except *The Last of the Mohicans* or *The Wept of Wish-ton-Wish*, could present a more moving picture of the Red Man's plight than this passage from Jackson's message:

Our conduct towards these people is deeply interesting to our national character. Their present condition, contrasted with what they once were, makes a most powerful appeal to our sympathies. Our ancestors found them the uncontrolled possessors of these vast regions. By persuasion and force, they have been made to retire from river to river, and from mountain to mountain; until some of the tribes have become extinct, and others have left but remnants to preserve, for a while, their once terrible names. Surrounded by the whites, with their arts of civilization, which, by destroying the resources of the savage, doom him to weakness and decay; the fate of the Mohegan, the Narragansett, and the Delaware, is fast overtaking the Choctaw, the Cherokee, and the Creek.

Was this passage inspired by a reading of the favourite novels of America's favourite novelist? *The Wept*, with its tragic story of the passing of the Narragansetts, Mohegans, and Delawares, was published shortly before Jackson's message. In any case,

[16] Cf. Meyers, *The Jacksonian Persuasion* (Vintage ed.: New York, 1960), pp. 3-32, 57-100. I am much indebted to Professor Meyer's brilliant analysis of Cooper's ideological affinities with Jackson.

Cooper must have been mightily pleased to suppose that part of the gospel expounded by the President came straight out of *The Wept* or *The Mohicans*. It is a sad irony that the humane attitude exhibited by Jackson here led eventually to measures which proved as inhumane as possible—forced migrations in which thousands of Indians died.[17]

Other passages in the President's message would have appealed to Cooper on non-Jeffersonian grounds. As we have seen, Cooper was a maritime nationalist, a 'Big Navy' man. Jackson, too, though a soldier, saw the importance of a strong navy:

Constituting, as it does, the best standing security of this country against foreign aggression, it claims the especial attention of government. In this spirit, the measures which, since the termination of the last war, have been in operation for its gradual enlargement, were adopted; and it should continue to be cherished as the offspring of our national experience.

Related to the need for a manifestly powerful navy was a need for firmness in foreign policy. As the conqueror of the English at New Orleans, Jackson promised to win some respect for the United States in his dealings with European nations. Though his menace is muffled by deliberate restraint and circumlocutory prose, Jackson's message is confident and unyielding:

Our foreign relations, although in general character pacific and friendly, present subjects of difference between us and other powers, of deep interest, as well to the country at large as to many of our citizens. To effect an adjustment of these shall continue to be the object of my earnest endeavors: and notwithstanding the difficulties of the task, I do not allow myself to apprehend unfavorable results. Blessed as our country is, with every thing which constitutes national strength, she is fully adequate to the maintenance of all her interests. In discharging the responsible trust confided to the executive in this respect, it is my settled purpose to ask nothing that is not clearly right, and to submit to nothing that is wrong; and I flatter myself, that, supported by the other branches of the government, and by the intelligence and patriotism of the people, we shall be able, under the protection of Providence, to cause all our just rights to be respected.

In Cooper's view, this was exactly what was wanted: 'it has done, both him and us credit, all over Europe'.[18]

[17] Cf. Glyndon Van Deusen, *The Jacksonian Era* (New York, 1959), pp. 48–50.
[18] *op. cit.*

No reader of Cooper's tracts, prefaces, and letters on political subjects can fail to discern how closely he approximates the humourless, moralistic rhetoric of Jackson's message. This was not because he consciously imitated it, but because his own mind and character were curiously like Jackson's—and became more so as a result of his living in the phantasmal political world of conspirators and crusaders created, in large measure, by the Old Hero's rhetoric. Though he was often disappointed in Jackson and eventually lost faith in many of the Jacksonian doctrines, the embattled Cooper of the 'thirties and 'forties was a truly Jacksonian figure, in many ways like the Old General as unforgettably described by Marvin Meyers:

Because he was a commanding figure, and a man of simple, thundering judgments who found things right or wrong and made disputants friends or enemies, the war against the Bank became a general struggle to preserve the values of the Old Republic. A general of the best Roman breed—as partisans saw him—sworn to his people, instinctively just, had come in righteous wrath to strangle a conspiracy with tentacles in every vital part of American society.

One cannot think of Jackson in this situation as the doctrinal counsellor, or as the architect of policy. His affirmations and especially his fierce denials have the force of elemental acts: one feels Old Hickory throwing himself into the breach. In his own estimate, and the favorable public's, Jackson was the guardian of a threatened republican tradition which demanded not adjustment or revaluation but right action taken from a solid moral stance.[19]

How Jackson would have approved of this judgment by Cooper:

My whig friends . . . say 'join *us*, and see what we will do for you'. I have no answer for them but to say they would support the devil, and *do* I believe, if he would turn Whig.[20]

But it would be a mistake to suppose that Cooper's Jacksonian stance was exclusively political and an even greater mistake to assume that it could be defined in the narrow terms of Democratic party policies. Virtually every book Cooper wrote between 1834 and the year of his death was Jacksonian in the broad sense that it was the work of a man who saw himself as 'the guardian of a threatened republican tradition which

---

[19] *Jacksonian Persuasion*, p. 17.
[20] Letter to William Gilmore Simms (5 Jan. 1844), *Letters*, vol. IV, p. 438.

demanded not adjustment or revaluation but right action taken from a solid moral stance'. This is true not only of such openly anti-Whig works as *Home as Found* and *The Autobiography of a Pocket Handkerchief*,[21] but also of works like *The Redskins* and *The Crater*, which, because of their irreverent handling of 'the people', might appear to be anti-Jacksonian. Of all these books it is true to say that Cooper's 'affirmations and especially his fierce denials have the force of elemental acts'. This political style, invented by Jackson to satisfy urgent personal and social needs, was translated by Cooper into a literary style: it is in this sense especially that Cooper may be said to have been deeply and permanently influenced by the Old Hero.

2. *Home as Found*

The high-water mark of Cooper's political liberalism was probably reached in 1834 when he wrote to his wife, 'Every hour I stay at home, convinces me more and more, that society has had a summerset, and that the élite is at the bottom!' [22] He was then thoroughly disillusioned with the reading, i.e. the upper, classes and continued to be so to the end of his life. An ex-Federalist himself, he now believed that some of the Federalist leaders had conspired to destroy the Republic:

It is not at all necessary to believe that the great body of the political party with which Mr _____ was connected, meant revolution and a monarchy . . .: although, that many among them did contemplate both, I do not now entertain the smallest doubt. You know I was educated in the particular opinions of this political sect; that I had every opportunity of ascertaining their real sentiments; and I cannot but know, that, while the great majority of them dreamed of no more than arresting what they believed to be the dangerous inroads of democracy, some of their leaders aimed at a return, in principle, to the old system.[23]

One such leader, certainly was Hamilton—a great man, in Cooper's view, but one who had been mesmerized by the

---

[21] *The Autobiography of a Pocket Handkerchief* (1843), though negligible as a literary work and never included in the collected novels of Cooper, has some interest as an attack on the commercial values of New York society. For an able discussion of this short novel, see Grossman, *James Fenimore Cooper*, pp. 170–5.

[22] Letter to Mrs Cooper (12 June 1834), *Letters*, vol. III, p. 42.

[23] *Excursions in Switzerland* (Paris, 1836), p. 267.

supposed grandeur of the British aristocracy.[24] By 1834 he was convinced that England, the American Whigs, and the Devil were in league to destroy American political principles; it was in this spirit that he undertook to complete one of his most misguided efforts—*The Monikins* (1835).

In the politico-literary critical language of the 'thirties and 'forties, 'Monikins' was synonymous with dullness and perversity. And although various twentieth-century critics have found things to admire in it,[25] I believe that the critical consensus still is that, as a whole, *The Monikins* is well-nigh unreadable and certainly does not deserve a revival. The history of the composition of this Swiftian allegorical satire furnishes a clue to the nature of its failure. It was begun well before Cooper started work on *The Headsman* but was not completed until after Cooper's return to America. He alludes as follows to this change of plans in a letter to S. F. B. Morse: 'I am caught by local things here, and shall probably bring out a Swiss tale before the Monnikins which requires time and thought—On Monday I am to go on the Great St Bernard with Mr Cox. We shall see if the mountain cannot be worked up in the way of romance.' [26] Hence the glut of particularized descriptive passages in *The Headsman*, which, though they interrupt the progress of that novel, must have afforded Cooper a welcome relief from the unremittingly dry, abstract allegory of *The Monikins*. In the latter, though Cooper employs the Swiftian device of a voyage to an unknown territory—to the lands of 'Leaphigh' (Britain) and 'Leaplow' (the U.S.), populated by 'monikins' (monkeys who act and think like Englishmen and Americans)— he deliberately refrains from giving his readers a concrete picture of these strange lands:

The monikins were by far too polished to crowd about when we landed, with an impertinent and troublesome curiosity. So far from this, we were permitted to approach the capital itself without let or hindrance. As it is less my intention to describe physical things than to dwell upon the philosophy and other moral aspects of the Leaphigh world, little more will be said of their houses, domestic

---

[24] Entry in Journal (24 Sept. 1830), *Letters*, vol. II, p. 32.
[25] e.g. Yvor Winters, *In Defence of Reason*, pp. 183–4, and James Grossman, *James Fenimore Cooper*, pp. 93–7.
[26] Letter to S. F. B. Morse (21 Sept. 1832), *Letters*, vol. II, p. 337.

economy, and other improvements in the arts, than may be gathered incidentally, as the narrative shall proceed. Let it suffice to say on these heads, that the Leaphigh monikins, like men, consult, or think they consult—which, so long as they know no better, amounts to pretty much the same thing—their own convenience in all things, the pocket alone excepted; and that they continue very laudably to do as their fathers did before them, seldom making changes, unless they may happen to possess the recommendation of being exotics; when, indeed, they are sometimes adopted, probably on account of their possessing the merit of having been proved suitable to another state of things.

Among the first persons we met, on entering the great square of Aggregation, as the capital of Leaphigh is called . . .

In fact, Leaphigh and Leaplow are not concretely imagined at all. The Monikins are not even monkeys who act like men, they are heavily caricatured men who exhibit (in the most repetitive fashion) some of the physical properties of monkeys. Cooper shows rather more ingenuity in some of the subordinate political allegories. One of these, a great moral eclipse in Leaplow, which occurs when Pecuniary Interest intervenes between the country and light of Principle—an allegory inspired by the Whigs' activities on behalf of the Bank of the United States—promises for a time to achieve a sombre grandeur reminiscent of the conclusion of *The Dunciad*. But even this conceit fails to assume the concrete reality necessary for it to become a thing of interest in itself. Indeed, though critics have often disparaged Cooper by saying that he was mainly an author of books for boys, the trouble with *The Monikins* is that no boy could possibly take any interest in it, in spite of its monkeys and hitherto unknown lands. On the other hand, the adult historian of Cooper's social and political views, though proof against boredom maybe, will find little in this book that is not stated elsewhere with far greater clarity and vigour. This is, in fact, the period of Cooper's most brilliant works of non-fiction: the delightful and shrewd travel books (1836-8); that lucid and, though tough-minded, liberal political treatise *The American Democrat* (1838); and the expert, still quite readable *History of the Navy of the United States* (1839). By almost any standards, these works are superior to the works of fiction discussed in this chapter. Had Cooper never written a single novel, these works would have assured him a distinguished, if minor, place in the history of American letters.

Cooper did not produce another work of fiction until, in 1838, he published the two Effingham novels—*Homeward Bound* and *Home as Found*. These novels, particularly the latter, mark new departures in his work, from the standpoints both of form and socio-political alignment. As there is good cause to believe that the formal innovations issued out of changed socio-political circumstances, I shall deal with the latter at once.

The Jacksonian rhetoric, with its explicit appeals to 'the people' and its implicit Jeffersonian appeal to a liberal, cultivated gentry, proved an irresistible political force. The political creed of the Democratic party was at once more democratic and, in the good sense, aristocratic than that of its rival: as such, it suited Cooper remarkably well. But the harmonious relationship it promised between Jeffersonian *aristoi* and 'the people' was in many respects illusory. Though a sincere Jeffersonian, Jackson was an uncultivated man of action much of whose popular appeal was due to his *not* being a Boston or Virginia gentleman like all the previous Presidents. The cultivated, intellectual elements in the Democratic party, such as Cooper and Jackson's successor Martin Van Buren, were therefore encouraging and riding a political force which could easily be turned against them. After being trounced in three successive national elections (1828, 1832, and 1836), the Anti-Jacksonians, led by the New York state Whig boss Thurlow Weed, decided that they would have to steal Jackson's fire from the Democratic party. Cooper was one of the first victims of the Whigs' revised electoral strategy, which in 1840 would carry General William Henry Harrison ('Old Tippecanoe') into the Presidency on a platform of Log Cabins and Hard Cider.

As executor of his father's estate, Cooper held in trust a small piece of land known as Three Mile Point. Though owned by the Cooper family, it was a natural recreation spot for inhabitants of Cooperstown and had been kept open to the public for many years. Newcomers to Cooperstown, and some more established residents, actually supposed that the Point was public property. By an unfortunate series of incidents in 1837, Cooper was led to forbid trespassing on the property; he was promptly denounced at a special meeting of local citizens for his 'arrogant pretensions' in 'denying to the citizens, the right . . . they have been accustomed to from time immemorial'. The local Whig press picked up the story and retold it in misleading and abusive terms: here was the way your true Democrat behaved—like an oppressive, usurping European Aristocrat! When the editors refused to retract, Cooper sued for libel. This controversy might have died down had Cooper been able to regard the whole affair as a lamentable but not very significant lapse of 'the people' and the popular press. But the Three Mile Point incident obviously stung him to the quick and he extracted from the incident the maximum social and political significance it could yield. To be denounced, and that too in the village his father had founded, by the very class of citizens whose interests he had fought for—this was intolerable, and that the citizens in question were mostly new residents merely proved that the unsettled state of American life was undermining civilized values. Translated into political terms, this restlessness was Whiggish: men on the move, who respected neither truth nor tradition were men in search of dollars; they were Whig small fry who hoped to grow into Wall Street sharks. Viewed in regional terms, these transients were mostly New Englanders—once the masters of religious, now of political, cant: levellers who took their hats off only to Daniel Webster and Gold.

Besides suing the Whig editors, Cooper took two other, closely related, remedial actions. One was to write *The Chronicles of Cooperstown* (1838)—'the simple and brief annals of the place, from the time when the site of Cooperstown was a wilderness, down to the present moment. . . .' [27] The other was to write a sequel to *The Pioneers*, in which the later fortunes of the Effingham family are described. Cooper originally intended to write but one Effingham novel, in which an expatriate American family returns home for the first time in eleven years. But his plan to begin the action with the arrival of the Effinghams in America was changed by popular (i.e. his family's) demand: 'As a vessel was introduced in the first chapter, the cry was for "more ship", until the work has become "all ship"; it actually closing at, or near, the spot where it was originally intended it should commence.' The result is that *Home as Found* is, for all

[27] *Chronicles of Cooperstown* (Cooperstown, 1838), pp. 85–6.

practical purposes, the novel Cooper first intended to write, while *Homeward Bound* is scarcely more than an entertaining but dispensable preliminary.

Before dispensing with it, however, I should point out that *Homeward Bound* is something more than a tale of nautical adventure. Nautical adventure is the right vehicle to reveal the virtues of one of Cooper's good New England sailors: John Truck, Captain of the *Montauk*, is a sturdy, courageous, self-reliant man of skill who embodies most of the things Cooper admired in the Democratic Man. Opposed to him is one Steadfast Dodge, Esq., Editor of the *Active Enquirer*—a cowardly, sneaking, lying fictional descendant of Hiram Doolittle of *The Pioneers*, a 'Man of the People'. As is all too frequently the case in Cooper's fiction, these two subordinate characters, rather than the Effinghams and their genteel friends, provide the fictional centre of interest in *Homeward Bound*. The action of the novel, though highly improbable, does at any rate exhibit the characters of these two American types in a glaring yet not patently unfair light. By contrast, the light in *Home as Found* is unfair to the lower-class American characters: in a novel of manners, these characters can only exhibit their gaucheries, never the practical virtues which might win the reader's respect.

None the less, the practical American virtues which Cooper's fiction had done much to make honourable in the eyes of the world—virtues so necessary during the heroic phase of American development—might after all prove unattractive and undesirable once the nation settled down into a more or less civilized condition. That this had proven to be the case is the central, and not obviously unreasonable, thesis of *Home as Found*. To do any critical justice to this novel, therefore, we must view it, not as the sequel to *Homeward Bound*, but as the sequel to *The Pioneers*. The chief characters, John and Edward Effingham and Edward's daughter Eve, are descendants of Oliver Effingham and Elizabeth Temple: in Cooper's eyes they are the flower of American civilization, Jeffersonian gentry who make use of their inherited material wealth to cultivate themselves and then spread their culture among their provincial neighbours. Returning to Templeton, they find what to them is a new social situation, but what in fact is little more than a logical extension of the social situation in *The Pioneers*. Viewed without nostalgic indulgence, Richard Jones is substantially the same type of person as Aristabulus Bragg, the manager of Effingham affairs in *Home as Found*. Translated into an editor, Hiram Doolittle is Steadfast Dodge, Esq. Multiply Jotham Riddel a thousand times and you have the floating population of Templeton in *Home as Found*. So true is this that everything I have already said about Jones, Riddel, and Doolittle as embodiments of Plato's Democratic Man, held in check by Judge Temple, may be applied to Bragg, Dodge, & Co.: the difference is that Judge Temple is no more, only the law stands in the way of mob rule.

This central perception—that yesterday's imperfect yet beloved pioneers are today's hated mob—is almost the only moving thing about *Home as Found*; it justifies Cooper's otherwise irritating attempt to make this labour of hate a sequel to an earlier labour of love. But there was another reason why Cooper yoked these two novels together. Confronted, so he believed, with a society abandoned to speculation and change, he became more than ever convinced that the old country families, like the Jays, the Rensselaers, and the Coopers themselves, were the only hope for a civilized and dignified America —one in which the obsession with space would not entirely destroy the awareness of time. In *Home as Found* he hit upon the proper literary form, the family chronicle novel, to record and praise what, in his view, they stood for—filial piety and paternal care. While this novel is far from a success, it is at least a precursor of the Littlepage trilogy; it opens up a new vein in Cooper's fiction.

It is also the first American novel of manners. To the literary historian or social historian it must always, therefore, be an interesting book. But a bad book it nevertheless is. Though Cooper had a former naval officer's obsessed interest in etiquette, he was remarkably insensitive to nuances of tone and manner. A man capable of writing, in all seriousness, 'rustic seats were *improvisés*, and the business of restauration proceeded'—is hardly to be trusted to discriminate accurately between what is elegant and what is not. His Eve Effingham, who is supposed to be elegant beyond the comprehension of most of his stay-at-home American characters, is in fact such an arrogant cosmopolite, so deficient in tact and insensitive to the feel-

ings of her cousin Grace Van Cortlandt, that she is easily
the most loathsome of Cooper's heroines. One of her tricks is
to take advantage of her countrymen's ignorance by ridiculing
them in French while they are standing by. Another is to
compare everything she encounters in the state of New York
with what she has seen in Europe: apparently she is incapable
of trying to understand anything before she pronounces it,
comparatively speaking, inferior. Occasionally, Cooper seems
to sense that something is wrong with his heroine, but usually
he speaks ecstatically of her moral, intellectual, and physical
perfection. Meanwhile, his reader must reflect with grim irony
that it was for this that the Indians were dispossessed of their
lands and Natty Bumppo driven west.

On the other hand, Eve Effingham is impressively (oppres-
sively) real; so are John Effingham and Aristabulus Bragg. John,
the middle-aged cousin of Eve's father, is a disillusioned upper-
class Whig critic of America to whom Cooper entrusts his most
sardonic asides. Though blind to the faults of Eve, Cooper
recognizes that John Effingham's aristocratic contempt is excessive and self-isolating. At the same time, he puts so much of
himself into John that he becomes a figure attractive for his
irascible integrity and masculine understanding of the strengths
as well as the weaknesses of American character. John alone
appreciates the abilities of Aristabulus Bragg, who is certainly
the most impressive of Cooper's characters in *Home as Found*.
From the moment he first appears in the novel, when at first
glance he coolly determines to make Eve his wife, to the
moment when, having been rejected by Eve (in one of Cooper's
few successful courtship scenes), he marries her French maid
and departs for the West, Aristabulus is the epitome of Whiggish go-aheadism. 'I rejoice', says Aristabulus, 'in being a
native of a country in which as few impediments as possible
exist to onward impulses.' So far as local attachments are concerned—to some tree which seems more pleasant than another,
to the house he was born in—Aristabulus takes an emancipated
view:

'. . . a human being is not a cat, to love a locality rather than its
own interests. I have found some trees much pleasanter than others,
and the pleasantest tree I can remember was one of my own, out of
which sawyers made a thousand feet of clear stuff, to say nothing of

middlings. The house I was born in was pulled down shortly after my birth, as indeed has been its successor, so I can tell you nothing on that head. . . . In the way of houses, Mr Effingham, I believe it is the general opinion you might have done better with your own, than to have repaired it. Had the materials been disposed of, they would have sold well, and by running a street through the property, a pretty sum might have been realized.'

'In which case I should have been without a home, Mr Bragg.'

'It would have been no great matter to get another on cheaper land. The old residence would have made a good factory, or an inn.'

'Sir, I am a cat, and like the places I have long frequented.'

All of this is of course startlingly relevant to the situation in the United States today. For all his lack of finesse, all the petty personal grievances which prey upon and probably motivated the writing of this novel, Cooper described the emerging pattern of American life with devastating accuracy. In a world dominated by the values of Aristabulus Bragg, Cooper, like Natty Bumppo in *The Pioneers*, had become obsolete.

That Cooper was indeed obsolete was the joyous cry of the Whig press when they received *Home as Found*. 'Handsome' Edward Effingham, recently returned from Europe, looked remarkably like an infatuated self-portrait; Templeton looked astonishingly like Cooperstown; and Lake Otsego, after all, was Lake Otsego. Worse, Cooper included in the novel a thinly disguised account of the Three Mile Point affair. Within a few weeks of the publication of *Home as Found* the 'aristocratic Mr Effingham' became a target of the national Whig press. Cooper's cranky Jeffersonian critique of American society was tortured into the unpatriotic ravings of a self-styled nobleman who dreamed of castles and coats of arms. James Watson Webb, for example, accused Cooper of

aristocratical pretensions; and publishing a book to demonstrate that he is a scion of a noble English family living on 'the estate of his father', in a kind of baronial style, consonant alike with the early education, noble descent, and habitual tastes of the 'mild and thoughtful Mr Effingham', whose 'well regulated mind', had pointed out to him the moral grandeur of such a man gradually descending into the vale of years surrounded by a dependant peasantry. . . .[28]

[28] Webb, *Morning Courier and New York Enquirer* (13 Sept., 1839), quoted from

This was of course a grotesque caricature of Cooper's real position, but editors like Webb, Horace Greeley, and Thurlow Weed specialized in attacks of this kind. Weed in particular, who was already masterminding the Whig presidential campaign strategy for 1840, was building up the Whigs as the Party of the People, the Democrats as the Party of the Aristocracy. In fact, the attacks on 'Mr Effingham' were but the opening shots of a giddy campaign which reached its absurd climax in mid-1840 when Whig lithographs exhibited Old Tippecanoe welcoming the People at the door of his log cabin, while Van Buren was damned for living a life of degenerate aristocratic ease in the White House, which was depicted in Whig campaign literature as a 'PALACE *as splendid as that of the Caesars, and as richly adorned as the proudest Asiatic mansion*'.[29] Harrison carried nineteen of the twenty-six states.

Cooper prosecuted the Whig editors for libel with remarkable success, but the Three Mile Point affair and the victory of Harrison undermined his recently acquired belief that 'the élite is at the bottom'. More than ever, Whiggery seemed to him the party of the Devil, combining as it did the worst elements of both the upper and lower classes in an unprincipled rush for money and power. Evidence of his hatred of the Whigs is scattered throughout his later novels. In *The Deerslayer*, for instance, which seems remote enough from contemporary politics, one of the villains is the rough backwoodsman Henry March, otherwise known as 'Hurry Harry'; the novel was partly written during the presidential campaign of 1840, and there can be little doubt that the portrayal of Harry is to some extent Cooper's caustic commentary on the virtues of the 'Log Cabin Democracy' of William Henry Harrison. More important than such reflections of party politics in his novels, however, was the major shift in his socio-political alignment. Between 1828 and 1836 Cooper saw himself as the defender of 'the rights of the mass' in Europe and America; after 1837 he became the defender of individual or minority rights. Up to 1837 he had been a

[29] Charles Ogle, *The Royal Splendor of the President's Palace*, cited by Schlesinger *Age of Jackson*, p. 293. The Whig pre-campaign strategy and the campaign itsel, are vigorously described in *Age of Jackson*, pp. 267–305.

Ethel R. Outland, *The 'Effingham' Libels on Cooper* (Madison, 1929), which reprints the whole of Webb's article on pp. 232–41.

cautious believer in social and political progress in America, recognizing and approving of the 'two changes of administration, that have involved changes of principles, or changes in popular will;—that which placed Mr Jefferson in the seat of Mr Adams, senior, and that which placed Mr Jackson in the seat of Mr Adams, junior. . . .' [30] But the Three Mile Point controversy and its aftermath brought home to him how easily the noble democracy of Jefferson might be transmogrified into the crass egalitarianism of the Whig press. A late convert to Jeffersonianism, he could not make another radical adjustment of his social and political philosophy. Increasingly an isolated and archaic figure, he developed an embittered awareness of the historical processes which had left him stranded; out of this awareness, especially in *The Deerslayer*, *Afloat and Ashore*, and the Littlepage trilogy, he was to create some of his greatest fiction.

[30] *A Residence in France* (1836), pp. 204–5.

X

THE PATHFINDER:
LEATHERSTOCKING IN LOVE

The Wigwam   *vs.* My Hotel
Chingachgook   *vs.* My Wife
Natty Bumppo   *vs.* My Humble Self
—D. H. Lawrence, *Studies in
Classic American Literature*

The Pathfinder (1840) is the only Leatherstocking tale in which Natty Bumppo at all resembles the wavering hero of a Scott novel. Here for the first and only time we see him waver between the life he has always led—untrammelled by property, responsible only to his own strict code and conscience, free to follow his own bent away from white European society—and the life of a border family man with all that that implies in terms of a wife who must be kept content with her lot, children who must be properly educated, property which must be acquired and protected. Yet *The Pathfinder* is not in the least like a Waverley Novel. It is not even very much like one of the earlier Leatherstocking tales. Why, more than a decade after burying the Leatherstocking in *The Prairie* (1827), did Cooper revive him again? And why revive him in this particular way?

Three of the Leatherstocking tales are more or less intimately connected with scenes and events which were important in Cooper's own life. *The Pioneers* (1823) was, among other things, a nostalgic portrait of Lake Otsego and early Cooperstown. In *The Deerslayer* (1841), written when he was disillusioned with the progress of Cooperstown and the United States generally, Cooper turned back to a time when his beloved Lake Otsego and its surroundings were almost a virgin wilderness, almost undefiled by white settlers. *The Pathfinder* is not concerned with Lake Otsego, but it does hark back to scenes which Cooper knew as a young midshipman shortly before his marriage in 1810. In his preface to the novel Cooper wrote proudly that

> In youth, when belonging to the navy, the writer of this book served for some time on the great western lakes. He was, indeed, one of those who first carried the cockade of the republic on those inland seas. This was pretty early in the present century, when the navigation was still confined to the employment of a few ships and schooners. . . . Towns have been built along the whole of the extended line of coasts, and the traveller now stops at many a place of ten or fifteen, and at one of even fifty thousand inhabitants, where a few huts then marked the natural sites of future marts.

Though Cooper disliked the unheroic service at Fort Oswego (the fort in *The Pathfinder*) and soon obtained an extended furlough which terminated eventually in his resignation, there can be no doubt that the U.S. naval service always held a place in his affections which no other occupation could rival. Not only did he retain many naval officers among his closest friends, but also, in such novels as *The Pilot* and the *Red Rover*, he acted as a propagandist for a strong U.S. Navy.[1] In 1839, just as he was embarking on *The Pathfinder*, he published his monumental *History of the Navy of the United States*. Some of the most important battles described in that work (and mentioned in the preface to *The Pathfinder*) were those fought on the Great Lakes just a few years after Cooper left the navy: battles in which young Cooper himself might have joined had he not been kept home by domestic circumstances—which included, almost certainly, a pledge to his new wife to abandon the navy.[2]

Though likely, it is not at all sure that Cooper's work on the *History of the Navy* inspired him to set the scene of a new Leatherstocking tale on the Great Lakes. Even as early as 1831 he planned to write what he described cryptically as a tale of 'Lake Ontario, with scenes on the Great Lakes, with Indians inter-

---

[1] For a full account of Cooper's interest in the sea and the U.S. Navy, see Thomas Philbrick, *James Fenimore Cooper and the Development of American Sea Fiction* (Cambridge, Mass., 1961).

[2] Cf. Letter to Smith Thompson (8 Jan. 1823), *Letters*, vol. I, p. 90. Professor Beard suggests, I think rightly, that Cooper's pledge to resign from the navy was probably made before his marriage. *Letters*, vol. I, p. 25.

mingled. . . .'[3] But probably the ebullient, enormously successful Fenimore Cooper of 1831 had no intention of resurrecting a
hero whom he had buried just a few years previously. It was left
to the disillusioned, economically harassed Cooper of 1839 to
try to bring Leatherstocking back to life. For months he had
been abused by the Whig press because of the views expressed
in *Home as Found* (1838); already he was preparing the series of
libel suits which were to occupy him for the next several years.
Ever since *The Heidenmauer* (1832) critics had charged him with
betraying his gifts as a romancer; more than once he had
threatened to lay down the pen forever. But Fenimore Cooper
could not keep quiet, and in any case he had to write in order
to support a comparatively large and expensive family. No
doubt he hoped that a new Leatherstocking tale would be a
profitable venture, and no doubt too he longed to regain some
of the popular esteem and affection which works like *The
Monikins* and *Home as Found* had forfeited. But more important
than either of these factors, writing *The Pathfinder* must have
held out the prospect of a temporary escape from the complicated, infinitely exasperating world of *Home as Found*—a return
to the scenes of his youth when, unencumbered by family
responsibilities and the uncomfortable though self-assumed role
of social critic, he was still true to his naval vocation.

Intrinsic to the very conception of the Leatherstocking
character is the idea of truth to vocation. From his first appearance in *The Pioneers*, where his bumpkinish manners and appearance are offset by his obvious skill and knowledgeableness,
Natty acts in accordance with the Platonic principle stated by
Judge Temple: 'that a man is to be qualified by nature and
education to do only one thing well'. The bungling ways of
Judge Temple's settlers, and of the Judge himself, serve to confirm the old hunter's sense of his own dignity: aside from woods-
man Billy Kirby, they are all of them fish out of water; Leatherstocking, we feel, could not be other than he is, and, more important, he could not wish to be other. He exhibits the same
traits in *The Last of the Mohicans* and *The Prairie*; especially in
the latter, where he is degraded to the status of a trapper, he

---

[3] Letter to Henry Colborn (1 Feb. 1831), *Letters*, vol. II, p. 53. Cooper also
mentions this early plan for a novel about the Great Lakes in his preface to the
first edition of *The Pathfinder* (London, 1840), vol. I, p. v.

laments that he has fallen from the dignity of a hunter. Leather-stocking's vocation, however, involves a commitment to an entire way of life and not merely the ability to do one thing superlatively well (though the one is dependent on the other). In *The Prairie* as in *The Pioneers* grateful and well-meaning friends attempt to lure the old man away from the wilderness, but his answer is invariably the same:

Ay, if kind offers and good wishes could have done the thing, I might have been a congress-man, or perhaps a governor, years agone. Your gran'ther wished the same, and there are them still living in the Otsego mountains, as I hope, who would gladly have given me a palace for my dwelling. But what are riches without content?

It is true, of course, that habit speaks here as much as, or more than, vocation. But in the case of Leatherstocking habit and vocation are much the same thing, since, as Henry Nash Smith has observed, 'Leatherstocking was, so to speak, intrinsically aged.'[4] Aged and true to his 'gifts' Leatherstocking was from the beginning: traits which Cooper could exploit in *The Pathfinder* and *The Deerslayer*, but which he could not essentially alter.

In fact, the discontented novelist had the strongest personal motives, unconscious though they must have been, for stressing these traits in *The Pathfinder* and taking 'truth' (in the sense of fidelity) as his main theme. For Leatherstocking is not the only character in this novel who is tempted to betray something. Mabel Dunham, out of a sense of gratitude to Leatherstocking and devotion to her father, is tempted to prove false to her own heart by marrying Leatherstocking rather than the handsome young sailor Jasper Western. The treacherous Indian Arrowhead would like to be false to his loyal Indian wife by absconding with Mabel. Jasper Western is suspected of treason to his country; Lieutenant Muir is in fact guilty of treason. Even the great chief Chingachgook, though still movingly true to the traditions of his extinct tribe, is reported to be tempted by the soothing doctrines of the white man's religion. At the centre of the novel, however, is the triangular relationship between Path-

[4] H. N. Smith, *Virgin Land: The American West as Symbol and Myth* (Vintage ed.: New York, 1957), p. 74.

finder, Mabel Dunham, and Jasper Western. It is here that the autobiographical element in *The Pathfinder* is most clearly revealed.

Though Jasper is not permitted to say much for himself, he more than rivals Pathfinder in action. Second only to the hunter as a marksman, he greatly excels him as soon as the action moves on to the water. Nick-named 'Eau-douce' because of his mastery of all that pertains to sailing on the great fresh-water lakes, Jasper Western, as his surname implies, is a magnificent frontiersman and worthy competitor for the hand of Mabel Dunham. His true friend Pathfinder is well aware of these qualities and, measuring his own against them, is the more convinced of his own unworthiness. Worse, he fears that whatever good qualities he does indisputably possess would be destroyed if he married Mabel:

With you in danger, for instance, I fear I might become foolhardy; but before we became so intimate, as I may say, I loved to think of my scoutin's, and of my marches, and outlyings, and fights, and other adventures; but now my mind cares less about them; I think more of the barracks and of evenings passed in discourse, of feelings in which there are no wranglings and bloodshed, and of young women, and of their laughs, and their cheerful soft voices, their pleasant looks, and their winning ways! I sometimes tell the sergeant, that he and his daughter will be the spoiling of one of the best and most experienced scouts on the lines!

And:

I trouble myself but little with dollars or half-joes, for these are the favourite coin in this part of the world, but I can easily believe by what I've seen of mankind, that if a man *has* a chest filled with either, he may be said to lock up his heart in the same box. I once hunted for two summers during the last peace, and I collected so much peltry that I found my right feelings giving way to a craving after property; and if I have concern in marrying Mabel, it is that I may get to love such things too well, in order to make her comfortable.

That these fears were not groundless is strongly implied by the conclusion of the novel, after Pathfinder's last visit to Jasper and Mabel:

Neither Jasper nor his wife ever beheld the Pathfinder again. They remained on the banks of the Ontario for another year; and then the pressing solicitations of Cap induced them to join him in New York, where Jasper eventually became a successful and respected merchant.

The gallant and intrepid sailor Eau-douce, the vigorous frontiersman Jasper Western—reduced to a 'successful and respected merchant'! Clearly these few sentences are meant to suggest that marriage would have been the 'spoiling' of Pathfinder, as it was of Jasper; but it is impossible to tell precisely—one can only guess—how much unconscious bitterness and irony they also express. At the same time, if we continue to read *The Pathfinder* as, on one level, an autobiographical document, Cooper must have found some consolation in the fate of Pathfinder. For if Pathfinder remained true to his vocation, he did so only because Mabel finally rejected him; his sense of loss, so Cooper emphatically tells us, was both deep and permanent. As for Cooper himself, discontented though he was with his occupation as a writer, he must have been aware that, in returning to Leatherstocking, he was again being true to his own best gifts.

But even if *The Pathfinder* has the kind of relevance to Cooper's personal history that I suggest it has, how does this novel differ from the earlier Leatherstocking tales? *The Pioneers* in particular is much more obviously and directly autobiographical than *The Pathfinder*. But in *The Pioneers* Cooper carefully excludes anything that could be construed as a self-portrait; the portrait, rather, is of a community; and the issues of the novel are primarily communal issues. Whereas in *The Pathfinder* we are mainly concerned with the fate of individuals who are pressed by the strongest personal feelings to abandon or greatly modify their old patterns of life, in the early Leatherstocking tales we are concerned with the fate of rival cultures, rival societies. In *The Pathfinder* almost nothing is said about the destruction of the red men and the inexorable movement westward of white civilization: but this is the general theme which unites *The Pioneers, The Last of the Mohicans,* and *The Prairie.* Equally new and important in *The Pathfinder*, the pathos with which Leatherstocking is invested has nothing to do with the pathos of a vanishing way of life. In short, the early tales are variants of the historical novel created by Scott; *The Pathfinder* does not belong to this genre.

As Henry Nash Smith has pointed out, a novel, according to the canons which Cooper adhered to, was a love story in which the hero was the male lead in the courtship. And since in the early Leatherstocking tales Leatherstocking himself was not the romantic lead, he could not be, technically, the hero. The hero was a genteel Oliver Effingham, Major Heyward, or Captain Middleton. Therefore, according to Professor Smith, Cooper's most vital character occupied a technically inferior position both in the social system and in the form of the sentimental novel as he was using it. The store of emotion associated with the vast wilderness in the minds of both Cooper and his audience was strikingly inharmonious with the literary framework he had adopted.

And Professor Smith goes on to argue that in *The Pathfinder* Cooper set out deliberately to make Leatherstocking the romantic lead so as to elevate him to a status commensurate with his importance as a 'symbol of forest freedom and virtue'.[5] I believe, on the contrary, that the idea of Leatherstocking in love, conceived as a test of his vocation, very likely preceded and motivated Cooper's reform of the novel as he had previously used it; i.e. roughly as Scott had used it. For Scott as for Cooper the novel was essentially a love story, but Scott transformed the genteel hero into a comparatively mediocre figure who was overshadowed by, and caught in between, more vigorous and firmly defined personalities. The great novelistic virtues of a hero like Edward Waverley were his lack of firm political commitment and his remarkable social and physical mobility: these allowed him not only to view the opposed socio-political forces of Jacobites and Hanoverians with an open mind, but also to visit them in their native habitats, whether they be a London house, Holyrood palace, or a robber's cave. Quite different characters were called for to act as spokesmen and leaders of the opposed factions: these must be vital, committed, firmly in place. One of the important features of such characters (e.g. Fergus Mac-Ivor in *Waverley* or Burley and Claverhouse in *Old Mortality*) is their monkishness; for they represent their respective factions the more purely and uncompromisingly because their passions are political, religious, or social rather than romantic. The same is true of Leatherstocking, particularly in

[5] Smith, *Virgin Land*, pp. 70-1.

167

The Pioneers, where he occupies a strictly analogous role as the spokesman and representative of the old wilderness way of life. To be sure, in *The Last of the Mohicans* and *The Prairie* Cooper abandoned the wavering hero (though he kept the genteel suitor) and relied on Leatherstocking's ambivalent status to provide the link between whites and Indians, at the same time retaining him in his role of spokesman and representative. This stroke of economy had unfortunate consequences: in order to bring the necessary variety of white characters into the presence of the wilderness-loving old hunter, Cooper had to resort to the most absurd fictional dodges and abductions. None the less, so long as Cooper's aims were similar to Scott's, he had little to gain by exhibiting Leatherstocking in love. Moreover, in novels which were designed to compare and contrast the virtues of rival cultures, Cooper inevitably wished to exhibit the courtship of genteel upper-class characters who—whatever we may think of them—were in Cooper's eyes the flower and justification of usurping white civilization.

The Pathfinder, with its less ambitious scope and its focus on personal rather than communal or even national problems, presented a new though less severe challenge to Cooper's ability to unify and structure his fictional materials. He met this challenge by creating a heroine who could replace the wavering hero of *The Pioneers* and the Waverley novels. Almost all the action in *The Pathfinder* takes place in the presence of Mabel Dunham. In this respect, Mabel is like one of Scott's wavering heroes. But in other respects her role in the novel is precisely the opposite of that of a wavering hero. She has none of Edward Waverley's mobility; the representatives of various stations and walks of life must come to her. Her drawing power (she is nicknamed 'Magnet') is of course limited by her social background and personal qualities. Young, beautiful, humble, yet educated above her station as the daughter of Sergeant Dunham, Mabel easily and plausibly attracts such varied suitors as Pathfinder, Eau-douce, and Lieutenant Muir. As a young girl without a mother (like nearly all of Cooper's heroines), she is regarded as more than usually vulnerable—especially in the wilderness—and so numerous protectors naturally flock around her. Her presence in fact unifies the novel: no character is permitted to remain very long in the foreground of *The Pathfinder* unless he has some direct relationship with her either as suitor or protector. Chingachgook, for instance, has nothing to do with *that* side of Leatherstocking's life. Not the least beautiful thing about this most unified of the Leatherstocking tales is the way Natty's inseparable Indian companion is made to fade out and then reappear at the end, waiting at the edge of the clearing by the path that leads into the wilderness.

There seems to be a critical consensus that *The Pathfinder* is neither the best nor the worst of the Leatherstocking tales. This must be partly because Pathfinder does not figure in this novel as the representative of a doomed way of life and therefore does not achieve his full mythic stature. Moreover, none of the other characters in *The Pathfinder* has the vigour and complexity of Judge Temple in *The Pioneers* or Ishmael Bush in *The Prairie*. There are, as well, other deficiencies in the novel. Yet these are not half so serious as similar deficiencies in novels which are much more admired, e.g. *The Prairie* or *The Deerslayer*. The inescapable fact about the Leatherstocking tales is that their chief source of power is Leatherstocking himself. In *The Pathfinder* he is quite simply not himself. It is not merely that he is apologetic and unsure of himself in his new role; he does not even take the lead in much of the physical action. Now this is not a defect in the novel; on the contrary, it is a necessary part of Cooper's artistic design that Leatherstocking should not be his old heroic self. But the loss of vitality is a real loss, not to be fully compensated for by a real gain in unity and in the development of Leatherstocking's character. So far as the sequence as a whole is concerned, however, *The Pathfinder* is an indispensable part in a way that *The Last of the Mohicans* is not. For the effect of *The Pathfinder* is to humanize Cooper's secular saint and to make his victimization by the forces of white civilization the more complete and irreparable.

XI

THE DEERSLAYER

I

D. H. LAWRENCE considered *The Deerslayer* 'the most fascinating' of the Leatherstocking tales.[1] I think he was right. Yet I
shouldn't wish to endorse Marius Bewley's judgment that *The
Deerslayer* is 'probably the best thing Cooper ever wrote'.[2] For
the fascination of this novel is in some respects the fascination
of a puzzle: how can a work of art that is so often gauche, improbable, crowded, bigoted, puerile—how can such a work
form, as I believe *The Deerslayer* does, an aesthetic whole which
is intensely moving and convincing? Certainly *The Pathfinder*
seems to be a much better novel, so far as artistic unity and
design are concerned. None of the characters in *The Deerslayer*
can match Ishmael Bush or (at his best) the old trapper in *The
Prairie*. And although Mr Bewley praises *The Deerslayer* for its
'vividly realized circumstantial detail' and for the profundity
and accuracy of Cooper's moral perceptions in creating the
American backwoodsman Hurry Harry,[3] the same qualities are
to be found—multiplied fivefold—in *The Pioneers*. Yet the fact
remains, in my experience at least, that *The Deerslayer* is the
most moving of all the Leatherstocking tales. No extant critical
discussion accounts at all satisfactorily for the power and
quality that I and other readers have felt when reading the
novel, though there are excellent analyses of some of its parts,
notably of its seventh chapter.[4] These, alas, are only parts, and

---

[1] Lawrence, *Studies in Classic American Literature* (1924). *Selected Literary Criticism*,
ed. Anthony Beal (London, 1956), p. 326.
[2] Bewley, *The Eccentric Design*, p. 88.   [3] *ibid.*, pp. 98 and 95.
[4] Cf. Yvor Winters, *In Defense of Reason*, pp. 187–90, and R. W. B. Lewis,
The American Adam (Chicago and London, 1955), pp. 104–5.

judged by its parts *The Deerslayer* is no less uneven and unsatisfactory in the main than *The Prairie*. What is wanted is some guide to the labyrinth which can suggest, if not fully explain, why *The Deerslayer* is, as a whole, a more powerful and ultimately more coherent book than *The Prairie*. I do not wish to claim that I can provide such a guide; for me *The Deerslayer* remains the most elusive and fascinating, though not the best, of the Leatherstocking novels.

2

Perhaps the surest ground is to be discovered by examining two characters—Hetty Hutter and Hurry Harry—who are developments of types already encountered in the Leatherstocking tales. It is often said that the continuity of the sequence depends almost entirely on the presence of Leatherstocking, whose life story the five novels trace from his early manhood in *The Deerslayer* to his death in *The Prairie*. This is true; but another sort of continuity is provided by the repetition of certain character types throughout the series. Thus Hurry Harry belongs to a line of American backwoodsmen which begins with Billy Kirby in *The Pioneers* and continues with Paul Hover and Jasper Western. These types vary according to the needs of each story—Jasper Western, for instance, is refined to the point of disappearance as a credible backwoods personality—but basically they are the same handsome, healthy, handy young males. Cooper could get along without them, as he did in the *Mohicans*; but young America could not, since they supplied the energy, brawn, and skills necessary to a developing country in the nineteenth century. Therefore they constitute a socially significant constant factor in the world of the Leatherstocking tales, giving the sequence more continuity than it is usually supposed to have. At the same time, Cooper's modifications of the type, from novel to novel, serve to throw surrounding objects into a new relief—a relief which should help us to interpret each succeeding novel with increased precision.

I shall return to Hurry Harry shortly, but I believe it is best to begin with a close examination of the feeble-minded girl Hetty Hutter. D. H. Lawrence was one of the first to call attention to the similarity between Judith and Hetty Hutter and the two contrasted sisters of the *Mohicans*, Cora and Alice Munro:

> The two girls are the inevitable dark and light. Judith, dark, fearless, passionate, a little lurid with sin, is the scarlet-and-black blossom. Hetty, the younger, blonde, frail and innocent, is the white lily again. But alas, the lily has begun to fester. She is slightly imbecile . . .
>
> Thomas Hardy's inevitable division of women into dark and fair, sinful and innocent, sensual and pure, is Cooper's division too. It is indicative of the desire in the man. He wants sensuality and sin, and he wants purity and 'innocence'. If the innocence goes a little rotten, slightly imbecile, bad luck!. . . .
>
> Hetty, the White Lily, being imbecile, although full of vaporous religion and the dear, good God, 'who governs all things by his providence', is hopelessly infatuated with Hurry Harry. Being innocence gone imbecile, like Dostoievsky's Idiot, she longs to give herself to the handsome meat-fly. Of course he doesn't want her.[5]

Certainly Lawrence is right to call attention to the traditional division of light and dark in Cooper's portrayal of these two pairs of heroines. Such a division was of course ready-made in the minds of most nineteenth-century novelists, who (often in the absence of genuine Christian belief) automatically sorted their women characters into the eternal categories of the damned and the saved. Yet this is by no means the whole story. Predisposed as Cooper was to see things in black and white terms, he inevitably preferred to work with bold moral and social contrasts and with nakedly contrived juxtapositions of character. But when reading a novel like the *Mohicans*, one cannot help suspecting that Cooper sometimes became a prisoner of his own fictional methods. For as the novel develops, the two sisters become progressively unlike each other, until in the end Cora has assumed all the attributes of robust womanhood and Alice has been reduced to frail, fainting juvenility— to a creature quite unlike any other supposedly marriageable female character in Cooper's fiction, though she has plenty in common with the heroines of Poe or *The Blithesdale Romance*. Lawrence was right to shiver with disgust at the thought of Alice Munro becoming the mate of any man, even Major

[5] Lawrence, *Studies in Classic American Literature. Selected Literary Criticism*, pp. 327–8.

Heyward. But was he right to identify child-like Alice with child-like Hetty Hutter—Alice's innocence gone 'a little rotten, slightly imbecile' in the later heroine?

I think not. The contrast between Hetty and Judith is not a contrast between two marriageable women. At one point, Deerslayer askes Hetty whether she believes herself to 'have enough mind to become a wife and a mother'. Clearly it is his opinion that she does not. Equally important, the imbecility which prevents her from marrying also shields her from the lust of Indians and white backwoodsmen alike:

'God knows, Hurry, that such poor things be defenceless enough with all their wits about 'em; but it's a cruel fortun' when that great protector and guide fails 'em.'

'Harkee, Deerslayer,—you know what the hunters and trappers, and peltry-men in general be; and their best friends will not deny that they are headstrong and given to having their own way, without much bethinking 'em of other people's rights or feelin's,—and yet I don't think the man is to be found, in all this region, who would harm Hetty Hutter, if he could; no, not even a redskin.'

'Therein, fri'nd Hurry, you do the Delawares, at least, and all their allied tribes, only justice, for a redskin looks upon a being thus struck by God's power as especially under his care.'

To be sure, Cooper is careful to stress that Hetty is not unattractive physically: 'Nor was there anything in Hetty Hutter's appearance, as so often happens, to weaken the interest her situation excited. . . . Her person, too, was agreeable, having a strong resemblance to that of her sister, of which it was a subdued and humble copy.' But the point is, not that Hetty is sexually attractive, but that her imbecility has no repulsive physical side-effects. Lawrence was closer to the truth when he associated Hetty with Dostoievsky's Myshkin, though he would have shown more critical tact by connecting her with such inferior Cooper characters as David Gamut in the *Mohicans*, Obed Bat in *The Prairie*, or even Cap in *The Pathfinder*. All of these characters, especially Gamut, are regarded by Cooper's Indians as weak in the mind, harmless, and therefore under God's protection. Unlike Hetty, however, none of them is supposed to be truly mentally deficient; rather, each is such a specialized product of white society—a psalmodist, a pedantic natural scientist, a salt-water sailor—that he would seem odd

even in white society, while in the wilderness he is no better
than imbecile. These characters are introduced partly for the
sake of comic relief, of course. But as I have already pointed
out, they are also included in the tales in order to enhance the
effect of Leatherstocking's cool wilderness expertise and to
make the Indians seem, by way of contrast, eminently sane and
normal. Hetty, on the other hand, really is one of God's Fools.
Her presence in the novel cannot be accounted for in terms of
major cultural contrasts or (in the case of *The Prairie*) contrasting vocational patterns: she is not of any society, white or red;
she is not of this world. The issues her presence in the novel
raises are, consequently, strictly ethical and spiritual; as Cooper
says of her after her accidental death, she was 'one of those
mysterious links between the material and immaterial world,
which, while they appear to be deprived of so much that is
esteemed and necessary for this state of being, draw so near to,
and offer so beautiful an illustration of the truth, purity, and
simplicity of another'.

Cooper was a convinced Christian, and he took Hetty's truth,
purity, and simplicity as seriously as possible. But what, precisely, is her function in the novel? Is she seriously offered as a
model of behaviour and outlook by which other (mentally
competent) characters in the novel are to be judged? R. W. B.
Lewis, for one, takes her to be a false rather than impractical
model:

And beneath the comedy of poor Hetty's visit to the Iroquois
camp and her attempt to preach the captors into releasing their
prisoners is a profoundly suggestive distinction between the quality
of Hetty's innocence and that of Hawkeye's; Hetty has an innocence
which is, in fact, a self-delusive helplessness, a half-witted conviction
of universal goodness, which exposes her to every physical and moral
danger and finally kills her. It is partly by contemplation of that
hapless girl, by conversations with Hetty and about her, that
Hawkeye arrives at a more durable kind of innocence and at the
insight that it must be bounded by an observation of ethical differences. Cooper skilfully exposes the solid core of Hawkeye's
Adamism by setting it alongside the flimsy hopefulness of Hetty
Hutter.[6]

---

[6] Lewis, *The American Adam*, p. 105. D. E. S. Maxwell, *American Fiction* (London,
1963), p. 136, objects to part of Lewis's reading on grounds similar to mine but

In the first place, nothing in the text of *The Deerslayer* suggests that Hetty's death was other than an accident which might have happened to any of the other characters, whether saint or sinner, full- or half-wit. As for her having a 'half-witted conviction of universal goodness', she is, though ingenuously trustful, too much of a literal-minded Christian to hold any such heretical belief. She has, indeed, a naive conviction that the truth of the Gospels is so manifest and persuasive that it need only be expounded to the Indians to be accepted by them. She is, as well, a dupe of fair appearances, lacking the wit to perceive that the handsome exterior of Hurry Harry is no reflection of interior worth. On the other hand, as Cooper insists throughout the book, Hetty is blessed with an innocent reliance on the moral precepts she was taught as a child and with a sure intuitive understanding of what is good, what is evil, in human conduct. As to her being exposed to 'every physical and moral danger', Cooper explicitly states that 'Providence . . . shielded her from harm by a halo of moral light, as it is said "to temper the wind to the shorn lamb".' The point, of course, is that Providence does not temper the wind to the other lambs: Hetty's chief function in *The Deerslayer* is to expose, by way of contrast, the extreme physical and moral vulnerability of the other characters, who, as they have greater natural gifts and powers to protect themselves, are subjected to greater trials and dangers. Meek, humble Hetty is safe from all molestations; but poor Judith, so beautiful and intelligent, so proud, is considered fair game by Providence—and by every man she has ever known except Deerslayer. In a like manner, every other character except Hetty is tempted to his physical or moral destruction by excessive pride in his best natural gift: Hutter, in his cunning; Hurry Harry, in his great physical strength; and Deerslayer, in his marksmanship. This Christian scheme of things may seem to bear heavily on the competent and comely, but it is the moral scheme of *The Deerslayer*.

Hetty Hutter is not much admired by twentieth-century critics; neither she nor her function in the novel seems to be much understood. Hurry Harry, however, has fared rather

accepts Lewis's contention that Hetty's innocence is a 'half-witted conviction of universal goodness'.

better. Marius Bewley, in particular, has given a favourable and perceptive account of this character:

In Hurry and his moral vision of life we have an early representative of a type that was to become a dominant element in American civilization as it moved along towards the Gilded Age—a type that could supplant moral motives by motives of commercial expediency, and pretend, even to itself, that the substitution had never been made. Cooper's perceptions in creating Hurry Harry are profound and accurate. Although he does not perceptibly wince at the idea of scalping Indian children for the bounty, he is a pattern of the forthright, impulsive, attractive young America. Much of Cooper's genius is shown in the way he effectively suggests the squalid reality behind the romantic figure of the woods. And it is well to bear in mind that this brand of American romanticism was partly cultivated in Cooper's day for the sake of putting some colour of attractive decorum on the crimes of the American wilderness, without which the expansion of the frontier would have notably lagged, or so it seemed.

And Mr Bewley goes on to point out that, unlike those of Deerslayer, Hurry's 'true roots are in the settlements, and the wilderness exists for him essentially as a business that he may make periodic visits to "civilization" with his pockets jingling'.[7] It is helpful to have Hurry placed in this way, both in relation to Deerslayer inside the novel and to American society outside it. In particular, Mr Bewley is right to associate Hurry's values with those of the Gilded Age; for as I have already suggested, Cooper's conception of the character was almost certainly influenced by the Whig election campaign of 1840, which began by starring 'Harry of the West' (Henry Clay) and ended by electing a 'Log Cabin President'—William Henry Harrison. The Whiggery of 1840, an alliance of raw Western agrarianism and Eastern industrialism, clearly foreshadowed the Republicanism of the Gilded Age.[8] Hurry is an 1840 Whig—a man with a frank Western manner but with the conscience of a cut-throat city man. Neither is it too far-fetched to connect Hurry's spurious personal glamour with the spurious political glamour of that pseudo-Jackson figure, General Harrison. And the election of Harrison marks, not only the cynical exploitation of

[7] Bewley, *The Eccentric Design*, pp. 95–6.
[8] Cf. G. G. Van Deusen, *The Life of Henry Clay* (Boston, 1937), pp. 424–5.

the Jacksonian popular appeal, but also the total vulgarization of the Jeffersonian agrarian ideal. Much of the disillusionment evident in *The Deerslayer* must surely be traced to the electoral effectiveness of Log Cabins and Hard Cider.

Our problem with Hurry, then, is not so much to define his function in the novel, or to establish his relevance to American social and political life as to determine whether he functions effectively. Donald Davie maintains that he does not:

And yet for this opposition to function as a real not a schematic underpinning to this action, Cooper would have to have created Harry as richly and comprehensively, in as much depth, as Leatherstocking, who is opposed to him. I cannot find in Cooper's portrayal of Harry that 'concrete richness', and 'superbly solid physical embodiment' which Mr Bewley finds. And surely he gives his own game away when he defines the genre of *The Deerslayer* (usefully and rightly) as 'fictional hagiography'. For it is characteristic of hagiography that it cannot give the devil his due; and Cooper gives Harry less than his due, not in the sense that there is anything more to be said for his side of the case, but in the sense that he is, most of the time, a man of straw, two-dimensional, all too rigidly in character whenever he opens his mouth.[9]

This is suggestive, and even more suggestive is a remark made later by Mr Davie to the effect that Billy Kirby in *The Pioneers* does possess the qualities which are lacking in Hurry Harry. But who is right about Hurry Harry, Mr Bewley or Mr Davie? I agree with Mr Bewley that Hurry is 'a thoroughly realistic character', though I should wish to drop some of the superlatives Mr Bewley lavishes on him. I also agree with Mr Davie that 'Cooper gives Harry less than his due'. The trouble with Hurry Harry is not that he lacks 'concrete richness' or that he isn't sufficiently realistic but that in spite of his representative political significance, he isn't sufficiently mythic. Mr Bewley gives us the clue when he says that 'Deerslayer exists on a different level of the imagination than Hurry. He is essentially a poetic evocation, and his conception inevitably incorporates an element of myth in so far as myth may be defined as the incarnation of racial aspiration and memory.'[10] Exactly. If we consider such a figure as Billy Kirby, however, or the

[9] Davie, *The Heyday of Sir Walter Scott*, pp. 126–7.
[10] Bewley, *The Eccentric Design*, p. 96.

patriarchal Ishmael Bush in *The Prairie*, we have to do with a character who, without sacrificing any concreteness, confronts Leatherstocking on his own mythic plane. As Kirby is clearly a character of the same general type as Hurry Harry, we shall be repaid if we look at him more closely.

If Leatherstocking is the epic hero of the American wilderness, Billy Kirby is the epic hero of the American frontier. He assumes these epic proportions when he is first introduced in *The Pioneers*:

> For days, weeks, nay months, Billy Kirby would toil, with an ardour that evinced his native spirit, and with an effect that seemed magical, until, his chopping being ended, his stentorian lungs could be heard emitting sounds, as he called to his patient oxen, which rung through the hills like the cries of an alarm. He had been often heard, on a mild summer's evening, a long mile across the vale of Templeton; when the echoes from the mountains would take up his cries, until they died away in feeble sounds from the distant rocks that overhung the lake. His piles, or, to use the language of the country, his logging ended, with despatch that could only accompany his dexterity and Herculean strength, the jobber would collect together his implements of labour, like the heaps of timber, and march away, under the blaze of the prostrate forest, like the conqueror of some city, who having first prevailed over his adversary, applies the torch as the finishing blow to his conquest.

And he never ceases to be a sort of frontier demigod, even when we learn that he is noisy, boisterous, reckless, and none too bright. As one to whom 'chopping comes quite natural', Billy is the natural opponent of Leatherstocking. Yet it is no accident that they like and, in a way, respect each other, and that when Billy is tricked into serving the warrant on Leatherstocking, he protests:

> 'He is a harmless creater, and I must say that I think he has as good right to kill deer as any man on the patent. It's his main support, and this is a free country, where a man is privileged to follow any calling he likes.'
>
> 'According to that doctrine,' said Jotham, 'anybody may shoot a deer.'
>
> 'This is the man's calling, I tell you,' returned Kirby, 'and the law was never made for such as him.'

But the sympathy that exists between Leatherstocking and

Billy does not prevent the latter from being the leading spirit in the general waste and destruction of the former's beloved wilderness. The author of *The Pioneers* was able to create such a complex relationship because the points at issue in the novel, though ethical in nature, were not so narrowly ethical that they could be reduced to a simple choice between defying or obeying the commandments of the New Testament. Almost equally important, the large gallery of characters in *The Pioneers* made it unnecessary for one or two of them to provide all the moral contrast and thus become obviously contrived foils for Leatherstocking.

When Hurry Harry is introduced to us in the opening pages of *The Deerslayer*—

It would not have been easy to find a more noble specimen of vigorous manhood than was offered in the person of him who called himself Hurry Harry. His real name was Henry March; but the frontiermen, having caught the practice of giving *sobriquets* from the Indians, the appellation of Hurry was far oftener applied to him than his proper designation, and not unfrequently he was termed Hurry Skurry, a nickname he had obtained from a dashing, reckless, off-hand manner, and a physical restlessness that kept him so constantly on the move, as to cause him to be known along the whole line of scattered habitations that lay between the province and the Canadas. The stature of Hurry Harry exceeded six feet four, and being unusually well proportioned, his strength fully realized the idea created by his gigantic frame. The face did no discredit to the rest of the man, for it was both good-humoured and handsome. His air was free, and though his manner necessarily partook of the rudeness of a border life, the grandeur that pervaded so noble a physique prevented it from becoming altogether vulgar.

—he promises to become a character no less powerful than Ishmael Bush. If, on closer inspection, he turns out to be a racist and a bit of a bully, these are qualities that might comport perfectly well with a hero of the rough-and-tumble school. But as Mr Bewley says, Hurry is denied any romantic trappings; indeed, he isn't even permitted to achieve any of the triumphs for which he seems to have been created. There is one point in particular in the novel where we can see very clearly how the demands of realism (*pace* Mark Twain) deprive Hurry of any mythic stature. In Chapter XX, after undergoing ignominious capture and release at the hands of the Indians, Hurry encounters them, outnumbered seven to one, in hand-to-hand combat. After a magnificent struggle, Hurry is again overcome:

Thus were the tables turned, in a single moment; he who had been so near achieving a victory that would have renowned for ages, by means of tradition, throughout all that region, lying helpless, bound, and a captive. So fearful had been the efforts of the paleface, and so prodigious the strength he exhibited, that even as he lay, tethered like a sheep before them, they regarded him with respect, and not without dread.

This may seem sufficiently heroic to establish the defeated Harry as a border champion. Yet why does Cooper deprive him of his legendary victory? Shortly after this defeat, Harry experiences a harrowing escape which leaves him a chastened, but not an ennobled, man. Seeing that the situation is more than he bargained for and that he stands to gain nothing by remaining, he virtually abandons the other characters to their fate. Now no doubt this is sound, if not subtle, realistic psychology; and it can scarcely be argued that, according to the law of probability, Harry should have licked the seven Indians. But realism and probability are applied in this novel only when they suit Cooper's convenience; apparently it is not convenient to suspend them in the case of Hurry Harry, who must on no account be allowed to rival Deerslayer—even as a man of action.

And this is bad fictional strategy. Leatherstocking's moral superiority to Billy Kirby or Ishmael Bush is not impaired by lending them the grandeur appropriate to their peculiar roles. On the contrary, Leatherstocking seems all the grander for being measured against figures cast from a less perfect but almost equally epic mould. Can one imagine Ishmael being dismissed from the scene, as Harry is dismissed by Judith and Deerslayer, with contempt? For Harry turns out to be such a completely hollow man that only poor Hetty could fail to find his presence an embarrassment. It seems likely that it was Cooper's intention from the first, as Mr Bewley implies, thoroughly to de-romanticize the American backwoodsman in the person of Hurry Harry. Yet the process is taken to such extremes that one wonders whether Cooper might not have been led astray, as I believe he was in the *Mohicans*, by his own fictional methods. Once Tom Hutter is despatched, Harry is the only available male foil for the virtuous Deerslayer, and it is at this point that Harry, under the cover of realism, begins to deteriorate most rapidly.

One thing is certain: the centre of fictional interest in *The Deerslayer* does not lie in the conflict between Hurry Harry and Deerslayer. This is not, however, to suggest that Hurry's presence in the novel is unnecessary. Stated in the baldest possible manner, the subject of the novel is the way people bear up under the responsibilities imposed on them *as Christians*. This definition may seem at once too abstract and too narrow, as such definitions invariably are. But clearly, it is with the fortunes of the white characters—i.e. the Christians, nominal or otherwise —that we are mainly concerned in *The Deerslayer*. The Indians are important (they are more convincingly here than in any other Leatherstocking novel); but they are important primarily because they create trials for the Christian characters and because they are themselves exempt from Christian responsibilities, though not from the responsibilities of their own culture. Cooper's problem was to localize his universal theme so that it didn't remain inertly abstract. In Hurry Harry he created a thoroughly local and realistic character who, motivated by *cupiditas*, takes advantage of typically American racist theories to exempt himself from his Christian duties to other men. In this way he does serve to localize Cooper's theme: but this isn't quite good enough. We cannot feel that Harry fairly represents the American backwoodsman. For Cooper's theme to have been firmly embedded in a border context, Harry would have had to exhibit some of the notable virtues as well as vices of his kind. As he stands, in spite of his concrete local identity, Harry slips all too neatly into his allotted place in the scale of moral being which Cooper has contrived for his white characters in *The Deerslayer*. And as the novel progresses, it is increasingly in terms of his place in this abstract scale, rather than of his place in frontier America, that we think of him.

3

The living centre of *The Deerslayer* is the relationship between Deerslayer and Judith Hutter. This life seems to have been kindled almost contrary to Cooper's intentions, since sinful Judith develops into a much more sympathetic character (to Cooper as well as the reader) than he probably planned her to become. In the closing pages of the novel, there are many signs that Cooper's heart and mind were pulling him in different directions when the time came for him to consign Judith to oblivion. That he succeeded in so consigning her usually enrages readers of *The Deerslayer*—a sure sign that Judith has a great deal more vital humanity than most other female characters in Cooper's fiction.[11] And the very notion of a 'fallen woman'—one false step and you are forever expelled from Eden, from Good Society, and maybe from Heaven too—seems monstrous, as well as un-Christian, to us. Did Cooper subscribe to such a doctrine? I suppose that, like most Victorian upholders of female purity, Cooper rarely examined or questioned the doctrine—he simply took its truth for granted. But in *The Deerslayer*, so it seems to me, Cooper's worst prejudices came into collision not only with his better feelings but also with his deeply held Christian belief in the possibility and efficacy of repentance; so that, although the conclusion seems cruel, the treatment of Judith is, as a whole, far from uncompassionate or unintelligent.

More than in any other Leatherstocking tale, including *The Prairie*, characters in *The Deerslayer* are conscious of standing on the brink of eternity: death may, and indeed is likely to, come suddenly, cut short the period of one's earthly probation. This happens to Hetty and Thomas Hutter, both of whom experience brief glimpses of Heaven and Hell before they depart from this world. The other white characters are left at the end of the novel still undergoing their probation. Of his role in this Christian drama of salvation, Hurry Harry seems to have no awareness whatever. This is one of the reasons why, in a novel so insistently Christian in outlook, Harry soon ceases to be an interesting character. But Deerslayer and Judith, in their different ways, are acutely aware of their roles. For Deerslayer the problem is simple enough: 'I strive to do right, here, as the

---

[11] Cf. Donald Davie, *The Heyday of Sir Walter Scott*, p. 127: 'For Cooper's portrayal of Judith is not to be judged in terms of literary skill; what is wrong with it is its inhumanity, a cramped littleness, prurience and meanness, the complete lack of magnanimity.'

surest means of keeping all right, hereafter.' He has always done right and, after witnessing his conduct in this novel, we know that he always will. For Judith, however, the past is shameful and the future terrifyingly uncertain. The words and deeds of Deerslayer, the special immunity to moral and physical danger of Hetty, the threat of sudden death, the revelation of her family's sordid past—all these conspire to jolt Judith out of her obsession with trivialities into a state of fearful apprehension for the future of her own soul.

Summarized in this fashion, the development of Judith's character may sound like nothing more than a standard piece of nineteenth-century novelistic piety. But this is not the case. No matter how shaken she may be, she never ceases to be the spirited, intelligent, and beautiful girl she was at the beginning of the novel. She exhibits such resourcefulness and presence of mind in the face of danger that even Deerslayer, who is strongly prejudiced against her, cannot withhold his admiration. Deerslayer's reluctant admiration is, in fact, the secret of Cooper's success in convincing us that Judith really is an extraordinarily winsome woman. Like the elders of Troy (Deerslayer is equally sexless and censorious), he can but praise her, he can but disapprove of her. A compulsive truth-teller, he can hide neither his admiration nor his disapproval.

What is most moving, and central to the novel, is the way Judith comes to feel that marriage with Deerslayer offers her perhaps her only hope for spiritual as well as social salvation:

'Talk of your sins, Hetty! If ever there was a creature on earth without sins, it is you! I wish I could say or think the same of myself; but we shall see. No one knows what changes affection for a good husband can make in a woman's heart.'

This perception that in Judith's case (though not in Deerslayer's or Hetty's) the future of a soul is at stake in the wooing gives the courtship in *The Deerslayer* an urgency and seriousness which is altogether absent from the romantic episodes in the rest of Cooper's novels. If this perception were the author's only, it might seem no more than a nineteenth-century advertisement for the sanctifying properties of matrimony. But it is Judith's perception too, based on a newly awakened realization of her own failings and a grim awareness that, in the absence of the awakening and sustaining presence of Deerslayer, she may well return to her previous condition. It scarcely matters whether we share Judith's and Cooper's Christian vision of life: it suffices that Judith does believe and that she is an attractive human character, for her predicament to be as poignant as it is morally significant. Cooper himself clearly was moved, and his treatment of her proposal to Deerslayer (an act of which Cooper would normally disapprove as being un-womanly) is handled with respect and compassion:

This indomitable diffidence, which still prevented the young man from suspecting the truth, would have completely discouraged the girl, had not her whole soul, as well as her whole heart, been set upon making a desperate effort to rescue herself from a future that she dreaded with a horror as vivid as the distinctness with which she fancied she foresaw it. This motive, however, raised her above all common considerations, and she persevered even to her own surprise, if not to her great confusion.

Or earlier in the novel:

Although far from unfeminine or forward in her feelings or her habits, the girl was goaded by a sense of wrongs not altogether merited, incited by the helplessness of a future that seemed to contain no resting place, and still more influenced by feelings that were as novel to her as they proved to be active and engrossing.

Poor Judith! To save herself she is willing to burn all her fancy clothes and live what would be virtually a conventual exist-ence with Deerslayer. But when we learn that, in the end, she has once again given herself to the callow beauty-fancier Cap-tain Warley, we know that she was right to dread the future—right, too, to fear for the state of her soul.

By thus linking together, in Judith's mind, Judith's fate as a social and spiritual being, Cooper not only invests the courtship in *The Deerslayer* with a moral importance proportional to the space and attention devoted to it (something almost unheard of, so far as Cooper's fiction is concerned), but he also translates his Christian theme of probation into concrete personal terms, the force of which every reader must feel. In a similar way, Deerslayer's trials on the lake—trials which constitute his initiation into full manhood—are something more than a mere analogue of the trials by which the Christian soul is tested for

admission into Heaven: they are in most instances trials of
Deerslayer, not merely as a warrior, but as a Christian. What
happens on Lake Glimmerglass is a series of concrete moral
tests so exacting and so impeccably passed that the successful
outcome of Deerslayer's life-long probation as a Christian soul
is scarcely left in doubt. The implied contrast between Judith
and Deerslayer, in this respect, is particularly sharp and painful.

4

More than in any other novel, Cooper is concerned in *The
Deerslayer* with the moral and social significance of the names
attached to people and things. So true is this that one might say,
without absurdity, that the main action of the novel concerns
Deerslayer's winning a name and Judith's losing one. Quite
early in *The Deerslayer* Cooper indicates how much significance
may lie hidden in a name:

'Have the Governor's or the King's people given this lake a
name?' he suddenly asked, as if struck with a new idea. 'If they've
not begun to blaze their trees, and set up their compasses, and line
off their maps, it's likely they've not bethought them to disturb
natur' with a name.'

To give a thing a name is of course to assert one's mastery over
it. Not to have a fixed name for a thing is, in a very practical
sense, not to have power over it, since this may mean that one
doesn't know of its existence, or, if one does know, it means that
one cannot communicate one's knowledge or ask precise
questions:

'I'm glad it has no name,' resumed Deerslayer, 'or, at least, no
pale-face name; for their christenings always foretell waste and
destruction. No doubt, howsoever, the red-skins have their modes of
knowing it, and the hunters and trappers, too; they are likely to call
the place by something reasonable and resembling.'

And so the lake is named 'Glimmerglass', the mirror of Heaven,
just as Natty Bumppo is named successively (so he tells Hetty)
'Straight-tongue', 'The Pigeon', 'Lap-ear', 'Deerslayer'. 'Reasonable and resembling' is the criterion for such names: they are
intended to fix the moral identity of the individual by means of
generic attributes which tell one in an instant who or what one

has to deal with. Such names also have the power to modify or direct behaviour, since they give one something to live up to or to live down. At the same time, however, the individual has the power to modify the associations connected with a name. Although feeble-minded Hetty cannot ignore the 'not so pretty' associations that go with 'Lap-ear',[12] Deerslayer himself has learned to like the name Chingachgook, in spite of its unpleasant associations:

'Now, I'm nat'rally avarse to sarpents, and I hate even the word, which, the missionaries tell me, comes from human natur', on account of a sartain sarpent at the creation of the 'arth, that outwitted the first woman; yet, ever since Chingachgook has 'arned the title he bears, why the sound is as pleasant to my ears as the whistle of the whippoorwill of a calm evening—it is. The feelin's make all the difference in the world, Judith, in the natur' of sounds; ay, even in that of looks, too.'

In his speech Deerslayer suggests what Judith knows all too well: that as names are appearances—external signs of interior qualities—they can be deceptive. Uncomely and provincial though Deerslayer is, Judith discovers she would be glad to be named Judith Bumppo.

In the famous seventh chapter of the novel, Natty earns the name 'Hawkeye'. Considering the impressiveness of his exploits later in the action, Hawkeye hardly seems an adequate name for the hero. However, it is a particularly apt title in the context of this novel, since it signifies the hero's powers of penetrating through appearances of all kinds (or at least most kinds: for he becomes almost unbelievably obtuse whenever Judith tries to court him). These powers, whether applied to moral or military problems, are his best assurance that he will pass safely through all the trials of the future years.

Judith's fate is to discover that her real name is not Hutter—Hutter is itself a pseudonym—and that she cannot trace her true family name. Her Christian name has a neat ironic appropriateness, since the biblical Judith was famed for her

---

[12] It is of course in connexion with Hetty herself that Cooper is most concerned with the problems of association. Reviewers of Wordsworth's poetry (and Coleridge in the *Biographia*) had censured him for trying to overcome disgusting associations in 'The Idiot Boy'; Cooper, with less courage than Wordsworth, was careful to avoid such associations in his portrait of Hetty.

daring and resourcefulness—and for her chastity. It has a
further appropriateness in that Judith's mother, who bore her
out of wedlock, bequeathed her own Christian name but no
family name to go with it: Judith was the nearest thing to a
family name she could give. At first Judith is delighted to find
that her surname is not Hutter: the name is not only that
adopted by an ex-pirate, but it is also a name which symbolizes
Judith's membership in a social class which she considers beneath her. But it soon becomes apparent that not to have a
family name means a total lack of social identity, an apartness
from civilized society that is far more fearful than her sister
Hetty's apartness from the human race generally; for Judith's
outcast lot makes her especially vulnerable to all the dangers
against which Hetty, because of *her* outcast lot, had been especially protected. Considering the importance which Cooper
attaches to names throughout this novel (my discussion is by
no means exhaustive), his final words on the subject of Judith
clearly carry a greater weight of meaning than is likely to be
apparent on a casual reading:

The same fate attended Judith. When Hawkeye reached the
garrison on the Mohawk, he inquired anxiously after that lovely, but
misguided creature. None knew her—even her person was no
longer remembered. Other officers had again and again succeeded
the Warleys and Craigs and Grahams; though an old sergeant of the
garrison, who had lately come from England, was enabled to tell
our hero that Sir Robert Warley lived on his paternal estates, and
that there was a lady of rare beauty in the lodge, who had great
influence over him, though she did not bear his name.

5

After observing that the plot of *The Deerslayer* lacks unity of
action and taking note of Marius Bewley's definition of the
genre of this novel as 'fictional hagiography', Donald Davie
gives this account of the form of its action:

The Deerslayer by contrast has the only plot appropriate to a saint's
life; a succession of incidents each providing an opportunity for the
saint, by resisting temptations and surmounting obstacles, to prove
his saintliness. At this point Cooper is quite out of touch with the
novel as conceived of and written by Scott. Marius Bewley once

thought Cooper's achievement in *The Deerslayer* was to have rid the plot of the inconsequent picaresque elements still to be found in Scott; so far is this from the case that it would be truer to say that Cooper worked his way (or was pushed by the American reality) out of the world of Scott to a point where a picaresque plot, in the guise of a series of exacting tests, was once again possible and necessary.[13]

It is certainly true that some of the incidents of the novel, such as Hetty's being befriended and escorted by the bears, might well have been taken directly from a saint's legend; and it may be that we shall be unable to better Mr Bewley's classification of this novel as 'fictional hagiography'. Yet it is an odd picaresque novel or saint's legend which adheres strictly, as *The Deerslayer* so strikingly does, to the unities of time and place.

Why does Cooper pay so much attention to these lesser unities and so little to the crucial unity of action? It does not seem to be the case (as it so often was with hapless neoclassical playwrights) that observance of the unities of time and place forced him to neglect unity of action. On the contrary, there is ample evidence to show that he quite deliberately crowded as many incidents as possible into the space of a few days. Whether this procedure was a wise one is, of course, another matter; but we must try to understand why he did it before we damn him or take refuge in a theory that he was reviving picaresque or hagiographic forms.

These are the opening words of the novel:

On the human imagination events produce the effects of time. Thus, he who has travelled far and seen much is apt to fancy that he has lived long; and the history that most abounds in important incidents soonest assumes the aspect of antiquity. In no other way can we account for the venerable air that is already gathering around American annals. When the mind reverts to the earliest days of colonial history, the period seems remote and obscure, the thousand changes that thicken along the links of recollections, throwing back the origin of the nation to a day so distant as seemingly to reach the mists of time; and yet four lives of ordinary duration would suffice to transmit, from mouth to mouth, in the form of tradition, all that civilized man has achieved within the limits of the republic.

[13] Davie, *The Heyday of Sir Walter Scott*, pp. 125–8.

Not once but several times in the course of the novel does Judith express the view that, although she has known Deerslayer but a few days, he seems to her an old and proven friend. The principal expression of this view that events produce the effects of time occurs quite late in the novel, when Judith proposes to Deerslayer:

'You are not an acquaintance of a week, but it appears to me as if I had known you for years. So much, and so much that is important, has taken place within that short time, that the sorrows, and dangers, and escapes of a whole life have been crowded into a few days; and they who have suffered and acted together in such scenes, ought not to feel like strangers.'

This is not the pretext of an impulsive girl, but a view of human experience which the author himself endorses. Normally, of course, Cooper would deplore what might seem a hasty as well as unwomanly action; but this is a special case; what Judith says is true. So far as Deerslayer is concerned, the action of this novel, by crowding the trials of an average lifetime into a few days, does initiate him into manhood in the fullest possible sense: he has already lived through whatever lies before him as a Christian warrior. It is as a novel of initiation, if at all, that the crowded, episodic form of *The Deerslayer* can be explained and justified.

In this novel Cooper is aware of the time in several of its aspects. As we should expect of a work whose main theme is Christian probation, all the action takes place against the backdrop of eternity:

'I don't know what you mean by future, Judith,' she at length suddenly observed. 'Mother used to call heaven the future, but you seem to think it means next week, or tomorrow!'
'It means both, dear sister; everything that is yet to come, whether in this world or another. It is a solemn word, Hetty, and most so, I fear, to them that think the least about it.'

Time, however we manipulate it in imagination, manipulates us in our physical being:

'Yes, good looks may be sarcumvented, and fairly outwitted, too. In order to do this, you've only to remember that they melt like the snows; and, when once gone, they never come back ag'in. The seasons come and go, Judith; and if we have winter, with storms and frosts, and spring, with chills and leafless trees, we have summer, with its sun and glorious skies, and fall, with its fruits, and a garment thrown over the forest that no beauty of the town could rummage out of all the shops in America. 'Arth is an eternal round, the goodness of God bringing back the pleasant when we've had enough of the onpleasant. But its not so with good looks. *They* are lent for a short time in youth, to be used and not abused. . . .'

The Deerslayer is a novel in which all things stand trembling on the edge of some other condition. This is obviously true of Deerslayer and Chingachgook, who are on their first warpath; but it is no less true of all the other characters, especially of the marriageable young men and women. Lake Glimmerglass itself, as yet unnamed by the white men, stands on the threshold of history. All this must change, but for a brief period we see the lake, the brave young men and the beautiful young girls with their freshness still upon them.

Though much happens during a few days in this novel, Cooper resorts but rarely to summary; the action is rather presented, often in such detail that the happenings, especially the interviews, take up about as much time in the telling as they would have in fact. This makes *The Deerslayer* a long and sometimes tedious work, but it also makes its conclusion unusually effective. After the long and poignant last interview between Judith and Deerslayer, in which the minutest gestures and inflexions are carefully observed, Cooper switches fairly abruptly into the summary mode of the historian:

The war that then had its rise was stirring and bloody. The Delaware chief rose among his people, until his name was never mentioned without eulogiums; while another Uncas, the last of his race, was added to the long line of warriors who bore that distinguished appellation. As for the Deerslayer, under the *sobriquet* of Hawkeye, he made his fame spread far and near. . . .

Fifteen years had passed away, ere it was in the power of the Deerslayer to revisit the Glimmerglass. A peace had intervened, and it was on the eve of another, and still more important war, when he and his constant friend, Chingachgook, were hastening to the forts to join their allies. A stripling accompanied them, for Hist already slumbered beneath the pines of the Delawares, and the three survivors had now become inseparable. They reached the lake just as the sun was setting. Here all was unchanged; the river still rushed through its bower of trees; the little rock was wasting away by the slow action of the waves in the course of centuries; the mountains stood in their native dress, dark, rich, and mysterious; while the sheet glistened in its solitude, a beautiful gem of the forest.

This sudden change of pace in the narrative is precisely adapted to the change in tone and point of view. Nothing in the whole of Cooper's fiction is so intensely elegiac as the last few pages of *The Deerslayer*:

The ark was discovered stranded on the eastern shore, where it had long before been driven, with the prevalent northwest winds. It lay on the sandy extremity of a long, low point, that is situated about two miles from the outlet, and which is itself fast disappearing before the action of the elements. The scow was filled with water, the cabin unroofed, and the logs were decaying. Some of its coarser furniture still remained, and the heart of Deerslayer beat quick as he found a ribbon of Judith's fluttering from a log. It recalled all her beauty, and we may add, all her failings. Although the girl had never touched his heart, the Hawkeye, for so we ought now to call him, still retained a kind and sincere interest in her welfare. He tore away the ribbon and knotted it to the stock of Killdeer, which had been the gift of the girl herself.

In spite of some of Cooper's most maiden-auntish qualifications ('and we may add, all her failings' or, better yet, 'still retained a kind and sincere interest in her welfare'), Deerslayer's reactions and gestures are exactly as they should be. Well might the ageing Hawkeye knot Judith's ribbon—still, no doubt, unfaded —to the stock of the marvellous rifle he had embraced instead of her body. It is a breathtaking poetic stroke, and one can only wonder whether Cooper even half-guessed what he was doing.

XII

THE LATE SEA NOVELS

I

THOMAS PHILBRICK'S STUDY of Cooper's late sea novels is so thorough and so illuminating that my first act in this chapter must be to advise my reader to do as I have done: use Mr Philbrick as his chief guide to these novels and also to the vast body of early nineteenth-century nautical fiction which forms their background.[1] Yet authoritative as Mr Philbrick's work is and must remain, it is not altogether free from the biases which we should expect to find in a study of Cooper's sea fiction considered mainly, not in relation to the rest of his novels, but in relation to the same kind of fiction written by his contemporaries. The most obvious danger inherent in such an approach is that the critic is likely to overrate Cooper's sea novels, as seems to be the case when Mr Philbrick pronounces *The Sea Lions* 'without doubt, his most complex and yet fully integrated fiction'.[2] Another danger is that the critic bent on discussing the sea novels as a distinct kind and therefore peculiarly open to the influence of other writers of sea stories, will tend to underestimate the homogeneity of Cooper's fiction.[3] It might well be argued, for instance, that *The Pathfinder* is positively more nautical and aquatic than *The Two Admirals*: Cooper had a liking for water, in fact and fiction, which embraced rivers and lakes as well as oceans, so that the characteristic action of a 'land story' like *The Deerslayer* is not, after all, so very different from that of a 'sea story' like *Jack Tier*. More important, the

[1] Philbrick, *James Fenimore Cooper and the Development of American Sea Fiction.*
[2] *ibid.*, p. 209.
[3] This is a question of bias and stress rather than of neglect. Mr Philbrick does not, of course, ignore the place of Cooper's sea fiction in his total *œuvre*.

themes and characters of Cooper's novels tend to repeat themselves irrespective of setting. It is a curious and important fact
that *The Deerslayer*, not the sea romances of the same period,
most fully anticipates the characteristic attitude and themes of
his last sea novels. To be sure, the character in *The Deerslayer*
who especially prefigures the Daggetts and Captain Spikes of
the last sea novels is Tom Hutter, the ex-pirate. But if you read
the sea romances contemporaneous with *The Deerslayer*, you
discover that their villains are all, properly speaking, landsmen.

Cooper's development as a novelist (and not merely as a sea
novelist) during the last decade of his career falls into two
sharply differentiated phases. The completion of the *History of
the Navy* (1839) seems to have had a great liberating effect on
his creative powers. During the next three years, in spite of his
involvement in numerous lawsuits and public controversies, he
produced five historical romances: all of them, except *The
Deerslayer*, of a largely nautical character; all of them, except
Mercedes of Castile (1841), of substantial though uneven literary
merit. The final phase of his literary career opened in 1843
with three very unromantic works, the disenchanted novels
Wyandotté and *The French Governess* and the nautical memoir
Ned Myers (of which Cooper was scribe and editor rather than
author). During this final period his deepening social and religious disillusionment with man, particularly mid-nineteenth-
century American man, affected everything he wrote. In the
nautical anti-romance *Jack Tier* (1846-8) no less than in the
anti-utopia *The Crater* (1847) he set out to expose the ugliness
and depravity of men, seamen and landsmen alike. The New
Englanders of this period, whether landsmen like the Newcomes
of the Littlepage trilogy (1845-6) or seamen like the Daggetts
of *The Sea Lions* (1849), are nearly all of them hypocritical,
avaricious rogues. And the major representative work of this
period, *Afloat and Ashore* (1844)—representative because, as its
title implies, it effectively combines many of the concerns of
Ned Myers and *The Sea Lions* with those of the land-bound
Littlepage trilogy—exposes rascality afloat and rascality ashore
with scrupulous impartiality.[4]

---

[4] *Afloat and Ashore* was published as a double novel, the first part which was
issued under the title *Afloat and Ashore*, the second under the title *Miles Wallingford*.
As the two parts cannot stand by themselves as separate novels and were never

Still, though it is right to stress the interrelatedness of Cooper's fiction and insist that his development as a sea novelist is not clearly distinct from his development as a novelist generally, it must be owned that there is a strong case for considering the sea novels separately. For the middle-aged Cooper, whose writing of the *History of the Navy* seems to have re-aroused at the same time that it partially satisfied many of his non-literary aspirations, the fluid element became the area of unexplored personal possibility—where anything might have happened. The sea, for him, was the road not taken. By contrast, the land now became, not merely tame and familiar (which it always had been in his sea fiction), but distressingly unstable—unstable, however, in ways which had been personally experienced and which could be charted in the known circumstantial facts of American social history. This is not to suggest that Cooper now presented the land in a prosaic light, the sea in a romantic one. On the contrary, as I have insisted, his writing is pretty much of a piece within any given period. Still it remains true that a certain view of the sea cuts across the last two phases of his literary career. From the time of *Mercedes of Castile* (1841) Cooper and his leading characters tend to regard the sea as *par excellence* the area of possibility: the area whose limits are unknown, where moral and physical dangers are most acute, and where the potential rewards and punishments are most prodigious. Given this view of the sea, no amount of muck-raking or social and religious pessimism in the last novels could rob the sea and seamanship of their glamour—though they could and did make that glamour sinister in ways that went beyond the Byronic glitter of the *Red Rover*. The land novels of the same period lack this sinister quality; their glamour, when they have it, is the glamour of nostalgia.

Mercedes of Castile is essentially a narrative of Columbus's first voyage to the New World on to which Cooper has soldered an absurd and puerile love story. Nobody, I believe, has ever maintained that *Mercedes* is anything but a very bad book. Nevertheless, it has the distinction of being (with the partial exception of *The Monikins*) the first of Cooper's novels in which the sea, rather than the land, is the field for exploratory or pioneering

intended to, I shall follow the usual practice of referring to them as a single work entitled *Afloat and Ashore*.

ventures. Indeed, it comes as rather a shock to find that, important as the Renascence voyages of discovery had been to the European literary imagination, the greatest sea novelist before Melville established his pre-eminence with novels which might have been written in total ignorance of Hakluyt or the Icelandic sagas. The fact is that by the time of Cooper's birth the continental peripheries and even most of the remoter islands of the Pacific had already been explored by seamen; the great voyages of discovery of his time and country were inland. Not Drake or Cook, but Daniel Boone or Lewis and Clark were the heroes who penetrated the unknown, furnishing Cooper and his countrymen with the myth and circumstantial details out of which the Leatherstocking saga sprang. At the same time, it is true, the vastness, irreclaimable wildness, and—to landsmen—strangeness of the ocean made it perhaps the most potent Romantic symbol of sublimity. But the same ocean was also a regular commercial highway. Given these conflicting associations, it is easy to see why writers like Scott, Byron, and Cooper seized upon piracy and smuggling as the maritime activities that best expressed the complex meaning of the sea. This is not to deny that the voyages of discovery undertaken by Columbus or—that archetypal trespasser of human boundaries—Dante's Ulysses, have something in common with smuggling and piracy, in so far as all these activities place their nautical actors outside the pale of human society. No such resemblance, however, should be permitted to obscure the essential differences between Columbus's voyage of discovery and the Red Rover's voyage of plunder. After *Mercedes* the characteristic voyage in Cooper's sea novels is made in pursuit of plunder and discovery. This shift of focus may appear to be slight, but it is of major importance.

Whatever may be said of the value of *Mercedes* as a novel, Cooper took his role as naval historian with great seriousness. His description of the voyage was as accurate as he could make it. More interesting than his description of the voyage itself, however, is his presentation of the various contemporary attitudes to it. The worldly King Ferdinand regards it as a merchant would: a foolish gamble and yet, possibly, a way to incredible riches; for him, it is a voyage of plunder, as it is for most of Columbus's crew. Isabella shares Columbus's pious conviction that he is on God's mission: the conquest of Granada achieved, Christendom appears to them to be on the eve of a great expansionist phase. To the 'fiery' young romantic hero of the novel it is an opportunity for adventure and fame. In the eyes of many, however, the projected voyage is the work of the Devil: not only does Columbus's theory of the roundness of the world seem to contradict apparent fact, but the journey seems to be an impious transgression of the limits set to human knowledge and power. And though Cooper is careful to emphasize throughout *Mercedes* that Columbus is the most humble of mortals in his relations with God, the superstitious Spanish peasants and sailors are not wrong in sensing something heretical in the Genoese navigator. As befits the discoverer of America, Cooper's Columbus is indifferent to the claims of hereditary rank; in all but spiritual matters, he accepts or rejects received opinions according to their usefulness or conformity with the conclusions he has reached through the exercise of reason. But once remove his habitual respect for the mysteries of religion, and the navigator of the long voyage—who in the absence of landmarks must rely on the deductions of reason—becomes the lost freethinker.

Raoul Yvard, captain of the beautiful lugger Le Feu-Follet in *Wing-and-Wing* (1842), is such a freethinker. He is not, as a matter of fact, a sailor of the long voyage; rather he is a corsair in the employment of the French Republic not long after Nelson's great triumph at the Nile. Though he has imbibed the atheistical doctrines of the Revolution, he is every bit as frank and manly as the earlier Cooper seaman—Tom Tiller of *The Water Witch*—after whom he was obviously modelled.[5] Raoul loves Ghita, a pious Italian girl who returns his love but who will not marry a man who differs from her on so vital a matter as religion. This, if not the most interesting, is certainly the most central human relationship in the novel. Cooper's problem was somehow to integrate this relationship and its attendant issues

[5] James Grossman, *James Fenimore Cooper*, pp. 173–5, stresses the resemblance of *Wing-and-Wing* to *The Water Witch* and much prefers the later novel, in which Cooper abandoned 'its predecessor's bold fantasy and elaborate and rather vulgar magical apparatus for a more modest effect'. That the magical apparatus of *The Water Witch* is somewhat vulgar is doubtless true; but the fantasy seems to me as successful as it is bold—and therefore more valuable than the more modest success of *Wing-and-Wing*.

with the main action of a nautical romance. In this he was partially, but only partially, successful. Like Tom Tiller, Raoul delights in clever deceptions of all kinds; given the vast naval superiority of the English, he can survive only by his wits. Ironically, this master of delusion is himself deluded on the most important point of all—the extent to which man can or should wish to comprehend the mystery of the godhead. By way of symbolic contrast, the simple Ghita, who has spent most of her life in a lonely watch-tower, takes a longer and clearer view than does the clever Raoul. This moral-intellectual contrast is mirrored in a comic fashion in the Cervantesque relationship between the intellectually pretentious *vice-governatore* of Elba and his unimaginative underling, the *podestà*. To the stubbornly matter-of-fact mind of the *podestà*, the philosophical idealism propounded by the *vice-governatore*, as a way of accounting for the baffling exploits of Le Feu-Follet, is the height of folly and human pride. Innocent and amusing as the *vice-governatore's* speculations are, and wrong-headed as are the *podestà*'s objections, they supply a biting commentary on Raoul Yvard's enthronement of reason in the place of God.

Unfortunately, the main action of *Wing-and-Wing* is not a suitable vehicle for dealing with the seaman as lost freethinker. Though a corsair fighting for what was then regarded as a renegade nation, Raoul holds a regular commission from the French Republic and feels the most ardent patriotism: only in the most superficial sense could he or his actions be considered outside the bounds of any law, human or divine. Moreover, though Raoul may be metaphorically adrift on 'the sea of speculation and conceit',[6] the sea he actually sails on is the pleasant, familiar Mediterranean, which offers neither mysteries nor difficulties to the skilful mariner. Cooper did a great deal better when, in *The Sea Lions*, he placed his nautical freethinker among the shifting ice and weird lights of the Antarctic Sea.

Critics of *Wing-and-Wing* usually ignore the issues raised by the Raoul–Ghita relationship and concentrate on a quite different set of issues raised by the conduct of the British navy and its opponents. They are doubtless right to do so; for Cooper's own interest in *Wing-and-Wing* seems to have been more deeply and complexly engaged by problems of moral behaviour than

[6] Preface to *Wing-and-Wing*.

by the more important, but less novelistically rewarding, problems of faith and intellectual pride. Courageous, high-handed, enormously efficient, Nelson's fleet inspired both great respect and great hatred. As a young sailor, Cooper himself had witnessed the impressment of American seamen by the British navy; it was an experience he never forgot or forgave. In *Wing-and-Wing* the injustice of the British navy has two victims: Admiral Caraccioli, summarily executed by Nelson on a trumped-up charge of treason, and one Ithuel Bolt, an impressed American seaman who (though his own country is neutral) has joined Raoul Yvard in order to revenge himself on the British. Raoul too very nearly dies at the hands of a British naval court. Yet, as Mr Grossman points out,[7] the extraordinary thing is that Cooper contrives to make us understand, if not completely sympathize with, the point of view of the British naval officers. It is Ithuel Bolt who makes this balanced and complex view possible. Though deeply wronged by the British, and for this reason the recipient of the author's and the reader's fullest sympathies, Bolt himself is one of the most hateful of Cooper's hateful New Englanders. Loveless, avaricious, cunning, hypocritical, Ithuel is as it were energized by Cooper's conflicting feelings until he becomes a character not much less remarkable than Malvolio. His presence is so real that Raoul and Ghita and their problems fade into insignificance. Alas, they cannot be made to disappear entirely, they are developed just enough to disrupt the unity of the novel.

The Two Admirals (1842), the second of Cooper's three nautical romances of the early 'forties, is the odd man out among all his sea stories. Much of the novel is given over to an account of a bastard's unsuccessful attempt to inherit an estate in England, the true heir to which is a young American serving in the British navy during the Jacobite rebellion of 1745. This part of the novel has only a loose though clever thematic connexion with the part of the novel in which Cooper himself was primarily interested, both as a novelist and as a propagandist for a certain type of organization in the American navy of his own day.[8] Cooper believed that navies should be organized in fleets under

[7] Grossman, *James Fenimore Cooper*, pp. 163–5. This is a most perceptive discussion of the novel or at any rate of part of it.

[8] Philbrick, *op. cit.*, pp. 126–7.

the command of admirals, and in *The Two Admirals* he set out to show the beauty and efficiency of fleet manœuvres. This doesn't sound like a promising subject for a novel, but Cooper's enthusiastic description of the ballet-like order and precision achieved by a well-disciplined fleet is surprisingly effective. What is more, he succeeded in humanizing the action by creating a complex personal and professional relationship between the two commanders of the British fleet, Admirals Gervaise Oakes and Richard Bluewater. Radically unlike in their personalities, talents, and political views, Oakes and Bluewater nevertheless enjoy a perfect understanding and confidence, the result of life-long friendship and service together. So it is with the fleet they command: individual differences of strength, speed, manœuvrability are made to complement rather than conflict with each other; the imperfect parts are joined together in a harmonious whole. But this harmony is threatened, personal and national tragedy seem imminent, when Bluewater's Jacobitical sympathies hold him back from engagement with a French fleet which Oakes, greatly outnumbered, has already attacked. Bluewater's eventual succour of his friend and subsequent death are both extremely moving.

No doubt this nautical portion of *The Two Admirals* has many affinities with boys' adventure fiction; the true friendship of Oakes and Bluewater, with its pronounced homoerotic overtones, especially belongs to that genre. But as Cooper had already shown in the Leatherstocking tales, physical adventure and male friendship might be the ingredients of great fiction. Though quite unlike any of his other sea stories, *The Two Admirals* in its nautical sections sometimes approaches the quality of his best land stories. Probably it is the best of the three nautical romances of this period. Unfortunately, it suffers from the same fatal disunity as the others do: the extensive land-bound action of this novel of 1745 is a bad pastiche of bad eighteenth-century English fiction—worthless in itself and improbably linked with the nautical action. Perhaps Cooper himself was aware of the disunity; for in his next piece of 'sea fiction', *Afloat and Ashore*, he took great pains to bring land and sea together in a plausible and mutually illuminating relationship.

Cooper's critics have always felt a sneaking affection and an admiration for *Afloat and Ashore* (1844), even though it seemed to them indefensible as a work of art. A richly historical portrait of New York at the end of the eighteenth century, an exciting panoramic view of American maritime activities all over the world, a great compendium of the author's often crotchety, often wise observations on mid-nineteenth-century American society and politics—*Afloat and Ashore* is all these things, and other things as well. Here if anywhere we have the true vintage Cooper. But can it be taken seriously as a novel? Thomas Philbrick maintains that it should be so taken, and his case is a formidable one.[9] He does not venture to say precisely how good a novel he thinks *Afloat and Ashore* is relative to Cooper's other novels; but he leaves us in no doubt that he considers it one of the best. And this judgment is wholly new, daring—and right. To say so is not to deny the novel is loose, uneconomical, and often documentary to no good fictional purpose. I think Mr Philbrick acknowledges these defects less frankly than he might. Furthermore, as will emerge later, his perception that *Afloat and Ashore* is not formless (as other critics had taken for granted) sometimes leads him to make the design of the novel appear much more schematic than it actually is. Still, these are venial faults in a truly pioneering work of criticism, and my own reading of the novel is, in a way, no more than an extended footnote to Mr Philbrick's.

On a quick first reading *Afloat and Ashore* is likely to seem aimlessly digressive and episodic. It is true that the narrator, Miles Wallingford, is a digressive old man whose point of view is itself quite consistent—consistent because, as many critics have noted, it is essentially the point of view of James Fenimore Cooper, only slightly modified to take account of Miles's belonging to a slightly earlier generation and lower social station than the author. (There is even a wonderful passage in which Miles takes sides with 'a writer of this country, one Mr Cooper' against Captain Marryat in a dispute over the eating habits of Americans!) Yet Miles is so digressive that one feels bound in critical self-defence to invoke Yvor Winters's fallacy of imitative form. It is true too that, episodic as the action is, all the events in the novel were either experienced by or (more rarely) reported to Miles Wallingford when as a young man he made four long ocean voyages and as many returns to his home in

[9] Philbrick, *op. cit.* pp. 131–65.

New York state. But Aristotle was right: you cannot achieve unity of action merely by reporting the diverse experiences of one man. And though there is more to the art of fiction than the theories of Winters and Aristotle, strictly interpreted, allow for, the fact is that *Afloat and Ashore* does ramble too much. Having said this, however, I wish to endorse Mr Philbrick's argument that it has as much shape and unity as it needs to have.

It has unity of tone but no unity of style. On the whole it is a melancholy book, not merely because Captain Wallingford regrets the many changes that have taken place in America between 1797–1804 (the time of the action) and 1844 (the time of the writing), but because the changes that took place between 1797 (when he still belonged to the secure, happy world of childhood) and 1804 (when he married and settled down) were themselves predominantly sad. What Wallingford regrets, with respect to his family circle in 1804 and with respect to the nation in 1844, is a loss of simplicity and roots. Though widely travelled, observant, and critical, old Miles is himself a comparatively simple man, as were his ancestors.

Given this theme and this narrator, Cooper's usual prose style—at once ponderous and slovenly, intermittently forceful and pointed—clearly would not do. He had already experimented with first person narrative in *Notions of the Americans* (1828), *The Monikins* (1835), and *The French Governess* (1843); but the narrators in these works were so feebly or uncertainly characterized that he did not feel the need to depart much from his ordinary manner of writing. In *Ned Myers* (1843), however, where he acted as amanuensis for a real old salt, he made a serious and successful attempt 'to adhere as closely to the very language of his subject, as circumstances [would] allow'. *Ned Myers*, subtitled 'A Life Before the Mast', was one of many books inspired by Dana's *Two Years Before the Mast* (1840) to provide a realistic account of the lives of American merchant seamen.[10] And as *Afloat and Ashore* too must be regarded as a fictional descendant of Dana's autobiographical account of his trading voyage around Cape Horn to California, there is some point in comparing the respective styles of the three books.

Though he wrote little of literary importance besides *Two*

[10] Cf. Philbrick, pp. 115–20.

Years Before the Mast, Dana was a brilliant though unambitious stylist. A good example of his work is this description of an albatross:

They look well on the wing; but one of the finest sights that I have ever seen was an albatross asleep upon the water, during a calm, off Cape Horn, when a heavy sea was running. There being no breeze, the surface of the water was unbroken, but a long, heavy swell was rolling, and we saw the fellow, all white, directly ahead of us, asleep upon the waves, with his head under his wing; now rising on the top of one of the big billows, and then falling slowly until he was lost in the hollow between. He was undisturbed for some time, until the noise of our bows, gradually approaching, roused him, when, lifting his head, he stared upon us for a moment, and then spread his wide wings and took his flight.

Here it is the fidelity with which the language lazily mirrors the movements of the bird that is most impressive. At his best, as in *The Pioneers* or *The Pathfinder,* Cooper could be equally or even more impressive in the same way. But Dana's characteristic diction—simple, relaxed, flexible—did not come naturally to Cooper. Yet it was the diction he himself consistently recommended to others, e.g. in *The American Democrat*:

The common faults of American language are an ambition of effect, a want of simplicity, and a turgid abuse of terms. To these may be added ambiguity of expression. Many perversions of significations also exist, and a formality of speech, which, while it renders conversation ungraceful, and destroys its playfulness, seriously weakens the power of the language, by applying to ordinary ideas, words that are suited only to themes of gravity and dignity.[11]

All these faults, of course, might be abundantly illustrated from Cooper's own writings: Dana writes as Cooper's American Gentleman should; Cooper generally does not. So true is this that, like R. W. B. Lewis, 'one is sometimes tempted to say that Cooper has no style at all'.[12] Yet if this is true of most of his books, it is only fair to add that he exhibited something very like 'negative capability' in a few of them. The pseudo-Elizabethan prose of *Lionel Lincoln* and *The Water Witch* is no inert imitation of dead prose forms: it has more life and true eloquence than he could normally achieve when he was trying

[11] *The American Democrat* (Vintage ed., 1956), p. 116.
[12] *The American Adam,* p. 101.

to write good nineteenth-century prose. A similar though less impressive success is the prose of *Ned Myers*.

Most of the colloquial vigour of *Ned Myers* must probably be attributed to Ned himself; Cooper, by his own admission, was little more than a midwife. A fair specimen of their work is this description of Ned's escape from an English customs cruiser:

As the English never employed any but the fastest cruisers for this station, we had a scratching time of it. The brig sailed very fast, and out-carried us; but our little schooner held on well. For two days and one night we had it, tack and tack, with her. The brig certainly gained on us, our craft carrying a balanced reefed-main-sail, bonnet off the foresail and one reef in, and bonnet off the jib. The flying-jib was inboard. At sunset, on the second night, the brig was so near us, we could see her people, and it was blowing fresher than ever. This was just her play, while ours was in more moderate weather. Our skipper got uneasy now, and determined to try a trick. It set in dark and rainy, and, as soon as we lost sight of the brig, we tacked, stood on a short distance, lowered everything, and extinguished all our lights. We lay in this situation three hours, when we stuck the craft down again for Tory Island, as straight as we could go. I never knew what became of the brig, which may be chasing us yet, for aught I know, for I saw no more of her.

Racy this language is, and incomparably more lively than Cooper's usual polysyllabic plodding. Nevertheless, even if Ned were as intelligent and sensitive to impressions as Dana, it is hard to believe that this relatively primitive prose could equal Dana's as a vehicle for moral analysis or description. Nor could it equal Cooper's. Indeed, when moral analysis is undertaken in *Ned Myers*, it is in the language of Cooper—probably not because Cooper was in these instances the 'author', but simply because Ned lacked the vocabulary and syntax to articulate his ideas with any precision or compactness:

It is seldom that a seaman cannot lay by a hundred dollars in a twelvemonth—oftentimes I have earned double that amount, beyond my useful outlays—and a hundred dollars a year, at the end of thirty years, would give such a man an independence for the rest of his days. This is far from all, however; the possession of means would awaken the desire of advancement in the calling, and thousands who now remain before the mast, would long since have been officers, could they have commanded the self-respect that property is apt to create.

Ned's language will do for dollars and cents, but for the analysis of motivation something more is needed. The same poverty of means limits Ned as a descriptive writer; not for a moment can he match or even come close to the descriptive passages of, say, *The Red Rover* or *The Deerslayer*. What Ned's language can do is to delimit the character of the narrator sharply and to lend an air of authenticity to his report: it is the language that makes this book what Cooper always generously insisted it was— 'Ned's book'.

With the exception of occasional discordant phrases or sentences, the prose of *Ned Myers* is pretty much of a piece; but the style is extraordinarily rigid, for all its appearance of colloquial ease. The same style could not possibly suit Captain Miles Wallingford, who is at once an old salt and a landed proprietor of considerable means and education. A relatively neutral style, like that of Dana, might have been appropriate; but *that* style, so deceptively simple, was nearly as far out of Cooper's as his own style was out of Ned Myers' reach. Consequently, the language of Miles Wallingford is—and quite convincingly— a medley of styles:

Could Nelson, after his victory of the Nile, have walked into the King of England's private cabinet with the news of his own success, his reception could not have been more flattering than that I now received. I was 'Captain Wallingforded' at every sentence; and commendations were so intermixed with inquiries about the value of the cargo, that I did not know which to answer first. I was invited to dine the very next day by both the gentlemen in the same breath; and when I raised some objections connected with the duty of the ship, the invitations were extended from day to day for a week. So very welcome is he who brings us gold!

We went alongside of a North River wharf, and had everything secure, just as the sun was setting. The people were then allowed to go ashore for the night. Not a soul of them asked for a dollar, but the men walked up the wharf attended by a circle of admiring landlords, that put them all above want. The sailor who has three years' pay under his lee, is a sort of Rothschild on Jack's Exchange. All the harpies about our lads knew that the Crisis and her teas, etc. were hypothecated to meet their own ten and twenty dollar advances.

I dressed myself hurriedly, and ordered Neb to imitate my example. One of the owners had kindly volunteered to see Major

Merton and Emily to a suitable residence, with an alacrity that surprised me.

From the stilted to the relaxed, from the pungently colloquial and wittingly allusive to the dully genteel, this language veers in accordance with the narrator's shifting attitude to the subjects he surveys. One can scarcely say that this is a flexible style, it is no style at all. Compare this passage, for instance, with a description of a similar event in *Two Years Before the Mast*:

About ten o'clock a sea breeze sprang up, and the pilot gave orders to get the ship under way. All hands manned the windlass, and the long-drawn 'Yo, heave, ho!' which we had last heard dying away among the desolate hills of San Diego, soon brought the anchor to the bows; and, with a fair wind and tide, a bright sunny morning, royals and skysails set, ensign, streamer, signals, and pennant flying, and with our guns firing, we came swiftly and handsomely up to the city. Off the end of the wharf we rounded to, and let go our anchor; and no sooner was it on the bottom than the decks were filled with people; customhouse officers; Topliff's agent, to inquire for news; others, inquiring for friends on board, or left upon the coast; dealers in grease, besieging the galley to make a bargain with the cook for his slush; 'loafers' in general; and last and chief, boardinghouse runners, to secure their men. Nothing can exceed the obliging disposition of these runners, and the interest they take in a sailor returned from a long voyage with aplenty of money. Two or three of them, at different times, took me by the hand; pretended to remember me perfectly; were quite sure I had boarded with them before I sailed; were delighted to see me back; gave me their cards; had a handcart waiting on the wharf, on purpose to take my things up; would lend me a hand to get my chest ashore; bring a bottle of grog on board if we did not haul in immediately; and the like. In fact, we could hardly get clear of them to go aloft and furl the sails. Sail after sail, for the hundredth time, in fair weather and in foul, we furled now for the last time together, and came down and took the warp ashore, manned the capstan, and with a chorus which waked up half North End, and rang among the buildings in the dock, we hauled her in to the wharf. The city bells were just ringing one when the last turn was made fast and the crew dismissed; and in five minutes more not a soul was left on board the good ship *Alert* but the old ship-keeper, who had come down from the counting-house to take charge of her.

Dana's style is truly flexible and urbane; it can absorb Latin quotations or seaman's jargon without affectation, and, as in this passage, it can render scenes and behaviour with remarkable immediacy. By any standard, the limpid and robust prose of *Two Years Before the Mast* is vastly superior to that of *Ned Myers* or *Afloat and Ashore*. And yet the odd mixum-gatherum prose of *Afloat and Ashore* is well adapted to the odd amphibious character of its narrator, and it is by no means certain that Dana's prose—the prose of Cooper's American Gentleman—would have suited him nearly so well. We may suspect that Cooper's success is due rather to accident than to art in this case, but a success it is and one that contributes much to the homely charm of the novel as a whole.

The action of *Afloat and Ashore*, as its title indicates, alternates between the land and the sea. More precisely, the action consists of voyages to foreign parts (to nearby New York City and all the world beyond) and homecomings to the prosperous Wallingford farm, Clawbonny. Lovely Clawbonny is the centre of existence to Miles and his sister Grace, as to a slightly lesser extent it is to their childhood friends Lucy and Rupert Hardinge. As heir to Clawbonny (his parents having died fairly recently), Miles has no practical reason for going to sea. At the commencement to his second voyage, he says:

> Man must be a stern being by nature, to be able to tear himself from such friends, in order to encounter enemies, hardships, danger and toil, and all without any visible motive. Such was my case, however, for I wanted not for a competency, or for most of those advantages which might tempt one to abandon the voyage. Of such a measure, the possibility never crossed my mind. I believed that it was just as necessary for me to remain third mate of the Crisis, and to stick by the ship while she would float, as Mr Adams thinks it necessary for him to present abolition petitions to a Congress which will not receive them. We both of us, doubtless, believed ourselves the victims of fate.

In other words, something idealistic, albeit quixotic, leads Miles to abandon home and friends in order to encounter the trials of the deep. Before his first voyage, however, when Miles has Rupert Hardinge as a companion, he finds plausible reasons for going to sea. In the first place, both boys simply long to see the world; the lure of the exotic pulls them away from the familiar world of Clawbonny:

'Yes,' said I, stretching myself with a little importance. 'I fancy an Indiaman, a vessel that goes all the way to Calcutta, round the Cape of Good Hope, in the track of Vasquez de Gama, isn't exactly an Albany sloop.'

'Who is Vasquez de Gama?' demanded Lucy, with so much quickness as to surprise me.

'Why, a noble Portuguese, who discovered the Cape of Good Hope, and first sailed round it, and then went to the Indies. You see, girls, even nobles are sailors, and why should not Rupert and I be sailors?'

As in *Mercedes* and later in *The Sea Lions*, the sea is the field of discovery and self-discovery; and sure enough, in the course of his travels, Miles does discover his *terra incognita*, an island in the Pacific, and discovers too the real value of Clawbonny. The sea is also the road to fortune—a factor which weighs much with the impecunious Rupert, but which weighs with Miles as well, since he has an ambition to build a splendid seat to replace the quaint old farmhouse inhabited and added to by four generations of Miles Wallingfords:

Nevertheless, there was something taking, to my imagination, in the notion of being the fabricator of my own fortune. In that day, it was easy to enumerate every dwelling on the banks of the Hudson that aspired to be called a seat, and I had often heard them named by those who were familiar with the river. I liked the thought of erecting a house on the Clawbonny property that might aspire to equal claims, and to be the owner of a seat; though only after I had acquired the means myself, to carry out such a project. At present I owned only a house; my ambition was to own a seat.

This enterprising but unfilial scheme is one of the first casualties of his maiden voyage: when beset by dangers, he recalls the old familiar place of childhood security and he decides that changes to Clawbonny, if they are made at all, must be organic: like his ancestors he will add a wing to the farmhouse, just as a tree adds a ring of growth each year. From the beginning, indeed, Miles's impulse to go to sea is not primarily a revolutionary impulse; quite the contrary. Miles's father, whose death occurred when Miles was thirteen, was himself owner and master of a merchant ship. So Miles will be too, even if he and Rupert have to run away from home to escape the paternal prohibition of Rupert's father, Miles's guardian. In Rupert's case, on the other hand, running away from home means precisely what it appears to mean: a wish to pull up roots and abandon the way of life of his fathers. It is no accident that later in the novel, having abandoned the sea in favour of the more genteel profession of the law, Rupert marries the English woman Emily Merton. Already, in 1844, Cooper was recording some of the symptoms of family and cultural break-up which were to be observed by Mann in *Buddenbrooks* and by Lawrence in *The Rainbow*.

And it turns out that Miles Wallingford was born to be a sailor. Shortly after joining his first ship, he is described by the chief mate, one Moses Marble, as 'the ripest piece of green stuff he had ever fallen in with'. By the end of his second voyage, aged twenty-one years, he is captain of a large ship. If this advancement seems improbably rapid, the fact is that Wallingford and his exploits quickly assume a legendary quality. Mr Philbrick points out that Miles

was born on 'the very day that Cornwallis capitulated at Yorktown'. He first goes to sea in 1797, a time when the shipping of America 'was wonderfully active, and, as a whole, singularly successful'. Throughout his nautical career Miles displays a marvelous affinity with events of great national interest. . . .[13]

After Miles's exciting and disastrous, but not improbable, first voyage, the nautical action of *Afloat and Ashore* becomes positively Odyssean as he visits strange lands and cities, experiences innumerable captivities and escapes, and encounters friends whom he had last seen in London now stranded on an unknown Pacific isle. While on his voyages, his beloved Lucy Hardinge is besieged by suitors, some attracted by her new fortune, others by her beauty. After his fourth and ruinous voyage, having mortgaged Clawbonny to purchase a cargo for his ship—both of which are now on the bottom of the Atlantic— Miles is recognized on his arrival in New York City by an old Wallingford family retainer and informed that Clawbonny has been sold to meet his debts and is now in the hands of a usurper. As for Lucy, Miles supposes that she, thinking him dead at sea, must have married one of her many suitors. Miles's recovery of Clawbonny and Lucy does not require the intervention of a god, and it may be that these similarities between the stories of

[13] Philbrick, *op. cit.*, p. 133.

Odysseus and Miles Wallingford are accidental. (I personally think it unlikely that they are.) In any case, these parallels will serve to enforce several points I wish to make about the novel. At the emotional centre of *Afloat and Ashore* is a powerful conflict between wanderlust and homesickness. Were the nautical action less fabulous, the rival claims of home would certainly put an end to Miles's voyages. Were Clawbonny and Lucy less magnetic—and their magnetism exerts remarkable force on the reader as well as on Miles—then such a bountiful, if in the end deceitful, mistress as the sea would certainly win all of Miles's love. Perhaps in no other novel by Cooper, not even *The Pathfinder*, is there a greater tension between his radical and conservative impulses, between the rival claims of adventure and domesticity. It is not for nothing that, as Cooper's biographers have pointed out, Lucy Hardinge and Susan De Lancy are strikingly alike, and Miles's career is in many ways a continuation in fantasy of Cooper's own brief career as a merchant seaman.[14]

However, it is misleading to suggest as Mr Philbrick does that there is a sharp discontinuity between Miles's experience afloat and Miles's experience ashore, or that, for Miles, the choice between land and sea is a simple choice between opposites:

Afloat, isolation and danger drive him back to his home, his family, and his friends. Ashore, frustration and artificiality make him 'all impatience to get to sea'.[15]

This sounds more like a description of Huckleberry Finn than like one of Miles Wallingford. We may be sure that Miles, son of Miles, would never have left Clawbonny had not his idolized father done so before him. Given his character, there is every reason to believe in his sincerity when he tells his first captain, 'though under no necessity to work at all, I wish to make this Miles Wallingford as good a seaman as the last, and, I hope, as honest a man'. This pious Telemachan wish hallows his nautical career and, in his own eyes at least, builds a bridge between his life as a seaman and his life as the heir to Clawbonny. At the same time, however, loyalty to his father's example (who left the sea when he inherited Clawbonny) demands that he should keep these lives distinct from each

---

[14] Grossman, *James Fenimore Cooper*, p. 195. [15] Philbrick, *op. cit.*, p. 162.

other. So long as he does, no matter how great his peril, his life and career on the water appear to be charmed, as his friend Moses Marble frequently remarks. It is when he mortgages his patrimony for the sake of a cargo that the charm is broken: Miles himself feels guilty and uneasy, and the reader knows that Clawbonny, the ship and cargo are doomed. This rather subtly developed relationship between Miles and his dead father thus greatly enriches the meaning of the action and helps to prevent Miles's experience from assuming a simple, lifeless antithetical structure.

Another enriching and at the same time defining factor in the novel is the presence of Miles's shipmate Moses Marble. Like Rupert Hardinge, whom he succeeds as Miles's closest companion and friend, Marble is clearly intended to be a foil for the young hero. But unlike Hurry Harry in *The Deerslayer*, Rupert and Marble seem to exist for their own sakes as well; they are among Cooper's most interesting characters. It is during Miles's second voyage that Marble comes fully to life and comes indeed to dominate the action. During a trading voyage to the north-west coast of America (one of the best episodes in the book), Miles's ship is captured and its captain murdered by Indians. After regaining the ship, Marble, now the captain, hangs the Indian leader Smudge as an act of revenge. In his new role, though still a fine seaman and just master, Marble exhibits the traits—arbitrariness and fecklessness—which have always prevented him from rising above the station of chief mate. Miles attempts to restrain him, but revelling in his new command Marble takes his ship off course to look for pearl fisheries: in fact, after coming close to wrecking the ship, Marble does blunder upon an apparently undiscovered and uninhabited coral island—only to be captured by a stranded French ship's crew. Embittered by this stroke of ill fortune, Marble now reveals his personal history: seemingly abandoned at birth by his parents in a New York graveyard (hence his name), Moses Marble has no home, family, or real name. Full of disappointment, he determines to become a hermit on the coral island:

'Just look at my situation, Miles, and decide for yourself, I am without a friend on earth—I mean nat'ral friend—I know what sort of friend you are, and parting with you will be the toughest of all—

but I have not a relation on the wide earth—no property, no home, no one to wish to see me return, not even a cellar to lay my head in. To me all places are alike, with the exception of this, which, having discovered, I look upon as my own.'

At this point we should recall Miles's earlier wish to be 'the fabricator of my own fortune' and to build a seat on the Clawbonny property. Poor Marble, become the prisoner of his own myth of himself, feels that he is compelled by fate to complete the myth by living in isolation on what he has himself christened Marble Island. Here Cooper is obviously reworking some of the themes of *The Deerslayer*; but there is a gain rather than a loss of power and clarity in the reworking. This gain is largely a result of Cooper's poignant and convincing characterization of Marble. Always colourful and shrewd in his observations, Marble in this dark night of his soul becomes epigrammatic and sternly honest about himself and others:

'And what shall I tell all your acquaintances, those who have sailed with you so often and so long, has become of their old shipmate?'

'Tell 'em that the man who was once found is now lost,' answered Marble, bitterly. 'But I'm not such a fool as to think myself of so much importance as you seem to imagine. The only persons who will consider the transaction of any interest will be the newspaper gentry, and they will receive it only as news, and thank you about half as much as they would for a murder or a robbery, or the poisoning of a mother and six little children.'

Eventually he finds his Robinson Crusoe-like existence on Marble Island unbearable: 'I just weathered Cape Crazy,' he later tells Miles, 'and that too in the white water.' In the end, Marble has the satisfaction of finding his own (quite blameless) family and comfortable home, but finds too that he cannot settle down. Unlike Miles, he returns to the sea and finally, at his own request, is buried in blue water.

This discussion of Miles's relationships with Marble, his own dead father, and Rupert Hardinge will suggest, I hope, how carefully and effectively the novel is designed. For other evidence of the ultimate coherence and shape of this superficially formless work, the reader should consult Mr Philbrick's brilliant defence. *Afloat and Ashore* does of course have major defects, even in addition to those I have already mentioned. One of these is the characterization of Miles's 'angelic' sister Grace. Another is the affectionate and yet consistently patronizing attitude towards the Wallingfords' negro slaves, an attitude which may perhaps be attributed to Miles rather than to Cooper himself but which is nevertheless annoying. Still, *Afloat and Ashore* is certainly one of Cooper's most rewarding and moving works. It is the one which gives me greatest pleasure when I re-read it, and I have no doubt that it is among Cooper's half-dozen most important novels.

2

If most of the action sequences of *Afloat and Ashore* have something fabulous about them, many of the particular incidents which they contain are harshly realistic and even well documented. If the sea is the area of possibility for Miles, he soon learns that seamen have their beastly and disreputable side and that the sea itself is full of treacherous currents. Nevertheless, *Afloat and Ashore* is not as a whole a harsh work, nor are the first two books of the trilogy which followed it. But by 1846, the year which marks the end of the Littlepage trilogy and the beginning of *Jack Tier*, Cooper seems to have become obsessed with the beastly and disreputable side of mankind; and during the last five years of his life he wrote about little else. It is impossible to like the misanthropic novels of this period, though in at least one of them, *The Sea Lions*, there is much to admire.

There is little to admire in *Jack Tier*. As both James Grossman and Thomas Philbrick have pointed out, this novel is a 'grab bag of characters and incidents gathered from *The Red Rover* and *The Water Witch*' [16]—with the crucial difference that the romantic qualities of strangeness, lightness, and elegance are replaced in *Jack Tier* with the anti-romantic qualities of lower-class familiarity, clumsiness, and ugliness. It is no accident that Captain Spike's old but still beautiful brigantine, now engaged in smuggling munitions to the Mexican enemies of the United States, should have been built during the War of 1812, which in Cooper's view was the last high point of national self-respect and effort. To drive home his thesis that the national

---

[16] Philbrick, *op. cit.*, p. 204.

character had deteriorated frightfully since then, Cooper virtually rewrote two of his most idealistic and patriotic sea romances; and as one of them, *The Red Rover*, had been one of his most popular works, he probably calculated on his reader recognizing the familiar features beneath the deformity. So wilful and formulary is this inversion of values that *Jack Tier* would be unreadable but for two things: the mate of the brigantine does, after much unmanly subservience, exhibit many of the more admirable traits of a Cooper seaman; and Captain Spike, though a thorough villain, is permitted to be a superlative professional sailor.

Cooper was evidently at some pains to dissociate Spike's moral and professional qualities, and as Mr Philbrick remarks, this was a new departure in his sea fiction.[17] Not unnaturally, though somewhat unrealistically, Cooper always liked to associate moral with professional excellence: the greatest example in his fiction of such a conjunction of qualities is, of course, Leatherstocking. But in the land fiction, unlike the sea fiction before *Jack Tier*, he frequently allows that the two qualities do not always go together. There are a number of reasons why Cooper should have taken it for granted that they always *did* go together in the case of seamen. (He was after all a sailor himself and an apologist for a strong American navy and merchant marine.) One of these reasons is particularly important in connexion with *Jack Tier*. The captain of any ship is responsible for the lives of his passengers and crew; their safety depends on his seamanship. By thus automatically assuming the role of protector, even when the mission of his ship is criminal, the professionally able captain almost automatically acquires heroic moral stature during moments of danger. And this is no less true of Captain Spike than of such noble fellows as Harry Wilder in *The Red Rover* or Tom Tiller in *The Water Witch*. At the end of *Jack Tier*, however, Cooper manages to get round this problem by exhibiting Spike's seamanship, not as the preserver, but as the destroyer of human life: trying to flee from a U.S. naval cutter in an overcrowded boat, Spike knows what he has to do to make his boat more swift and seaworthy; one by one the least useful, i.e. most helpless, passengers are thrown overboard to be drowned. This sequence is probably the most brutal

[17] Philbrick, *op. cit.*, pp. 207–8.

Cooper ever wrote, but it is a remarkably effective *dénouement* to an otherwise bad novel.

Like that equally avaricious, equally hardened sinner Tom Hutter in *The Deerslayer*, Captain Spike makes a bad end. So does Captain Jason Daggett in *The Sea Lions* (1849). One of those hardy sons of New England who have ransacked the world for gold, Daggett sails beyond the great barrier of Antarctic ice—'Cook's "Ne Plus Ultra" '—in search of an island whose virgin sealing grounds promise fabulous wealth. Though lacking accurate information about the location of the island, and contemptuous of all aids to navigation, Daggett as it were scents out the island and proceeds to fill the hold of the *Sea Lion* with booty. But trapped by the Antarctic winter, which is really to say trapped by his reckless attachment to worldly things, Daggett, his *Sea Lion*, and most of his crew all perish unredeemed. When the spring rains come, Daggett's body, like that of Spike in the earlier novel (and not unlike that of Tom Hutter in *The Deerslayer*), is washed out to sea, lost utterly, leaving the island rocks 'as naked and as clean as if man's foot had never passed over them'. Well might one of the characters in the novel ask, 'Ah! why cannot men be content with the blessings that Providence places within our immediate reach, that they must make distant voyages to accumulate others!'

But Jason Daggett is not the hero of *The Sea Lions*. The hero is young Roswell Gardiner, master of another and identical schooner named *Sea Lion*, bound on an identical voyage to the Antarctic sealing island. If Daggett is an embodiment of *cupiditas*, then Gardiner is an embodiment of *infidelitas*. He too, though with accurate charts and the aid of navigational science, will pass beyond the 'ne plus ultra of Cook' (the phrase is repeated) in order to discover the island for his avaricious owner. Gardiner's vice is an intellectual pride which leads him to deny what he cannot comprehend—he *will* not believe, as his beloved Mary devoutly does, in the mysteries of the Incarnation and Holy Trinity. The relationship between Roswell Gardiner and Mary Pratt in fact duplicates that between Raoul and Ghita in *Wing-and-Wing*; sometimes, indeed, and rather embarrassingly, the duplication of scenes and arguments goes so far that one suspects Cooper of writing *The Sea Lions* with the pages of the earlier novel open before him. However this may be, assisted by

Mary's Bible, the unctuous words of the Trinitarian old salt Stephen Stimson, and especially the overwhelming power and grandeur of the Antarctic winter world, Gardiner experiences a regenerating conviction of his own insignificance—the orthodox doctrines seem perfectly acceptable, the spring weather arrives almost simultaneously, and Gardiner is able to sail home soon after.

Thus, although their missions like their ships are superficially identical, the two masters of the *Sea Lions*, both of them unregenerate men at the commencement of their voyages, reach radically different ends. Summarized in this fashion, the allegorical structure and purpose of the novel may appear painfully schematic and obtrusive; but so far is this from the truth that until Thomas Philbrick published his exegesis of *The Sea Lions*,[18] most readers seem to have missed the allegory altogether! This failure to penetrate the surface of the novel must be attributed partly, I think, to sheer obtuseness, since at least a few of the coincidences in the action must appear gratuitous as well as inexplicable unless we discover another layer of meaning in the work to account for them. On the other hand, partly by inadvertence and partly by skill, Cooper does cover his tracks quite effectively; the highly realistic physical and psychological action is in its own right extraordinarily absorbing; the theological disputations, alas, which ought to direct our attention to the allegorical undercurrent of the action, are so hackneyed and doctrinaire that it is impossible to read them with any patience, let alone with any regard to their possible bearing on the action.

By virtue of his being the first person who may be said to have really read the novel (unless we cautiously except Herman Melville),[19] Mr Philbrick has surely earned the right to claim that *The Sea Lions* is Cooper's 'most complex and yet fully integrated fiction'.[20] But much as I share Mr Philbrick's view that *Afloat and Ashore* has not been sufficiently understood or admired, I cannot agree that *The Sea Lions* is yet another neglected masterpiece. It was ingenious of Cooper to place the rival *Sea*

[18] Philbrick, *op. cit.*, pp. 209–59.

[19] Melville's favourable, not especially illuminating review of *The Sea Lions* appeared in the *Literary World* for April 1849, p. 370. The best evidence that Melville grasped the inner meaning of *The Sea Lions* is to be found, as Mr Philbrick suggests, in the development of similar themes and techniques in *Moby Dick*.

[20] Philbrick, *op. cit.*, p. 209.

Lions side by side, superficially parallel, the one making a voyage of transgression, the other a voyage of ordeal. Thus conjoined are the two archetypal voyagers of the Western literary imagination—Homer's Odysseus and Dante's Ulysses. But the voyage of Cooper's proud freethinking Roswell Gardiner (the Ulysses figure) is almost exclusively a voyage of *ordeal*: the hardships he experiences (which assist his conversion) are not the result of reckless intellectual pride but of the charity he extends to the afflicted Daggett; and in so far as the fearful sublimity of the Antarctic winter is necessary to upset his spiritual complacency, the novel must be read as an argument in favour of expeditions beyond the *ne plus ultra*!

The chief transgressor, though he also passes unsuccessfully through an ordeal, is Daggett. Unlike the cautious Gardiner, Daggett in his rashness and sullen pride trusts to his luck and instincts; at heart, he is as contemptuous of reason as of danger. But as he seems to be intellectually incapable of recognizing any boundaries (he is more like Aristabulus Bragg than like Ulysses), he cannot be regarded as a criminal transgressor. In fact, avaricious and cunning as Jason Daggett is, it is not true that he is 'clearly evil, a brutalized hypocrite whose only motive is greed'.[21] Certainly, unlike Pathfinder, he is too much attached to the things of this world: to gold, to his ship, to his family:

'I'm afraid that I've loved money most too well,' he said to Roswell, not an hour before he drew his last breath; 'but I hope it was not so much for myself, as for others. A wife and children, Gar'ner, tie a man to 'arth in an unaccountable manner. Sealers' companions are used to hearing of misfortunes, and the Vineyard women know that few on 'em live to see a husband at their side in old age. Still, it is hard on a mother and wife to l'arn that her chosen friend has been cut off in the pride of his days and in a distant land. Poor Betsy! It would have been better for us both had we been satisfied with the little we had; for now the good woman will have to look to all matters for herself.'

Clearly, such a man is not altogether evil. Yet it is true that the austere New Testament moral code of *The Sea Lions* explicitly requires men and women to reject any worldly concern or affection which threatens to interfere with their Christian devo-

[21] Philbrick, *op. cit.*, p. 250.

tion or obedience. Bleak as the Antarctic landscape, this code consigns miserable devils like Daggett to perdition, but, strangely transmuted by the conventions of genteel fiction, rewards the regenerate Gardiner with a pretty wife and a fat fortune.

XIII

THE LITTLEPAGE TRILOGY

1. *Satanstoe*

THERE ARE AT LEAST four angles from which *Satanstoe* can be usefully approached. Most obviously, it can be approached as the first part of the Littlepage, or Anti-Rent, trilogy (1845-6), a series of novels which taken together form the first family chronicle novel in American literature. That it is the first part of a trilogy will have to be taken into account in any final assessment of the novel, or in any attempt to explain why, compared with some other Cooper novels, *Satanstoe* is rather less complex and powerful—but also much more disciplined. On the other hand, though *Satanstoe* prepares the way for *The Chainbearer* and *The Chainbearer* prepares the way for *The Redskins*, each of the three novels was designed to stand by itself as an independent work; moreover, though *Satanstoe* and especially *The Chainbearer* do deal in a general way with the issue underlying the Anti-Rent controversy—i.e. what are the rights and responsibilities of property?—they are so little concerned with the specific grievances and difficulties which attended that controversy in New York state in the early 1840's that there would be no need to discuss Anti-Rentism as such until one came to *The Redskins*. Indeed, it is important to stress at the outset that although the trilogy was occasioned by a particular controversy, Cooper chose to deal with it fictionally by devoting two of the three books to a 'background' so remote that they bear much the same relation to the third book as do *The Pioneers* and *The Prairie* to *Home as Found*. So like this earlier trio of novels is the Littlepage Trilogy, both individually and as a group, that a comparison between them helps one to see why *Satanstoe* is the sort of novel it is (a novel rather like *The Pioneers*) and why, in spite of a good beginning, Cooper failed to make the Littlepage Trilogy into a coherent and effective family chronicle novel. (He seems to have been content to imitate the fortuitous development and consequently loose 'internal' connexions of the earlier 'trilogy', rather than to work out the full artistic and social implications of the form he had stumbled upon.) This is an approach which reveals more about the trilogy than about *Satanstoe*, but which must be borne in mind when discussing the design and characteristic strengths of the novel.

But there are two other approaches which are more immediately helpful for an understanding of *Satanstoe* as an independent novel. First, the narrative technique of *Satanstoe* is quite clearly a development of the technique employed in *Afloat and Ashore*. Second, *Satanstoe* can be regarded as the last and best of a series of novels whose main theme is the emancipation of the American mind from a state of colonial dependence.

The Littlepage Trilogy is ostensibly a series of narratives written by members of succeeding generations of the Littlepage family with the disinterested object of describing 'American society, in its more familiar aspects'. Thus Cornelius (Corny) Littlepage, writing a few years afterwards about events which took place during the 1750's, does not foresee the Anti-Rent riots of the 1840's or even the revolutionary activities of the 1770's. Yet he does 'foresee that this country is destined to undergo great and rapid changes'—a prophetic insight which supplies him with the pretext for becoming an historian of the manners of his own time and place. In practice, of course, Corny Littlepage records just as much contemporary social history as suits Cooper's purposes as a novelist; and the reader who is chiefly interested in the factual details of mid-eighteenth-century New York colonial society will do better to consult, as Cooper himself did, such works as *Mrs Grant's Memoirs*. None the less, Cooper's purposes as a novelist and as a social historian are inseparable: the most important *datum* of social history in *Satanstoe* is the colonial mentality of its narrator.

The fictitious narrator is a device which lends itself almost equally well to highly impersonal or, by way of masquerade, highly personal art. Miles Wallingford in *Afloat and Ashore* is a fictitious narrator who is just sufficiently differentiated from the author to take responsibility for statements which, though they probably or certainly express the private views of the author, are put in such a way that James Fenimore Cooper, Esq., might not care to make them publicly. Cooper had less use for such *personae* than most authors do, because he had a great deal more moral courage than most authors. Still, when writing as James Fenimore Cooper, Historian and Gentleman, he found it necessary to invent an occasion for expressing his personal crotchets and also to produce some sort of rational and dignified argument to defend them. But a crusty, digressive old man like Miles Wallingford might be as crotchety and nostalgic as he liked when he wrote about the days of his youth and the evil changes that had taken place since that time. I have said that *Afloat and Ashore* is predominantly a melancholy book—a lament for a lost childhood, a lost youth, and a lost America; and so it is. But it is also a joyous book in so far as the author conspicuously feels that he can say any damned thing he pleases.

Corny Littlepage, however, is no *persona* for James Fenimore Cooper. So great a change did the Revolution make in opinions of educated upper-class New Yorkers that the point of view of Corny Littlepage is sharply differentiated from that of the author. It is further differentiated as a consequence of Corny's close association with the Dutch people who originally colonized New York and who were still, before the Revolution, numerically and culturally important. The post-revolutionary narrators of *The Chainbearer* and *The Redskins*, on the other hand, are forced to pass most of their time in the company of immigrant New Englanders, and their points of view tend to merge with that of Cooper.

Neither is *Satanstoe* a self-indulgent book in other respects. To be sure, Corny Littlepage's beloved York Colony is the ancestor of Cooper's beloved New York state; and the gusto with which old Dutch Albany customs are described reminds us that Albany was one of Cooper's own favourite places. In this respect *Satanstoe* is certainly a labour of love. It is also true that Corny Littlepage views the old Littlepage farm Satanstoe and the Mordaunt estate Lilacsbush through a haze of affection, since these were the places associated with his own childhood and with the beautiful Anneke Mordaunt. But Corny is never removed far enough from them, physically or temporally, to experience the aching nostalgia which Miles Wallingford feels for old Clawbonny when he is stranded on a Pacific island or when he is an aged man. By shortening and limiting the perspectives available to his narrator, Cooper not only reduces Corny's response to the emotionally charged materials of this novel, but he also creates a point of view—colonial, provincial, immature—whose very limitations provide us with good reasons for being glad that time does not stand still. With remarkable self-restraint, Cooper maintains this alien point of view throughout the entire novel, as Corny proceeds to express his provincial admiration for American architecture, his veneration for 'Home' (England), and his cheerful acceptance of political subservience:

It would seem that a party had been got up in town among the disloyal, and I might almost say, the disaffected, which claimed for the subject the right to know in what manner every shilling of the money raised by taxation was expended. This very obviously improper interference with matters that did not belong to them, on the part of the ruled, was resisted by the rulers, and that with energy; inasmuch as such inquiries and investigations would naturally lead to results that might bring authority into discredit, make the governed presuming and prying in their dispositions, and cause much derangement and inconvenience to the regular and salutary action of government.

After his sojourn in Europe, Cooper could not but be struck by the provincialism of the United States. It was a fact which hurt, baffled, and infuriated him as an American patriot: again and again he insisted that Americans grossly overvalued things of which they had no reason to be proud (such as American architecture, food, and higher education) but undervalued things in which they led the world (such as their political institutions, hospitality, or female beauty). What puzzled and enraged him was that American history had not taken the course which he considered natural and inevitable: clearly, almost by definition, colonial America was provincial in outlook; but political independence had been preceded by some large measure of intellectual independence; and it should have followed that having achieved its full political and economic majority, America would become no less mature intellectually and culturally— but when? Cooper was an impatient man, he did not see why the process should be so long and, to a travelled American Gentleman, so painful. But it would be a mistake to suppose that his assaults on American provincialism in works like *The Monikins, Home as Found*, and *Afloat and Ashore* represent some radically new development in his thought. On the contrary, as a student of Scott and the American Revolution, he was almost from the beginning of his literary career concerned with what may be termed the political provincialism of the American mind: no historical phenomenon interested him more than the mental shift from colonial allegiance to American independence. On this shift, or failure to shift, he based *The Spy, The Pilot, Lionel Lincoln*, and the later novel *Wyandotté* (1843). What interested him even more was the possibility of detecting signs of this mental shift during the period when, ostensibly and consciously, Americans were most loyal to 'home'. *The Red Rover, The Water Witch*, and *Satanstoe* are directly concerned with this incipient nationalism, as, somewhat incidentally, are *The Pathfinder* and *The Two Admirals*. Given this 'background' to his analyses of contemporary American cultural provincialism, it is not too much to say that he devoted the best part of his career to writing the history of American mental independence.

Cooper's qualifications to undertake the writing of this history were impressive. Thanks to his observations and research and conversations with those who had lived through the Revolution, he had a remarkable factual knowledge of American social and political life during the century preceding his death in 1851. Though married into the loyalist De Lancy family and thoroughly conservative in his social and religious feelings, he learned in time to venerate Jefferson as well as Washington, and he hated British politicians and political institutions with a vigour born of his conviction that they were the most fraudulent on earth. For the most part, these conflicting allegiances led to impartiality in his account of the battle between England and its colonies, between American Whigs and American Tories. So far as avowed political principles, as distinct from the secret motives of some of their human advocates, were concerned, he seems never to have seriously questioned the rightness of the revolutionists' cause; but he knew perfectly well that many of the American patriots were scoundrels. The Skinners in *The Spy*, for instance, are not so much rebels against Britain as against humanity. Even the disinterested patriot Harvey Birch is not free from moral taint. In *Wyandotté* a goodly number of the patriots are avaricious New Englanders who denounce their benevolent and pro-American (though English-born) landlord in order to steal his property. Such rogues are sufficiently historical and credible. But there is another type of mental rebel against British rule in Cooper's fiction which is more intriguing. I am thinking now of the madman Ralph in *Lionel Lincoln*, of the Rover in *The Red Rover*, and of Tom Tiller in *The Water Witch*. These characters are genuine patriots and at the same time men who live outside the pale of human society. That Cooper chose to make his prophets of American independence such morally ambivalent figures might seem to point to a secret and unconscious antipathy to *any* revolt against established authority. But this reading would be simple-minded as well as unverifiable. What is more to the point is that these three novels were heavily influenced by Shakespeare and Byron, and it was to them that he was indebted for the perception that the outlaw, the madman, the fool, occupy a vantage-point which sometimes enables them to see things more clearly than those who remain snugly within society. In the case of *Lionel Lincoln*, Ralph's madness is a personal affliction which has no generalizable political significance. But the outlawry of the Rover and Tom Tiller has political relevance because it is the result of their having had a foretaste of the oppression which later caused a majority of Americans to rebel against the established order.

And yet there is something showy and superficial about the Rover and Tom Tiller as precursors of the American Revolution; they really are eccentric figures whose grievances tell us only the most obvious things about the origins of the movement for American independence. Cooper came closer to the truth when, in *The Water Witch*, he depicted the unassimilated, avaricious Dutchman Van Beverout, and when in the same book he represented the heroine Alida wavering between the old Dutch manorial world represented by Van Staats and the new Anglo-Dutch colonial order represented by Ludlow. Whether consciously or not, the American colonists were gradually becoming a different people in their habits and values; and in the New York province, because of the large Dutch element, this process of alienation was not only more easily observed but also more easily dramatized by a writer working mainly in the tradition of Scott. Thus, of all Cooper's novels, it is *The Water Witch* which most clearly anticipates the main themes and methods of *Satanstoe*. In other respects, however, they are very different books, each a masterpiece of its particular kind and period.

In *Satanstoe* Corny Littlepage tells the story of his courtship of Anneke Mordaunt. The structure of the main narrative is extremely simple, consisting as it does of four large movements, the climax of each being achieved when Corny acts successfully as the protector of Anneke. The first movement concerns Corny's boyhood at Satanstoe and New York City, where, on a visit, he first encounters Anneke and defends her against a rude boy. In the second movement, now a young man fresh from college, Corny again encounters Anneke in New York, saves her from a mauling by a lion, and begins to court her. Then the action moves up the Hudson River to Albany, on the eve of Abercrombie's expedition against Ticonderoga; here Corny continues his courtship and saves Anneke from death when, during a sleigh-ride on the Hudson, the ice covering begins to break up. In the final movement, after fighting at Ticonderoga against the French, Corny joins Anneke at her father's wilderness estate Ravensnest, where he helps to protect her and the company from an attack by marauding French Indians.[1] At last, Anneke's knight is rewarded, he wins her hand as he had long since won her heart. Simple as this narrative structure is, it serves Cooper very well, and not merely because it gives him plenty of leisure and opportunity to describe a wide variety of York Colony customs.

As in *The Pathfinder* and, to a lesser degree, *The Water Witch*, the heroine of *Satanstoe* acts as a magnet, drawing to herself a wide variety of suitors. Like Corny, Anneke is of mixed Dutch and English ancestry. To two of her suitors, Corny's friend Dierck and Major Harry Bulstrode, she is fairly closely related. Corny, on the other hand, is only very distantly related to her. But it soon becomes clear that Corny and Anneke belong to a new breed with values and customs of its own. They may like and

---

[1] Dr Howard Erskine-Hill has pointed out to me that, at each major stage of the novel's development, there is an escalation of violence.

sympathize with their Dutch and English relations, but they do not wish to live with them. Roisterous and ill-educated, though manly and true, Cooper's Dutchmen belong to a different world. So does the English Bulstrode: worldly and supercilious, though fashionable, rich and brave, he is favoured by Anneke's Tory father but never touches Anneke's chaste provincial heart. So Anneke Mordaunt, though she calls England 'home' and never dreams of treason, chooses the Anglo-Dutch Cornelius Littlepage.

If in the marriage of Anneke and Corny like marries like, there is another pair of lovers in *Satanstoe* who are drawn together because they are so unlike each other. In Albany, Anneke's staid friend Mary Wallace, apparently of pure British descent, meets Guert Ten Eyck, a frolicsome Albany Dutchman. It is in connexion with this relationship that one begins to see the effectiveness of Cooper's narrative pattern. The journey in *Satanstoe* from lower New York, with its well-cultivated farms and growing metropolis, to the old Dutch town of Albany and the wilderness beyond, is, in effect, a journey into the past. The courtship of Anneke and Corny belongs, as they do themselves, to lower New York; and their marriage symbolizes the future development of America. But the painful and fruitless courtship of Mary Wallace and Guert Ten Eyck, of the British and the Dutch, belongs to Albany, to the past.

In reading *Satanstoe*, one is likely to regard Cooper's account of the abortive English expedition against Ticonderoga as a quite unnecessary digression from the main business of the novel. But this is not so. The main business of *Satanstoe* is to reveal something about the origins of the American independence movement. Certainly one of the principal causes of colonial loyalty was that the Americans regarded Britain as their protector against the French and Indians; and although the eventual victory of British arms in 1763 secured American loyalty for a few more years, the war that preceded it taught the colonials a good deal about their own military capabilities and about the vulnerability of British armies. Corny Littlepage's comments on the defeated Abercrombie are extremely relevant in this connexion:

A week before, and the name of Abercrombie filled every mouth in America: expectation had almost placed his renown on that giddy height where performance itself is so often insecure. In the brief interval, he was destroyed. Those who had been ready to bless him, would now heap curses on his devoted head, and none would be so bold as to urge aught in his favor. Men in masses, when goaded by disappointment, are never just. It is, indeed, a hard lesson for the individual to acquire; but released from his close, personal responsibility, the single man follows the crowd, and soothes his own mortification and wounded pride by joining in the cry that is to immolate a victim. Yet Abercrombie was not the foolhardy and besotted bully that Braddock had proved himself to be. His misfortune was, to be ignorant of the warfare of the region in which he was required to serve, and possibly to over-estimate the imaginary invincible character of the veterans he led. In a very short time he was recalled, and America heard no more of him. As some relief to the disgrace that had anew alighted on the British arms, Bradstreet, a soldier who knew the country, and who placed much reliance on the young man of her name and family whom I had met at Madame Schuyler's, marched against Frontenac, in Canada, at the head of a strong body of provincials; an enterprise that, as it was conducted with skill, resulted in a triumph.

It is surely unnecessary now to labour the point that the pattern of the action in *Satanstoe* is designed to exhibit Corny acting, with native daring and resourcefulness, as the protector of Anneke in a variety of American contexts. And Anneke makes no secret of the fact that her early preference for Corny was due to his valiant and effective protection.

I hope that this discussion of the design of *Satanstoe* does not make it seem dry, schematic, relentlessly didactic; for nothing could be farther from the truth. Not only is the narrative embedded in a rich and fascinating circumstantial reality, but it contains what is beyond dispute one of Cooper's greatest action sequences—the sleigh-ride on the Hudson River ice. Moreover, the tone of the novel, rather like that of *The Pioneers*, is usually genial and indulgent. Perhaps because Anneke is viewed through the affectionate eyes of her husband, she is one of Cooper's most attractive heroines. (The same is true, by the way, of Miles Wallingford's beloved Lucy in *Afloat and Ashore*.) In the permissive churchman Rev. Worden (the 'Loping Dominie'), the negro slave Jaap, and Dierck, *Satanstoe* has several excellent minor characters. But the finest characters in the novel—and they are among the finest Cooper ever created—are Guert Ten Eyck and the Danbury pedagogue Jason Newcome: here are Cooper's quintessential Dutchman and quintessential Yankee, carefully played off against each other and in the process becoming gigantic figures.

All this is to say, finally, that *Satanstoe* may well be Cooper's best, as it is certainly his most mature and finished, novel.[2] If I hesitate to say that it is his best, I do so because, for all its excellences, it lacks some of the qualities which one associates with Cooper's greatness. For one thing, the prose, while far from his unreadable worst, is scarcely up to the level of the prose of *The Pioneers*, parts of *The Pathfinder* and *The Deerslayer*, or, in a different vein, *Lionel Lincoln* or *The Water Witch*. But great fiction may be worse written than *Satanstoe*. What one does miss in *Satanstoe* (not as an inadequacy but as something unattempted and irrelevant to its design) is the mythic power and grandeur of conception that one frequently encounters in the Leatherstocking tales and especially in *The Pioneers*. In those works grandeur of conception is often coupled with a corresponding grandeur of expressive means, as though inspiration made Cooper write better than he knew how to write. There are few, if any, such moments in *Satanstoe*. Neither does this novel have any of the characteristic personal tensions—freedom *vs.* authority, progressivism *vs.* conservatism—which usually lie just below the surface of Cooper's best fiction. This is partly because Cooper's narrator, in spite of conflicting loyalties, is a relatively placid fellow. More important, perhaps, there was no reason why Cooper should try to express all his turbulent, contradictory feelings about American development in *Satanstoe*: there were two more books to record the loss of innocence that accompanied American independence. One can scarcely complain about the serenity of *Satanstoe*, but it is not Cooperesque. One is tempted to use the obsolete critical terminology of Cooper's contemporaries and predecessors and say that, while *Satanstoe* has all the beauty of a perfectly cultivated garden, the Leatherstocking tales at their best have the natural sublimity of the great American wilderness.

[2] I am here echoing the judgment of Robert E. Spiller, *Fenimore Cooper: Critic of his Times* (New York, 1931), p. 310. Professor Spiller has done more than any other critic to win recognition for *Satanstoe*, though others—notably George Sand, Lounsbury, and Yvor Winters—have made clear their admiration for this novel.

2. THE ANTI-RENT NOVELS

This is a convenient point to discuss a novel which not only anticipates many of the issues of the Anti-Rent trilogy but which in some measure fills in an important historical gap in that trilogy. *Wyandotté* (1843) appears to have been inspired, at least in part, by the early rumblings of the Anti-Rent controversy. As a personal friend of the Rensselaer family and frequent guest at their vast estate, where the Anti-Rent troubles began in 1839, Cooper must have been aware of the controversy almost as soon as it started. The controversy itself was extremely complicated, but its main points can be stated fairly simply. Many of the tenant farmers on the Rensselaer estate had been permitted to get into arrears in their rental payments; and when, on the death of the old Patroon in 1839, the heirs demanded payment of the arrears, the tenants formed Anti-Rent associations to resist evictions and forced sales of personal effects. Some of the tenants were certainly too impoverished to pay up; others, undoubtedly, were merely dishonest. But in either case, the Rensselaers, as owners of the property, were acting within their constitutional rights; and it soon became clear that the real aim of the tenant associations was, not to protect a few poor or evicted farmers, but to force the landlords to permit the tenants to own the land they now leased. It was argued that huge estates and tenant farming smacked of feudalism and were inimical to the spirit of a democratic republic. This feeling had existed long before 1839, but it now came out into the open and spread to other parts of New York, sometimes in the form of mobs and demonstrators disguised as Indians, after the patriotic fashion of the Boston Tea Party. Some of the state legislators sympathized with what they regarded as a democratic movement; others resisted it; and still others recognized it as a political opportunity. Legislation was passed which singled out the landlords for special taxes in order to induce them to sell. Other legislation was introduced to alter the laws of inheritance so that, upon the death of a landlord, his heirs would have to offer his lands for sale to the tenants. These measures Cooper rightly considered contrary to the spirit, if not the letter, of the federal constitution. Worse, he saw in this legislation the beginnings of mobocracy—nothing less than a national political crisis.[3]

When he eventually joined this controversy openly, in the prefaces to *Satanstoe* and *The Chainbearer* and in the whole of *The Redskins*, he became a well-nigh hysterical defender of the land-lords. But his basic case against the Anti-Renters was sound enough: in the first place, the Anti-Renters did not wish to abolish property; they merely wished to gain it for themselves. They agreed that property was sacred—except when it existed in quantities large enough to be leased. Given these assumptions about the nature and value of property, the tenants didn't have a moral, much less a legal, leg to stand on. But what infuriated Cooper most was that, in his view, the spirit which animated Anti-Rentism pretended to be that of patriotism whilst in fact it was that of cupidity. In the persons of the Skinners in *The Spy* he had already shown thieves of portable personal property masquerading as patriots. In *The Wept of Wish-ton-Wish* he had shown how, at great personal risk and expense, a retired English soldier and his family carved out an estate for themselves in the middle of the American wilderness. Now, in *Wyandotté*, he chose virtually to rewrite those two novels as one, this time exhibiting the English (but pro-American) landlord's hired agricultural labourers as land-thieves masquerading as patriots. *Wyandotté* does not refer directly to the Anti-Rent battles; its land-thieves are hired hands rather than tenants; but the appearance in the novel of unscrupulous white men disguised as Indians connects this tale of land piracy in 1775 with the unlawful activities of the early 1840's. As one might expect, the attempt to fuse *The Spy* and *The Wept* is unsuccessful: there are two separate, unrelated actions in the novel, one involving Captain Willoughby's relations with his (predictably Yankee) hired hands, the other involving his relations with the Indian Wyandotté (a rehash of Magua and Conanchet). Still, *Wyandotté* succeeds, as neither *Satanstoe* nor *The Chainbearer* do, in showing how the owner of an estate earns his right to it by virtue of his Crusoe-like hardships and resourceful actions. The reference to Defoe is Cooper's own, and it suggests how practical and primitive are the concerns of this 'border romance'.

[3] Cf. D. M. Ellis, 'The Coopers and New York Landholding Systems', *New York History*, vol. XXXV (1954), pp. 412–22.

But in this bleak, disillusioned work Captain Willoughby's Man Friday sticks a knife in his back.

The concerns of *The Chainbearer* are no less practical and primitive. Its plot can be dismissed as a mere mechanism designed to arrange a confrontation between Aaron Thousand-acres, a squatter on the Littlepage property, and Andries Coeje-mans *alias* Chainbearer, whose legendary honesty and accuracy have earned him a contract to survey that property. No reader of this novel can fail to recognize how closely Aaron Thousand-acres and his family are modelled after Ishmael Bush and his family or how closely Aaron's 'trial' of Chainbearer resembles Ishmael's 'trial' of Leatherstocking in *The Prairie*. So many of the novels of this period—*Wing-and-Wing, Wyandotté, Jack Tier* —reveal Cooper cannibalizing his own early work! Yet *The Chainbearer* is no mere rehash of *The Prairie*. The Bush family and the old trapper, it is true, are among Cooper's greatest and most original creations, and they win the reader's respect and sympathy to a degree that Chainbearer and the Thousandacres tribe never do. None the less, it is a weakness in *The Prairie* that Ishmael is wrenched out of his normal context and made to commit an uncharacteristic crime in order to bring together a variety of human types representing different stages of civili-zation. Aaron, however, is caught red-handed in his usual busi-ness of squatting on other men's property and harvesting their trees. Chainbearer, as the man who in advance of the owners establishes the true property boundaries, is the natural anta-gonist of one who, like Aaron, belongs to roughly the same stage of frontier development—a step ahead of civilization, a step behind savagery. Thousandacres sums up his relations with Chainbearer and Mordaunt Littlepage (son of Corny) neatly and poetically when he says to the former:

'You're woods, mainly; he's open country; and I'm clearin'. There's a difference atween each; but woods and clearin' come clussest; and so I'll say my say to you.'

What Aaron has to say is, in effect, that men should practise a sort of primitive form of communism in which use determines ownership and each man takes what he needs. Surrounded by the palpable evidence of his industry and having demonstrated his rude but ready hospitality, Thousandacres makes out a powerful case for himself and his loyal family, if not for the general applicability of his socio-economic principles.

Though the debate between Thousandacres and Chainbearer is sometimes tedious and the plot an altogether poor affair, *The Chainbearer* is remarkable for its effective use of symbolism. Cooper is quite conscious of the ambivalent meaning of the chains which old Andries drags through the free wilderness: how remote is this stern and righteous figure from old Leatherstocking, who would have shared so many of Aaron Thousandacres' views! But Chainbearer is none the less an impressive character. Cooper establishes his moral stature unforgettably by a single symbolic act early in the novel. The inhabitants of Ravensnest are about to raise a new 'meeting house':

The great body of the 'people' had just taken their stands at the first bent, ready for a lift, while trusty men stood at the feet of the posts, armed with crowbars, broad-axes, or such other suitable implements as offered, in readiness to keep those essential uprights in their places; for on the steadiness of these persons depended the limbs and lives of those who raised the bent. As this structure was larger than common, the danger was increased, and the necessity of having men that could be relied on was obviously so much the greater. Of one post, in particular, for some reason that I do not know, all the trusty men seemed shy; each declaring that he thought some one else better suited to take charge of it, than he was himself. The 'boss'—that Manhattanese word having travelled up to Ravensnest—called out for some one to take the delicate station, as nothing detained the work but the want of a hand there; and one looked at another, to see who would step forward, when a sudden cry arose of 'The Chainbearer!—the Chainbearer! Here's your man!'

Sure enough, there came old Andries Coejemans, hale, upright, vigorous, and firm-treading, though he had actually seen his three-score years and ten.

Other symbolic actions prepare the way for and conclude the debate at Thousandacres. Shortly before he first enters the squatters' secret clearing, Mordaunt Littlepage stumbles upon the bodily remains of a party of surveyors who, nearly thirty years earlier (in *Satanstoe*), were ambushed by the Indians who besieged Ravensnest—a memorial of the border during its earliest period and an omen of danger. Later, in the course of a furious argument, Chainbearer is mortally wounded by an

231

unidentified member of the Thousandacre family. The effect of this is to convict the entire family of murder—unfairly, of course, but not so unfairly as it might at first seem, since the joint criminality of the squatter family goes hand in hand with an admirable Old Testament family solidarity. Aaron himself, however, is the probable murderer; and he receives wilderness justice at the hands of the Indian Susquesus, who has befriended Chainbearer and the Littlepage family but retained the savage values of the aboriginal owners of the land.

Chainbearer has little of the circumstantial richness, still less of the human sweetness, of *Satanstoe*. It lacks the subtlety and finished design of that work. But by employing a concrete and unobtrusive symbolism and by sticking to the fundamentals of socio-economic debate, Cooper managed to write a highly didactic novel which retains its interest and power a century afterwards.

If *Chainbearer* is about half as good as *Satanstoe*, it is incomparably better than *The Redskins* (1846). This third member of the Littlepage trilogy is probably the only book Cooper ever wrote which can be justly termed contemptible. The narrator of *The Redskins* is Hugh Littlepage, a great grandson of Corny Littlepage, who returns to Ravensnest in 1845 (after a half-dozen years in Europe—all after the fashion of *Home as Found*) to find himself the victim of Anti-Rent agitation. Hugh's adventures in the guise of a German organ-grinder, the arsonist activities of Seneca Newcome (Jason's grandson), the dispersal of the Anti-Rent 'Injins' by a group of real Indians visiting one-hundred-and-twenty-year-old Susquesus—all these incidents are as crude as they are absurd. Hugh and his Uncle Ro Littlepage debate at great length and in great detail the rights of the landlords' and the wrongs of the tenants' claims. Their arguments are unbelievably repetitious and contradictory. The single truth which does emerge (unintentionally) from this barrage of propaganda—a truth which Judge William Cooper maintained and which James Fenimore must have accepted in his less hysterical moments—is that the leasehold system is inherently vicious. Cooper insists that cupidity is at the bottom of the troubles, and so it is. According to his own testimony, tenants, having no stake in the farms they till, build ramshackle houses and exhaust the soil; their improvements bring higher rents upon them; and though reinvestment will save the soil for posterity, that posterity might not be the actual descendants of the present tenants. Such neglect does not of course argue a moral right on the tenants' part to the property they abuse; but it does argue that no community can tolerate a system so wasteful of its present and future resources. As for Cooper's argument that large estates create the leisure necessary for culture and fine manners, which in turn set the tone for the community at large, his Hugh Littlepage, like his Eve Effingham in *Home as Found*, is the most damning refutation. An instance of Hugh's refinement is the following:

'I will pay the hundred dollars out of my own pocket-money, however, if that will buy it. Do say a good word for me, grandmamma!'
How prettily the hussy uttered that word of endearment, so different from the 'paw' and 'maw' one hears among the dirtynoses that are to be found in the mud-puddles!

But this precious fellow, so we are assured, plays the flute with rare skill. Alas, Cooper's ladies and gentlemen take such good care of their privacy that it is a little difficult to see how their pretty 'grandmammas' and melodies are to reach the improvable ears of their swinish neighbours. And as for the filial sentiments and noble sense of tradition which paternal acres are said to inspire in an 'old family', Uncle Ro Littlepage gives *that* show away:

' . . . I wish I had never parted with a foot of the old neck, though I did rather make money by the sale. But money is no compensation for the affections.'
'Rather make money, my dear sir! Pray, may I ask what Satanstoe was valued at, when you got it from my grandfather?'
'Pretty well up, Hugh; for it was, and indeed *is*, a first-rate farm. Including sedges and salt-meadow, you will remember that there are quite five hundred acres of it, altogether.'
'Which you inherited in 1829?'
'Of course; that was the year of my father's death. Why the place was thought to be worth about thirty thousand dollars at that time; but land was rather low in Westchester in 1829.'
'And you sold two hundred acres including the point, the harbor, and a good deal of the sedges, for the moderate-modicum of one hundred and ten thousand, cash. A tolerable sale, sir!'

'No, not cash. I got only eight thousand down, while thirty thousand were secured by mortgage.'

But he had done rather better with the old Mordaunt home Lilacsbush:

'I got three hundred and twenty-five thousand dollars, in hard cash. I would give no credit, and have every dollar of the money, at this moment, in good six per cent. stock of the States of New York and Ohio.'

And this is not all or even the worst. The worst, surely is that Cooper attempts to evade responsibility for the tone of *The Redskins*—for the endless sarcasm, the cheap jibes, the easy sneers, the pompous and self-righteous indignation—by blaming it all on his youthful narrator:

It may be well to add a word on the subject of the tone of this book. It is the language of a man who feels that he has been grievously injured, and who writes with the ardor of youth increased by the sense of wrong. As editors, we have nothing more to do with that than to see, while calling things by their right names, that language too strong for the public taste should not be introduced into our pages. As to the moral and political principles connected with this matter, we are wholly on the side of the Messrs. Littlepage, though we do not think it necessary to adopt all their phrases— phrases that may be natural to men in their situations, but which would be out of place, perhaps, in the mounts of those who act solely in the capacity of essayists and historians.

But this will never do. Hugh Littlepage is Cooper's *beau idéal*, Cooper's own advertisement for the advantages of great landed wealth; so far as this novel is concerned, Cooper must stand or fall by the way his narrator behaves. Moreover, it is very hard to believe that Hugh Littlepage does not mirror Cooper's own feelings. The moral blindness of *The Redskins* might be pardoned, but a compound of moral blindness and what looks remarkably like moral cowardice is something one supposed Cooper incapable of.

Thus in the Littlepage trilogy Cooper reaches the heights and depths of his fictional art. The trilogy fails to cohere, not merely because *The Redskins* is so appallingly bad, but because the generation between Mordaunt Littlepage and Hugh Littlepage is not accounted for, leaving a hiatus of something like sixty years. But taken together, *Satanstoe* and *The Chainbearer* do form an impressive, if incomplete, family chronicle novel which records the contrasting customs and attitudes of two generations of Americans, separated by the War of Independence. One wishes that the focus of *The Chainbearer* were not so narrow, since the contrast between the two generations is less rich and comprehensive than it might have been. Nevertheless, the contrast is sufficiently interesting—e.g. the prosperous and practised rascality of Jason Newcome in *The Chainbearer* differs from his fledgling covetousness in *Satanstoe*—sufficiently interesting to make it desirable to read the two novels as one. Read in this way, they form a work which is probably greater than any of his other works, always excepting the Leatherstocking saga.

XIV

THE WAYS OF THE HOUR

I. 'SEE-WISE'

WILLIAM HENRY SEWARD (1801–1872) is chiefly remembered as Lincoln's gifted if sometimes bumptious Secretary of State— as the adroit diplomatist who helped persuade England and France not to recognize the Confederacy, and as the prescient statesman who negotiated the purchase of Alaska. Certainly these were achievements of a high order, and it might well be argued that Seward never really came into his own until, under the steadying influence of Lincoln, he took charge of America's foreign relations. To his admiring contemporaries, however, he was primarily a great champion of domestic reform. As the first Whig Governor of New York (1838–42), he sought to end im-prisonment for debt, to improve schooling conditions for the children of immigrants, to assure trial by jury of fugitive slaves, and to end the Anti-Rent troubles by mediating between landlords and tenant farmers. Advocacy of such reforms placed him well to the left, not only of his own party, but of most Democrats as well. After his retirement from the governorship, he continued to gain fame as a liberal by acting as counsel for the defence in cases involving civil liberties. At least one of his defences, made on behalf of an imbecile negro murderer named Freeman, deserves to be remembered as a particularly coura-geous and eloquent plea for humanity—and one, too, which promised to be neither financially nor politically profitable.

For a time it appeared that Seward's political career was over; he was too far in advance of public opinion. But with the growth of Northern anti-slavery feeling, he began to emerge as a national leader of the 'Conscience-Whigs' (as distinguished from the 'Cotton-Whigs', North and South, who were interested in the growing or manufacturing of cotton). After the election of General Zachary Taylor as President in 1848, Seward became a U.S. Senator and one of Taylor's closest advisors. On the Senate floor he attacked both Calhoun's case for the extension of slavery into the U.S. territories, and the compromise measures advocated by Clay and Webster; behind the scenes he persuaded the President to think as he did on these issues. Taylor's death in the summer of 1850 allowed the Compromisers to triumph over Seward, but not before he had proven himself an outspoken and effective leader of the Free-Soil forces. During the ensuing decade he consolidated his position and, after joining the newly formed Republican party in 1855, became a strong contender for the presidential nomination. Indeed, his nomination in 1860 seemed a certainty, and had it not been for the place of the convention (Illinois) and the spiteful machinations of his old friend Horace Greeley, William Henry Seward might well have been the sixteenth President of the United States.[1]

Seward considered himself a disciple of John Quincy Adams —the foe of slavery, champion of the Union, and ardent friend of internal improvements. A graduate of Union College, he shared the ex-President's keen and informed interest in letters and sciences. No more than Adams was he an orator in the grand manner of Webster or Clay, but he had a felicitous style and a gift for memorable if ambiguous phrases: 'a higher law than the Constitution' and 'irrepressible conflict' stirred the nation in a way that old Quincy Adams's relentless logic never could. He also had what Adams notably lacked, a genial permissive temperament which made him one of the most personally attractive politicians of his era.

Unlike Adams, too, he was regarded by many observers as a shifty demagogue who espoused popular causes in order to achieve political power. Southern hatred of Seward was of course intense. (A nearly successful attempt on his life was made

[1] The important published sources for a study of Seward's career are Frederick Bancroft, *The Life of William Henry Seward* (2 vols., New York, 1900); Frederick W. Seward, *William H. Seward: An Autobiography* (3 vols., New York, 1891); *The Works of William Henry Seward*, ed. G. E. Baker (3 vols., New York, 1853–61). Also indispensable for a study of Seward is Thurlow Weed's *Autobiography* (2 vols., Boston, 1883–84).

shortly before the assassination of Lincoln.) But even among Northern Whigs of a certain class—the New York city bankers and Boston manufacturers in particular—he was considered a reckless, inflammatory character. American nativists, Cooper's old friend Samuel F. B. Morse among them, were horrified by Seward's warm relations with New York's Irish immigrants. As for Cooper himself, he regarded Seward as one of the most vicious and dangerous demagogues of the day. Almost with his last breath, in the last work he published during his lifetime, he took Seward as the model of what Americans had to fear most in their political affairs.

Cooper had good reason to be distrustful of the New York politician's motives and company. Seward was the personal friend and political protégé of the Albany editor and 'king-maker' Thurlow Weed, leader of the band of Whig journalists who libelled Cooper and then, as a revenge for defeats in court, refused to review his books. Unlike Seward, Weed was an un-cultivated, entirely political animal who desired one thing: the success of his party. As Weed shrewdly perceived, electoral success in post-Jacksonian America depended on cultivating the good will of two opposed factions: the affluent but conservative commercial classes, for their contributions to campaign funds; the newly enfranchised masses, for their votes. In his *Autobiography*, Weed openly boasts of his influence with New York City's 'merchant princes':

From year to year questions affecting the commercial interests of New York were introduced into the legislature. I made it my business to see that while wholesome laws were enacted, unjust or oppressive ones should be defeated, and ere long New York merchants, who never asked for anything that was wrong or opposed anything that was right, advised me of their wishes in reference to legislation, giving themselves no further trouble about it.[2]

He adds that 'suggestions of compensation' were made to him but declined. Why should the merchants pay double duty? They always paid 'liberally and cheerfully' when he came to them for campaign contributions. They must have contributed handsomely to the expensive campaign which Weed organized for the Whigs in 1840. Concerning the stunts and gimmicks which

[2] Weed, *Autobiography*, vol. I, p. 503.

replaced issues in the Whig campaign of that year, Weed comments cheerfully and cynically, 'To appeals of this character there was no answer, and for two or three weeks before the election intelligent Democrats saw that songs, log cabins, and hard cider were carrying the masses against Van Buren.' [3] Indeed, he was so sure of the gullibility of the people, and of his own ability to be the one who gulled them, that during the 1846 New York State Constitutional Convention he worked hard and successfully for such popular measures as an elective judiciary.[4] Weed may have had, probably did have, certain liberal inclinations: but he also knew that to profess liberalism, and even to practise it at times, was the ticket to political success in mid-nineteenth-century America.

If Seward's association with Weed was bound to be compromising in Cooper's eyes, his equivocating attitude to the Anti-Renters was positively damning. It was during Seward's first term as governor (in 1840) that the Anti-Rent troubles first became violent, and he immediately recognized that Anti-Rentism was an explosive issue. He had in the first place to restore order by calling out the state militia in the dead of winter. To placate the militia and other law-abiding citizens was his next task: he extolled their courage and self-sacrifice and asked the legislature to compensate them generously. But this was not enough: he had to placate the Anti-Renters too—deploring their recourse to violence but approving their brave opposition to the feudal, un-American institution of landlordism.[5] Seward himself was neither a rich man nor a member of the old ruling class of New York state, and it is likely that his disapproval of the Rensselaers and Morrises was perfectly genuine. But, as will emerge later, he was also well aware that it would be impolitic not to appease the Anti-Renters.

Cooper also had first-hand evidence of Seward's lack of candour—or perhaps he might have said, Seward's audacious disregard for the truth. One of Cooper's last libel suits was against Horace Greeley, editor of the New York *Tribune* and close

---

[3] *ibid.*, p. 493.
[4] G. G. Van Deusen, *Thurlow Weed: Wizard of the Lobby* (Boston, 1947), pp. 143-4. Van Deusen's is a scholarly and generally sympathetic study of Weed—more sympathetic, perhaps, than he deserves.
[5] Seward, *Works*, vol. II, pp. 354-69.

political associate of Seward and Weed. Greeley's editorial response to an action for libel brought against him by Cooper had been to add further libel: 'Mr Cooper will have to bring his suit *somewhere*. He will not like to bring it in New-York, for we are known here, nor in Otsego, for *he* is known there.' [6] The imputation is unmistakable: that among those who know them well Greeley has a good character and Cooper a bad one. Greeley's lawyer in this case was Seward, whose defence took the form of a lofty and not unimpressive plea for Freedom of the Press. But he condescended to a more particular defence of the most offensive passage:

> The libel reiterates and applies to the plaintiff a truism stamped with even divine truth, and if the sentiment complained of be *libelous*, then the Methodist Book Concern, and the Society for Propagating the Gospel, are dangerous engines. 'A prophet is not without honour but in his own country and among his own kin, and in his own house.'—*Mark* 6: 4. 'For Jesus himself testified that a prophet had no honour in his own country.'—*John* 4: 44.
> The sting of the libel in this case, if there be any, is in intimating that a party bringing an action would prefer a trial where the piques, the rivalries and prejudices which assail every man at home could not reach him.[7]

Seward's gloss on Greeley's text is patently disingenuous and even irreligious. So it would surely have seemed to Cooper. We may suspect, however, that Seward did not expect it to be taken seriously—it was an attempt to deflate Cooper by suggesting that he had made a fool of himself by assuming the roles of prophet and martyr. Self-righteous and humourless as Cooper was in his libel suits, he invited the witty thrusts of the Whig lawyer and the crude but often hilarious invective of the Whig editors. Seward's plea saved Greeley.

During the spring and summer of 1850 Seward was engaged in his battle with the Compromisers and Calhounites in the U.S. Senate. It was also during this period that Cooper wrote a short allegorical piece called *The Lake Gun* in which he attacked demagogues by means of an Indian fable of his own invention.

---

[6] Quoted from E. Outland, *The 'Effingham' Libels on Cooper* (Madison, 1929), p. 132. For Seward's defence of Greeley before the New York State Supreme Court on 14 May 1845, see Seward, *Works*, vol. I, pp. 391–408.

[7] Seward, *Works*, vol. I, p. 395.

The villain of the piece is a Seneca chief named See-wise who flatters the young braves and urges them to fish out of season and in various other ways to break divine and human laws. See-wise himself aspires to become the 'principal chief', but he is at last thwarted by the 'aged chieftains' who, with the connivance of the Manitou, transform him into a log condemned to float for a thousand years on Lake Seneca. Sometimes a noise like thunder is heard over the lake, and this, so we are told, is the voice of the Manitou forbidding See-wise to fish. Cooper's fable concludes with this moral:

There is a remarkable resemblance between this little incident in the history of the Senecas and events that are passing among our pale-faced race of the present age. Men who, in their hearts, really care no more for mankind than See-wise cared for the fish, lift their voices in the shouts of a spurious humanity, in order to raise themselves in the arms of those they call the people.[8]

After considering the possibility that 'Sea-wise' might be Clay or Calhoun (the frustration of See-wise on the lake corresponding to their frustration after failing to secure the presidential nomination in 1848), Professor Spiller identifies the countenance of the demagogue—'the forehead retreated, the face was hatchet-shaped, while the entire expression was selfish, yet undecided'—as belonging to William Henry Seward.[9] Clay and Calhoun are dismissed because, according to Professor Spiller, 'Cooper was not . . . much agitated by the problem of slavery and he had never taken a consuming interest in national politics.' [10] Seward, rather than Clay or Calhoun, is indicated because of his record as a state politician and his association with Weed and Greeley. As we now know, Cooper's interest in national politics was much stronger than Professor Spiller supposed in 1932.[11] None the less, he was almost certainly right to identify Seward with See-wise—for, from Cooper's political point of view, there was indeed 'a remarkable resemblance' between See-wise's career among the Senecas and Seward's among the Senators in Washington.

[8] Cooper, *The Lake Gun*, ed. by Robert E. Spiller (New York, 1932), pp. 53–4.
[9] *ibid.*, pp. 16–17.   [10] *ibid.*, pp. 15–16.
[11] It was Dorothy Whaples' brilliant dissertation *The Whig Myth of James Fenimore Cooper* (New Haven, 1938) which first fully revealed Cooper's consuming interest in national politics.

Always a strong Unionist, Cooper ridiculed the doctrine of States' Rights including of course the 'right' of secession. He also made short work of all the other Calhounite arguments in favour of the expansion of slavery, regarding them as obvious innovations on the Constitution.[12] At the same time, in spite of the strong anti-slavery influences exerted upon him by Lafayette, Jefferson, and the Jays, he had never been persuaded that domestic slavery was, of itself, a sinful institution. In 1838, following Jefferson, he was prepared to attack slavery on the grounds that it invited, and so was an accessory to, moral corruption;[13] but by 1850, irritated by the clamour of the abolitionists, he allowed one of his characters in *The Ways of the Hour* (the lawyer Dunscomb, Cooper's mouthpiece) to maintain that 'African slavery is an important feature in God's laws, instead of being disobedience to them.' Like a majority of Americans in 1850, he was as impatient with Northern as with Southern 'fanatics' and firebrands.

The political crisis of 1850, over whether slavery should be legalized in the U.S. Territories which were then seeking admission as states, at first found Cooper in the camp of those who held that California should be admitted *only* as a 'free' state. This at any rate is the position taken by lawyer Dunscomb in *The Ways of the Hour:*

As respects your Free Soil, it may be well to put down a foot; and so far as votes legally used can be thrown, to prevent the further extensions of slavery. In this respect you are right enough, and will be sustained by an overwhelming majority of the nation. . . .

It was also the position taken by President Taylor—and by W. H. Seward. Cooper seems to have admired the old Whig

---

[12] These refutations of the Southern pro-slavery spokesmen, chiefly Calhoun, are given their final and definitive form in Cooper's last work, a history of New York City which was to have been called 'The Towns of Manhattan'. After a weird publishing history, it survives only in a fragmentary way, the largest part of it in a short-lived daily periodical *The Spirit of the Fair* (New York, 1864), nos. for 5–9 April and 13–15 April. This part was reprinted in book form under the title *New York* (New York, 1930), with an introduction by Dixon Ryan Fox. Other fragments of the work, which Cooper himself did not complete, have been brought together in James F. Beard, Jr, 'The First of Greater New York: Unknown Portions of Fenimore Cooper's Last Work', *New York Historical Society Quarterly* (April, 1953), vol. XXXVII, No. 2, pp. 109–45. Cooper's main arguments against Calhounism are to be found in *Spirit of the Fair*, pp. 30–1 and 42–3.

[13] *American Democrat*, pp. 171–6.

general's firm stand on this issue, though he had originally
opposed his election;[14] but it was something new for Cooper
and Seward to be on the same side. The alliance did not last
long; for in his Senate speech of 11 March 1850, in which he
championed Free Soil, Seward also spoke ambiguously of a
'higher law than the Constitution' in such a way as to suggest
that the Fugitive Slave clause of the Constitution might be
violated with good conscience. The 'Higher Law' speech
created a national sensation, which Seward encouraged by
mailing out 100,000 copies of the speech. He then proceeded to
shuffle, giving various accounts of his meaning. In any event,
with Taylor's death not long afterwards, Seward's influence
dwindled; the compromise measures of Clay and Webster, by
which California was required to decide for itself whether it
wanted slavery, were pushed through Congress against Southern
and Free Soil opposition and signed into law by Seward's
enemy, President Fillmore. Cooper, giving his blessing to the
Compromise of 1850,[15] now found himself cheek by jowl with
the old Whig stalwarts Webster and Clay.

The Compromise of 1850 marked the triumph of the 'aged
chieftains' and, so far as Cooper was concerned, the eclipse and
frustration of a vicious demagogue. Cooper himself fervently
believed that there was a 'higher law than the Constitution',
but he also believed, almost as fervently, that the Fugitive Slave
clause should be enforced and would be were it not for the encouragement given to abolitionists by demagogues:

There might be a hope that the well-intentioned portion of these
people, and it is both numerous and respectable, could be induced
to adopt a wiser mode of procedure, were it not that dissolute
politicians, who care only for the success of parties, and who make a
stalking-horse of philanthropy, as they would of religion or
patriotism, or any other extended feeling that happened to come

---

[14] *Correspondence of James Fenimore Cooper*, ed. James Fenimore Cooper [II]
(New Haven, 1922), vol. II, pp. 667 and 594-8: Letters to Mrs Cooper (20 Feb.
1850) and Samuel Harris (5 Sept. 1848). Cooper's reasons for opposing Taylor
were on the familiar grounds that the General, as a Whig, favoured English
principles of government—i.e. legislative usurpation. In practice, however,
Taylor acted like a good Democrat by insisting on the prerogatives of the Executive. Cooper may also have suspected that Taylor would be the creature of Weed
and Seward.

[15] *Spirit of the Fair*, p. 54.

within their influence, interpose their sinister schemes to keep agitation alive for their benefit.[16]

Well did Cooper know that some abolitionists were both 'well-intentioned' and 'respectable', since his old and much-loved friend William Jay was one of the most famous anti-slavery writers.[17] But he had become convinced that Anti-Renters and the friends of fugitive slaves belonged, in the end, to the same party—the party which, in the name of liberty and humanity, violated divine commandments and the fundamental laws of society. The following words, though relating to violators of the Fugitive Slave clause, might equally well apply to the rebellious tenants of New York:

To us, it would seem that the portion of the people of this country, whom we should term the disinterested, or those who have no direct connection with slavery, on the one hand, or with fanaticism, and its handmaid demagogism, on the other, should turn their attention solely to the achievement of a single object. They have the strength to do it, if they only had the will. By compelling the disturbers of the public peace to submit to the control of the government, and to cease their meddling and wanton invasion of the security and property of their brothers and neighbors, the question of slavery would soon take care of itself.

Seward was the 'demagogue' both of Anti-Rentism and Abolitionism. As such, more than any other politician of his time he represented those forces in American public life which Cooper feared and hated most. It is perhaps worth remarking that the conclusion of *The Lake Gun*, though it refers to Seward's political defeat of 1850, foreshadows and virtually sanctions the attempted assassination of 1865.

2. COOPER'S LAST NOVELS

Nevertheless, the community will live on, suffer, and be deluded: it may even fancy itself almost within the reach of perfection, but it will live on to be disappointed. There is no such thing on earth,— and the only real question for the American statesman is, to measure the results of different defective systems for the government of the

---

[16] *Spirit of the Fair* p. 54.
[17] Cf. Louis Filler, *The Crusade Against Slavery* (New York, 1960), pp. 62 and 102-3.

human race. We are far from saying that our own, with all its flagrant and obvious defects, will be the worst, more especially when considered solely in connection with whole numbers; though we cannot deny, nor do we wish to conceal, the bitterness of the wrongs that are so frequently inflicted by the many on the few. This is, perhaps, the worst species of tyranny. He who suffers under the arbitrary power of a single despot, or by the selfish exactions of a privileged few, is certain to be sustained by the sympathies of the masses. But he who is crushed by the masses themselves, must look beyond the limits of his earthly being for consolation and support. The wrongs committed by democracies are of the most cruel character, and though wanting in that apparent violence and sterness that marks the course of law in the hands of narrower governments, for it has no need of this severity, they carry with them in their course all the feelings that render injustice and oppression intolerable.[18]

This unforgettable paragraph from Cooper's last work, his unfinished history of the towns of Manhattan, sums up the characteristic themes and attitudes of his last novels—and expresses them in a more dignified and moving way than do the novels themselves. The three novels which I have not already discussed—*The Crater* (1847), *The Oak Openings* (1848), and *The Ways of the Hour* (1850)—cannot be said to offer many surprises to the reader who is already familiar with other works of the same period. In all three novels we encounter the religiosity, or what can sometimes be called the religious vision, of *The Sea Lions*. In *The Crater* and *The Ways of the Hour* we are again shown how 'the people' are easily duped and how they abuse their freedoms, victimizing Cooper's genteel, well-heeled heroes and heroines. Yet if they are in this sense redundant, they are nevertheless remarkably energetic narratives; and *The Ways of the Hour* and *The Crater* show how, right up to the end, Cooper responded to the pressure of his materials by experimenting with new fictional forms.

Probably the weakest of the three novels is his last, *The Ways of the Hour*. Inspired by his own experiences in court and by his fears that the new elective judiciary would prove a feeble judiciary unable to counteract the credulousness of juries, *The Ways of the Hour* is a mystery-cum-courtroom novel which demonstrates the way class prejudices, hostile newspaper reports, and

[18] *Spirit of the Fair*, p. 114.

legal sharp practices could combine to convict the innocent. As a *demonstration* the work is almost entirely convincing; for Cooper's knowledge of the workings of the Press and the courtroom was both comprehensive and detailed. Moreover, the tone of the work is not cranky or irascible: Cooper is willing to admit that the judicial reforms of 1846, promoted enthusiastically by Weed and Seward, were not entirely evil. But as a novel *The Ways of the Hour* is a poor performance indeed: the characters are colourless stereotypes and the air of mystery surrounding the beautiful victimized heroine is as contrived and boring as such airs usually are. It is none the less impressive to find Cooper, in other respects so hardened in reaction, still trying out the possibilities of new fictional forms—seeking new ways of expressing and commenting on the shifting surface of American life.

In sharp contrast to *The Ways of the Hour* is the last of Cooper's Indian adventure stories, *The Oak Openings*. As an exciting tale of flight and pursuit in the wilds of Michigan during the War of 1812, it belongs to the genre which Cooper invented in *The Last of the Mohicans*. What is more, its central theme—genocidal conflict—is one which Cooper largely abandoned after *The Wept of Wish-ton-Wish* but which was crucial in the early Leatherstocking tales. At least one of the reasons why he returned to this theme must have been that the wholesale acquisition of new territories which occurred at this time, involving the United States in a brutal war with Mexico, gave fresh life and urgency to the moral questions inevitably raised by the American Westward Movement. Cooper, like a good Democratic supporter of President Polk, approved of the war and welcomed the addition of new territory. But how justify the war? Mexico had provoked it, Polk said and Cooper believed. In any case, like other American expansionists,[19] Cooper now openly identified Manifest Destiny with Divine Providence in such a way as to justify almost any white American oppression of other peoples:

The ways of Divine Providence are past the investigations of human reason. How often, in turning over the pages of history, do we find civilization, the arts, moral improvement, nay, Christianity itself, following the bloody train left by the conqueror's car, and good pouring in upon a nation by avenues that at first were teeming only

[19] Cf. Van Deusen, *Jacksonian Era*, p. 239, and H. N. Smith, *Virgin Land*, pp. 3–51.

with the approaches of seeming evils! In this way there is now reason
to hope that America is about to pay the debt she owes to Africa,
and in this way will the invasion of the forests and prairies and
'openings' of the redmen be made to atone for itself by carrying with
it the blessings of the gospel, and a juster view of the relations which
man bears to his Creator. Possibly Mexico may derive lasting benefit
from the hard lesson that she has so recently been made to endure.

This formula satisfied Cooper in 1848 as it had not twenty years
earlier, when in spite of his unclouded view of white American
civilization he was nevertheless deeply troubled by the destruction of the aboriginal American way of life—not to mention the
destruction of the aboriginal Americans themselves. Now, ironically, when bitterly disillusioned with his fellow white Americans,
he fell back without a qualm on the rationalizations of the *con-
quistadores*. It is difficult not to conclude that in his old age, as a
result of his friction with 'fanatics' and 'demagogues', Cooper
had grown morally callous. But something more than callous-
ness was involved. As his alienation from American society
increased, so did his commitment to religion: and as his religious
experience deepened, it also narrowed: he became what his
earliest writings explicitly condemned—a zealous and bigoted
Christian missionary. And so the long series of Indian tales
which began with *The Pioneers*, in which the aged Chingachgook
dies magnificently repudiating the white man's religion, ends
with *The Oak Openings*, in which the Magua-like Scalping Peter
experiences a spectacular conversion, assumes the white man's
garb, and learns in his old age to speak, as Leslie Fiedler has
pointed out,[20] remarkably like Uncle Tom:

'Stranger, love God. B'lieve his Blessed Son, who pray for dem dat
kill Him. Injin don't do dat. Injin not strong enough to do such a
t'ing. It want de Holy Spirit to strengthen de heart afore man can
do so great t'ing. When he got de force of de Holy Spirit, de heart of
stone is changed to de heart of woman, and we all be ready to bless
our enemy and die. I have spoken. Let dem dat read your book
understand.'

If Cooper could use the Christian religion to wash away the
white American's guilt, he could also use it (fictionally) to
expunge white American civilization. In *The Crater* Mark Woolston discovers a paradisal isle in the Pacific, colonizes it with

[20] Fiedler, *Love and Death in the American Novel*, pp. 195-6.

Americans, and established a stable republican government; after a few years, because of the divisive activities of ministers, editors, and demagogues, Mark's tiny state turns into an irresponsible mobocracy; bitterly disappointed, Mark leaves for a while and returns only to find that the island with all its inhabitants has disappeared in the ocean. Cooper repeatedly stresses the paradisal qualities of Vulcan's Peak. Like Natty Bumppo's or Judge Temple's America, it is God's Garden, bestowed on men to use and not abuse. Now the myth of the Garden of the New World is developed to its logical conclusion: given the opportunity to re-create society in a new Eden, men because of their fallen nature violate the clearest laws of God and man; they are ejected or destroyed; the new Eden disappears, leaving mankind more or less where it was. Here there can be no question of condemning the white colonists for destroying heathen tribes or justifying them because they introduced the blessings of the gospel; for in *The Crater* Cooper makes his paradise previously uninhabited. This eliminates the uncomfortable but novelistically fruitful ambiguities of the Garden myth as originally applied to America: Mark's settlers turn out to be nothing more than despoilers of the Garden, and can therefore be destroyed with a clear conscience.

The man who wrote *The Crater* and *The Oak Openings* was one who could no longer tolerate moral ambivalence or uncertainty. The effect of his personal sufferings, which though chiefly mental were real and acute, was to radically contract the range of his sympathies. His religion afforded him consolation: but we may question the purity, though not the intensity, of a religious vision which enabled him to see the crimes of his people punished or atoned for with so little inconvenience to himself.

The bulk of *The Crater*, however, is concerned with the discovery and colonization of Vulcan's Peak and adjacent islands. This part of the narrative, which owes much to *Robinson Crusoe*[21] and more to the author's early experience of Cooperstown, is a notable contribution to island literature. Mark's initial hardships on Crater Island, his laborious but ultimately successful efforts to introduce vegetation on the island, then his discovery of Vulcan's Peak (its secret Garden hidden behind a forbidding

[21] Cf. W. B. Gates, 'A Note on Cooper and Robinson Crusoe', *Modern Language Notes* (1952), vol. LXVII, pp. 421–2.

coast), and finally the colonization and establishment of government on the chain of islands which Mark has discovered—all these are described with the gusto and circumstantiality of Cooper's best work. Nothing was more congenial to his imagination than planning and 'improving': his profound interest in the early history of Cooperstown; a lifetime's correspondence on matters of naval reform; even an ambitious plan for revamping New York harbour[22]—these reveal how deeply and totally he could enter into utopian schemes. Despite the numerous reverses which his hopes had suffered, his was essentially an optimistic nature which had to find some creative outlet. It found that outlet—an almost unlimited one—in the fictional islands of *The Crater*, which seem not to be so much discovered by Mark as created by Cooper, one after another, according to the needs of his imagination. So much so that the creative phase of the novel surges through some twenty-eight chapters, while the reversal of fortunes is crowded into two. This abbreviated conclusion—caused probably by the exigencies of publishing—has a disastrous effect. Crammed into a single chapter, the account of the social and political decline of the island community is absurdly perfunctory—an allegorical caricature of the decline of the American republic. Having lavished so much attention on the slow, communal development of the colony, Cooper has built up something whose abrupt destruction in the final chapter cannot be accepted without a sense of cosmic injustice. This is the opposite of what he intended; and while it is a considerable achievement to have created a thing whose loss can be felt, the final effect of *The Crater* is one of moral chaos.

In his invaluable introduction to *The Crater*,[23] Thomas Philbrick argues persuasively that this utopia, or anti-utopia, was probably triggered off by the Fourierist rage of the 1840's, which had been given much encouragement by a series of articles in Horace Greeley's *Tribune*. Cooper's attitude to Fourier's socialist theories is brought out clearly in a passage which describes Mark Woolston's attempts to plan a more sensible, hence more durable, utopian community:

Mark Woolston was much too sensible a man to fall into any of the modern absurdities on the subject of equality, and a community

[22] Cf. Beard, *New York Historical Society Quarterly*, pp. 112–13.
[23] *The Crater, or Vulcan's Peak*, ed. Thos. Philbrick (Cambridge, Mass. 1962).

of interests. One or two individuals, even in that day, had wished to accompany him, who were for forming an association in which all property should be shared in common. . . . He was of opinion that civilization could not exist without property, or property without a direct personal interest in both its accumulation and preservation.[24]

And on the principle that 'so long as a man toiled for himself and those nearest and dearest to him, society had a security for his doing much',[25] Mark makes sure that each family in his community has its own private piece of ground. (Here, by implication, Cooper retracts his theoretical defence of the paternalistic landlord system!) This and other measures represent Mark's—and Cooper's—effort to do a better job of utopian planning than the American Founding Fathers had done. The failure of Mark's community is thus a pessimistic commentary, not only on the way American society and government seemed to be developing, but on the very possibility of planning a really successful community.

In a less apocalyptic but no less disillusioned mood than when he wrote *The Crater*, Cooper predicted in 1850–1 that one of three things might happen to the United States:

To us, it would seem that the future of this country holds out but three possible solutions of the tendencies of the present time—viz. the bayonet, a return to the true principles of the original government, or the sway of money. For the first it may be too soon, the pressure of society is scarcely sufficient to elevate a successful soldier to the height of despotism, though the ladder has been raised more than once against the citadel of the Constitution by adventurers of this character, through the folly and heedless impulses of the masses.[26]

The adventurers Cooper had in mind were, clearly, Taylor and Harrison, both of them the candidates of Thurlow Weed; but even Jackson may have been included in Cooper's vague indictment. He did not live to see General Winfield Scott defeated in the presidential election of 1852: in 1851 it did indeed appear that a successful general, no matter how unfit for the office, need only run to be elected. However, Cooper was less disconcerted by genuinely popular decisions—however misguided—than he was by the paralysis of the democratic system through the influence of parties:

[24] *The Crater, or Vulcan's Peak*, pp. 299–300. [25] *ibid.*, pp. 324–5.
[26] *Spirit of the Fair*, p. 102.

The people have yet to discover that the seeming throes of liberty are nothing but the breath of their masters, the demagogues, and that at the very moment when they are made to appear to have the greatest influence on public affairs, they really exercise the least. Here, in our view, is the great danger to the country—which is governed, in fact, not by its people, as is pretended, but by factions that are themselves controlled most absolutely by the machinations of the designing. A hundred thousand electors, under the present system of caucuses and conventions, are just as much wielded by command as a hundred thousand soldiers in the field. . . .[27]

That he was right goes almost without saying—what has been remarked about the activities and influence of Thurlow Weed indicates what Cooper had in mind.

But what happened when the national party system itself became paralysed?—

The particular form in which this imminent danger is now, for the first time seriously since the establishment of the Government, beginning to exhibit itself, is through the combinations of the designing to obtain a mercenary corps of voters, insignificant as to numbers, but formidable by their union, to hold the balance of power, and to effect their purposes by practising on the wilful, blind, wayward, and, we might almost add, fatal obstinacy of the two great political parties of the country. Here, in our view, is the danger that the nation has most to apprehend. The result is as plain as it is lamentable. In effect, it throws the political power of the entire Republic into the hands of the intriguer, the demagogue, and the knave. Honest men are not practised on by such combinations; but, with a fatality that would seem to be the very sport of demons, there they stand, drawn up in formidable array, in nearly equal lines of open and deriding hostility, leading those who no longer conceive it necessary to even affect the semblance of respect to many of the plainest and most important of the principles of social integrity that have ever been received among men.[28]

For the best part of twenty years Cooper himself had been a partisan Democrat: but he had long counted many important Whig politicians among his personal friends, and by 1851 he found himself endorsing the policies of Clay and Webster. The Whigs were, at any rate, infinitely preferable to the abolitionist-inspired Free Soil party or the Hell-inspired Anti-Rent party. 'Insignificant as to numbers, but formidable by their

[27] *ibid.*, pp. 54–5.   [28] *ibid.*, p. 90.

union', the Free Soilers in the national election of 1848 and the Anti-Renters in the state election of 1846 had in fact held the balance of power between the two major parties. Led by a renegade Martin Van Buren, the New York Free Soilers took enough votes away from the regular Democratic party nominee, Lewis Cass, to deliver the state to Taylor; the loss of New York gave the Whigs the election. A less important but much more striking instance of the power exerted by a minority party occurred in the 1846 state election, when the Anti-Rent party, rather than running their own candidates for the highest offices, endorsed the Whig candidate Young for the governorship and the Democratic candidate Gardiner for the lieutenant-governorship. Both won. Other factors undoubtedly played a part in the defeat of the incumbent Governor, Silas Wright,[29] but Seward, who was one of the shrewdest political observers of the period, believed that Anti-Rentism was at the bottom of Wright's failure to regain office:

> Today I have been at St Peter's and heard one of those excellent discourses of Dr Potter. There was such a jumble of the wrecks of parties in the church, that I forgot the sermon, and fell to moralizing on the vanity of political life. You know my seat. Well, half way down the west aisle sat Silas Wright, wrapped in a coat tightly buttoned to the chin, looking philosophic, which it is hard to affect and harder to attain. On the east side sat Daniel D. Barnard, upon whom 'Anti-Rent' has piled Ossa, while Pelion only has been rolled upon Wright.[30]

Barnard, like Hamilton Fish the defeated candidate for the lieutenant-governorship, was a Whig; both were friends of Cooper. Silas Wright, though he had not repressed the Anti-Renters savagely enough to satisfy Cooper, had acted firmly enough to cause the rebellious tenants to dislike him. Well might Seward moralize over the political mishaps of Wright, who was a more consistent and sincere liberal than himself: he, Seward, had managed things more adroitly, and, pray God, would do so in the future.

Cooper was not, therefore, without reasons for thinking that American democracy was breaking up. He still believed that

---

[29] Cf. J. A. Garrety, *Silas Wright* (New York, 1949), pp. 376–88.
[30] *Seward: An Autobiography*, vol. II, p. 34.

the Union would endure, and even at the end he could sometimes recover his old enthusiasm for the national destiny:

Then, the increasing and overshadowing power of the nation is of a character so vast, so exciting, so attractive, so well adapted to carry with it popular impulses, that men become proud of the name of America, and feel unwilling to throw away the distinction for any of the minor considerations of local policy. Every man sees and feels that a state is rapidly advancing to maturity which must reduce the pretensions of even ancient Rome to supremacy, to a secondary place in the estimation of mankind. A century will unquestionably place the United States of America prominently at the head of civilized nations, unless their people throw away their advantages by their own mistakes—the only real danger they have to apprehend; and the mind clings to this hope with a buoyancy and fondness that are becoming profoundly national. We have a thousand weaknesses, and make many blunders, beyond a doubt, as a people; but where shall we turn to find a parallel to our progress, our energy, and increasing power?[31]

But he had little hope that the nation would return to 'the true principles of the original government'; clearly, he expected that a licentious democracy would give way to 'the sway of money'. This eventuality no longer appalled him. So obsessed had he become with the need to defend Property that he now recognized commerce—Thurlow Weed's generous patron—as an acceptable ally in his fight against Fourierists, Anti-Renters, and violaters of the Fugitive Slave Laws. 'As has been already said, associated wealth will take care of itself.' [32] At one time in his career, these words would have conveyed a sinister implication of menace to the community: now they only communicated reassurance.

At the memorial gathering held in Cooper's honour in 1852, the chair was taken by Daniel Webster: it was something of a national occasion and the 'Godlike' Daniel was pleased to preside. There is a sad irony in this. For Cooper had, over a period of many years, attacked the Whig Senator's Anglophile interpretations of the Constitution; guessed (what was true) that he was in the pay of Wall Street; and even denied Webster's talents.[33] Yet there is a sadder irony in the fact that at the close

[31] *Spirit of the Fair*, p. 54.   [32] *ibid.*, p. 114.
[33] Cf. *Letters*, vol. III, pp. 84, 129–39, 177; vol. IV, p. 114. Webster's relations with Wall Street are explored in Richard Current, *Daniel Webster and the Rise of National Conservatism* (Boston, 1955).

of their careers, the dangers to Property and the Union crowding out all other issues and not a few principles, Cooper and Webster belonged to what was in fact (though not in name) the same party. Cooper must have approved of Webster's role in the Compromise legislation of 1850. Behind him Webster had a lifetime of well-paid if not exactly honourable service in defence of Property. Now, as Secretary of State, he was enforcing the Fugitive Slave laws with vigour; he meant to keep his bargain with the South. He had crushed Seward.

Both Cooper and Webster had worked hard to save the old America which they dimly and fondly recollected. Real as their differences had been, they agreed as to which political issues were important, which not. They also shared the same sense of political decorum. But the Compromise of 1850 was the last triumph of Cooper's political generation. That generation was swiftly passing: Jackson had died in 1845 and Calhoun in 1850; Clay and Webster were to follow in 1852. Many of the major issues of the Jacksonian era died with them or went underground. The year 1855 witnessed the disintegration of the Whig party itself, which had so inspired Cooper's hatred and Webster's loyalty. It is difficult to imagine Cooper lingering on the stage after 1851; but had he done so, all the evidence suggests that he would have remained a Democrat after all—his views of 1851 coincided closely with those of Stephen Douglas in 1860. Yet the Civil War would have found him loyal to the Union, working in uneasy alliance with Lincoln and Seward.

3. CONCLUSION

The changes in American life which Cooper witnessed between 1800 and 1850 were breathtaking in their scope and pace. Perhaps no comparable period in the history of any nation is so remarkable for its variety of revolutionary transformations. The transportation revolution, with all its economic and social consequences, had hit Europe somewhat earlier; but its impact on America was greater simply because American distances and resources were greater. For the same reason, the invention of the electric telegraph by Cooper's friend Morse was a more momentous event in America than in Europe. And yet it must have seemed that advances in transportation and communication, however revolutionary, could hardly keep pace with the actual territorial growth of the United States: in 1800 the states were still clustered along the Atlantic seaboard; in 1850 California had been admitted to the Union, and the nation (if we except Hawaii and Alaska) had assumed its present shape and dimensions. The population increased at an unparalleled rate too: migration west, urbanization in the East, immigration from Europe—combined to transform the basic pattern of life in a dramatic and visible way. Men who had been governed in 1800 by a Federalist élite, in 1848 elected, not for the first time, a 'People's President'. At the beginning of the century, slavery was a well-nigh universal institution in the states and was deplored by Southerners as well as Northerners; the Compromise of 1850 averted, for a time, the 'irrepressible conflict' between a free North and a slave-holding South.

New York was a focal-point of national change, as Cooper was well aware:

In 1790, the year in which the first census under the law of Congress was taken, the State already contained 340,120 souls, while New England had a few more than a million. It is worthy of remark that, sixty years since, the entire State had but little more than half of the population of the Manhattanese towns at the present moment! Each succeeding census diminished these proportions, until that of 1830, when the return for the State of New York gave 1,372,812, and for New England 1,954,709. At this time, and for a considerable period preceding and succeeding it, it was found that the proportion between the people of the State of New York and the people of the city, was about as ten to one. Between 1830 and 1840, the former had so far increased in numbers as to possess as many people as *all* New England. In the next decade, this proportion was exceeded; and the late returns show that New York, singly, has passed ahead of all her enterprising neighbors in that section of the Union. At the same time, the old proportion between the State and the town—or, to be more accurate, the *towns* on the Bay of New York and its waters—has been entirely lost, five to one being near the truth at the present moment. It is easy to forsee that the time is not very distant when two to one will be maintained with difficulty, as between the State and its commercial capital[34]

Less easily charted, but more poignantly felt by a man of

[34] *Spirit of the Age*, p. 6.

Cooper's class and generation, were the social and political changes which took place in New York state during this half-century. The political supremacy of the Federalists was already passing when Cooper was a young boy; but the city merchants and the rural squirearchy, while bemoaning the Jacobinical tendencies of the times, had little to fear from an electorate composed exclusively of property owners. With its vast estates and numerous good old Dutch and English families, New York was the most 'aristocratic' state north of the Potomac. But for this very reason the conflict between the Old and the New subsequently became more acute and more easily observed in New York than elsewhere: and the painful feelings it inspired were intensified by the fact that the new democratic tendencies came, or seemed to come, largely from outsiders—New Englanders in the country areas and European immigrants in the city. In fact, something like an invasion of his native state occurred during Cooper's lifetime, diversifying its population, altering its customs, and transforming its architecture.

Cooper lived in the midst of these changes, and he was equipped by his genius, his interests, and his social station to respond to them more deeply than other people. Inevitably, he lacked the cool detachment and philosophical temper of a foreigner like Alexis de Tocqueville. He tried desperately to retain his balance, even as late as *The Ways of the Hour*:

To tell you the truth, Ned, the state is submitting to the influence of two of the silliest motives that can govern men,—ultra conservatism and ultra progress; the one holding back, often, to preserve that which is not worth keeping, and the other 'going ahead', as it is termed, merely for the sake of boasting of their onward tendencies. Neither course is the least suited to the actual wants of society, and each is pernicious in its way.

It is probably true that at the end of his life his social and political views were middle-of-the-road, or no more than a little right of centre. But he reached this position only by moving steadily to the right during his last fifteen years, and it is in these terms that his reaction must be measured. Even so, these categories cannot express the degree of his confusion and disappointment. Once, as 'our national novelist', he had had access to every American ear; now, reduced to hack-work, he wrote political allegories like *The Crater* or *The Lake Gun*—works the form of which permitted him to indulge his violent emotions, and at the same time betrayed his uneasy awareness that he would not be listened to anyway.

It is true that he kept on trying to communicate, trying to bring Americans back to 'the true principles of the original government' and to remind them of what they had lost. Essentially a hopeful character, he continued to seek compensations for the losses, and attempted, as in his earliest work, to achieve a balance between hope and regret. This is evident in what remains of his final book, the unfinished history of the towns of Manhattan. On the one hand, he is exhilarated by the brilliant future of the city—by the thing it will become. Its present, still more its future, importance justifies his ambition to be its historian. On the other hand, this marvellous progress has already destroyed much of the city that he loved:

In the text of my own book, I say that it may be questioned if there be a single building now standing in New-York that was standing prior to the year 1750. Valentine, however, gives a picture of a dutch house and I am curious to ascertain if it still be standing. I recollect a great many of these houses myself and there were plenty of them to be found in the early part of the century. But I think nearly all, if not absolutely all have vanished.[35]

Vanished! Like the Mohicans, or like the trees felled in *The Prairie*:

As tree after tree came whistling down, he cast his eyes upward, at the vacancies they left in the heavens, with a melancholy gaze, and finally turned away muttering to himself with a bitter smile, like one who disdained giving a more audible utterance to his discontent.

But Natty Bumppo, the Mohicans, and the trees were supposed to make way, not merely for an incomparable material progress, but for the highest of national civilizations. For all his patriotism, Cooper could no longer share Jefferson's belief in a superior American civilization based on agrarian virtue and independence. It is significant that in his last work he should pin his hopes for civilization in America on a great city—one which, in time, might match or even excel the major European capitals.

---

[35] Letter to George Putnam (23 July 1851), quoted by Beard, *New York Historical Society Quarterly*, p. 112.

If this was the highest compensation he could find for the unparalleled wreckage and change of that half-century, we may
well forgive his final intransigence and his unfeeling attitude to
the aspirations of other Americans, many of whom had everything to gain by further change and few of whom could appreciate the quality of what men like Jay, Jefferson, Lafayette, and
Cooper had once envisaged for America.

Baffled and embittered as it made him, Cooper's awareness of
the dizzying scope and pace of change in American life was a
vital part of his genius as a novelist. He was, as we know, a rest-
less innovator himself and to this extent may be said to have par-
ticipated fully in the national mania. Some of his 'firsts' are not
very impressive, technically or historically: to say that he was
the first to write an American novel of manners (*Home as Found*)
or an American utopia (*The Crater*) is to say little more than
that he was the first in the field. His achievements as an innovator in the genre of sea fiction are much more substantial, as
Thomas Philbrick has shown. His extensive and effective use of
symbolism in *The Pioneers* is also, I believe, highly original. And
one might mention many other instances of his inventive genius.
But his most important innovations are to be found in his
development of the historical novel.

In Scott's hands, the novel registered complex historical
change by focusing on a brief but crucial period of transition.
In such novels as *Waverley* and *Old Mortality*, or Cooper's own
Pioneers and *Heidenmauer*, this method could open up vast perspectives backwards and forwards in time. What it did not
do was register the rate of historical change, and it was astonish-
ing rapidity of change that was so important and peculiar a
feature of American experience:

That which it has required centuries, in other regions, to effect,
is here accomplished in a single life; and the student of history finds
the results of all his studies crowded as it might be into the incidents
of the day.[36]

To this perception, however imperfectly grasped at first, we
probably owe the eventual unfolding of the Leatherstocking
sequence: a sequence of novels, tracing one man's passage
through time and space (American space), is the best possible

[36] *Spirit of the Fair*, p. 54.

way of showing how 'that which it has required centuries, in other regions, to effect, is here accomplished in a single life....' The same perception led Cooper, in *Afloat and Ashore*, to experiment with yet another variant of the historical novel—one in which the fictional narrator, as an old man recalling the adventures of his distant youth, constantly plays off the present against the past and in the process reveals the almost fantastic alterations that have taken place during his lifetime. His experiments with the family chronicle novel sequence, first in *Home as Found* (which was closely associated with his preparation of *The Chronicles of Cooperstown*) and later in the Littlepage trilogy, also derive from his awareness of the swift—and often heart-breaking—pace of economic and social change in America.

In these novels, if anywhere, Cooper's main achievement is to be found. Both as a man and as an artist, he was too much attached to certain conventions ever to carry through any formal revolution. But he understood the dynamic character of American society as few other writers have. At once exhilarated and appalled by what he saw, he developed fictional forms which, however clumsy and archaic in some respects, were nevertheless capable of expressing much that was typical and crucial in American experience. In many ways his opposite number in American literature is his contemporary, Poe; and no doubt he would have been a greater novelist had he shared Poe's ambition to be a fine artist. But at his best he was something better than a fine artist. He was a major novelist whose innovations were generated by a passionate need to be true, not only to his own experience, but to the experience of several generations of his countrymen. Americans in 1851 mourned the passing of their national novelist; in many respects he remains the most centrally American of novelists.

INDEX